Unforgettables

Winners, Losers, Strong Women, and Eccentric Men of the Civil War Era

John C. Waugh

SB

Savas Beatie
California

First edition, first printing

ISBN-13: 978-1-61121-665-3 (hardcover)
ISBN-13: 978-1-61121-666-0 (ebook)

Library of Congress Cataloging-in-Publication Data

Names: Waugh, John C., author.
Title: Unforgettables: Winners, Losers, Strong Women, and Eccentric Men of the Civil War Era / by John C. Waugh.
Other titles: Winners, losers, strong women, and eccentric men of the Civil War era
Description: El Dorado Hills, CA: Savas Beatie, [2024] | Includes bibliographical references and index. | Summary: "This book is a presentation of forty of the most memorable and impactful individuals the author has come across during his three decades of researching and writing about the American Civil War. Waugh's unique pen and spritely style bring to life a mix of the famous and the infamous, the little-known and the unremembered. The author's hope is that these sketches and word portraits rekindle that passion and hook a few non-believers on the undeniable drama that is history"-- Provided by publisher.
Identifiers: LCCN 2023043562 | ISBN 9781611216653 (paperback) | ISBN 9781611216660 (ebook)
Subjects: LCSH: United States--History--Civil War, 1861-1865--Biography.
Classification: LCC E467 .W37 2023 | DDC 973.4092/2 [B]--dc23/eng/20231004
LC record available at https://lccn.loc.gov/2023043562

SB
Savas Beatie
989 Governor Drive, Suite 102
El Dorado Hills, CA 95762
916-941-6896 / sales@savasbeatie.com / www.savasbeatie.com

All of our titles are available at special discount rates for bulk purchases in the United States. Contact us for information.

For the Unforgettables in the Tucson, Arizona, Senior High School class of 1947, with affection.

Books by John C. Waugh

The Class of 1846
Reelecting Lincoln
One Man Great Enough
Lincoln and McClellan
Lincoln and the War's End
On the Brink of Civil War
Surviving the Confederacy
Last Stand at Mobile
Sam Bell Maxey and the Confederate Indians
20 Good Reasons to Study the Civil War
Edwin Cole Bearss: History's Pied Piper
How Historians Work (co-author)

TABLE OF CONTENTS

TABLE OF CONTENTS (cont.)

TABLE OF CONTENTS (cont.)

ABBREVIATIONS

B&L: Battles & Leaders of the Civil War
CW: Collected Works of Abraham Lincoln
JAH: Journal of American History
JSH: Journal of Southern History
LOC: Library of Congress
MVHR: Mississippi Valley Historical Review
NA: National Archives
SHSP: Southern Historical Society Papers

In Appreciation

In this space, generally at the very end of first thanking everybody else who helped birth their book, authors generally think to thank their spouses. Husbands and wives generally deserve it, for their constant and loving support—moral and otherwise—during the research and writing process. This nod of gratitude is quite necessary. I nod, too. But wives and husbands are too often the last to be thanked, here at the very bottom of the appreciation page.

For this book I have moved my spouse, Kathleen D. Lively, up from last to first, because she performed acts quite above the call of spousal duty. What she did required a keen eye, grit, fortitude, a lot of love, immunity from frustration, and earplugs for the occasional outbursts of agony from her writer-husband. And after the big Source Search she was able to successfully intervene between me and my nemesis, 21st century technology. Tough work considering I am a 19th century person.

All the trouble began when I did not cite sources for most of these profiles at the time I was writing them. I didn't think they would ever appear in print this way. So Kathleen had to be drafted, out of matrimonial necessity, for the odious job of helping find what we thought might be long lost and forgotten sources and match them to their place in the text.

After they were all found and miraculously matched we made proper footnotes and then did it over and over and over again, again, and again. It was a needle in the haystack operation. To find and position these sources where they belonged took several months. Dirty work, but finally and magnificently done, with a heavy dose of thanks to Kathleen. I now footnote everything, instantly, including the weekly grocery list.

There are yet others who have won my gratitude as well, for thoughtful service in putting this book between covers.

Chris Mackowski, Professor of Communication at St. Bonaventure University, who is deeply acquainted with the Civil War and with the contents of this work, offered to introduce me to a publisher who might be interested in publishing it. You would not be holding the book in your hands but for Mackowski's intervention. He can't be thanked enough.

Another gentleman difficult to adequately thank is the publisher to whom Mackowski graciously introduced me—Ted Savas of Savas Beatie, a publishing house that specializes in books about campaigns in military history. This book is not about that. It is a book that profiles forty fascinating men and women of the Civil War era, some of whom might have fought in some of those campaigns. Savas might have thought this book a mite out of the Savas Beatie wheelhouse. But he took it and put it in his waiting line of books to be published.

When my book reached the head of the line, Savas assigned to it two seasoned freelance editors—Rebecca Hill to do the initial edit; and a copy editor, David J. Snyder, to do a final detailed edit before the manuscript headed for covers. These two editors helped make this a better book. For that they have my sincerest thanks.

Ted Savas is not the only one from Savas Beatie who needs to be thanked. He has a staff down in the trenches that transforms manuscripts into books. Among that group I had a typhoon of email exchanges with Veronica Kane, who coordinated the production of the book, and did excellent work, as did Elise Hess, who compiled the complete index. And I became acquainted with Sarah Keeney, the marketing director, and Sarah Closson, the media specialist, representing two forms of staff help closest to the heart of any author.

Finally, here at the end where spouses like Kathleen are usually thanked, I salute librarians. Those creatures, like elves to Santa Claus, are nearly as valuable to historians as wives and husbands are. From the Library of Congress in Washington to local and university libraries in Texas and elsewhere, librarians have helped guide my passage through the dozen other books I have written. They are never less than delighted to help any author doing serious research.

For everyone who has left a helpful imprint on this book, my sincerest thanks, again.

Prologue

All My Sources Are Dead

Historians are lucky. We get tickets in front row seats to the drama of history. We get to know as intimately as plausible the characters of the past.

I got hooked on history, and the unforgettable characters who made it, when I was just a kid. I discovered the past is a mother lode of drama with outstanding actors—century after century of terrific human stories. People who learn about the captivating history and human stories become hooked on the past for life. Just as I have been. Characters of the past are what this book is about. I have brought back a few friends from the Civil War era whom I have met in my three decades of researching and writing. They have all touched me in some way.

I have written word portraits of each of these individuals. Some sketches are long. Others are short. Some characters are famous and familiar, household names both then and now. Others are "little noted, nor long remembered"[1] in the pages of time. I could have picked a different cast entirely, and yet another and another, so rich is history's mother lode.

Great minds have attempted to define history through the ages. Automaker Henry Ford reportedly said, "History is bunk." He later claimed they misquoted him (a common dodge in all ages). Technically, Ford *was* misquoted. What he said was, "History is more or less bunk." Clearly, he thought it was bunk; who needs it?[2]

Carl Sandburg, the poet, folksinger, and Lincoln biographer, told us, "the past is a bucket of ashes."[3] Voltaire, the eighteenth century French Enlightenment writer and philosopher, believed history to be "nothing but a pack of tricks, which

1 A paraphrase of a phrase from Lincoln's Gettysburg Address, in Abraham Lincoln, *Collected Works of Abraham Lincoln*, Roy P. Basler, ed., 8 vols. (New Brunswick, NJ, 1953), 7:17-23. Henceforth this will be cited as *CW*.

2 *Chicago Tribune*, May 25, 1916.

3 Carl Sandburg, "Prairie" in *Cornhuskers* (New York, 1918), 11.

we play upon the dead."[4] The satire-tongued English playwright and novelist, Oscar Wilde, believed history is "merely gossip."[5] Ambrose Bierce, the American iconoclast writer and Union veteran, agreed indirectly with Wilde. A historian, Bierce grumbled, is but a "broad-gauge gossip."[6]

Winston Churchill, who was, among other things, a Civil War historian, said, "History stumbles along the trail of the past, trying to reconstruct its scenes, to revive its echoes, and kindle with pale gleams the passion of former days."[7]

I buy what Churchill said. I've written thirteen books about the Civil War era, hoping to help history reconstruct its scenes, revive its echoes, and rekindle its passion.

Writing history, at least narrative history, which I allegedly do, is strikingly similar to writing fiction. Neither differs from writing a feature story for a newspaper, which is what I did in much of my past professional life. I wrote stories for a newspaper, about twentieth century events and people. However, I discovered, nearly too late, that I was a nineteenth century person. So, I began writing news stories that broke a hundred and fifty years ago. For a time, I called myself a "history reporter." I'm nearly two centuries past my deadline.

When I started researching the Civil War, I discovered that writing about that era and its countless compelling characters was no different from writing about today's. I discovered history, when presented as it so often is, can be mind-numbing, dull, and sleep-inducing. Bad history is full of boring dates, facts, places, names, battles, wars, treaties, acts of Congress, with hardly a story line, drama, or humanity in it at all, and usually marching along with facts in lockstep, which must be memorized.

There is only one reason everybody doesn't love history in school and continues to love it throughout their lifetimes. That is because it isn't taught or written correctly. When done properly, as a great dramatic story driven by bewitching characters, it is everybody's favorite subject.

You can beam yourself down anywhere in the past, anywhere at all, and something dramatic, interesting, indeed riveting, is going on. Somebody amazing is doing something spectacular, and probably doing it to somebody else amazing. It ought to be written and taught that way. Good, readable, narrative history has

4 Quoted in Will Durant, *The Story of Philosophy* (New York, 1926), 168.

5 Oscar Wilde, *Lady Windermere's Fan.* Wilde says this about history in this play, in a line spoken by the character Cecil Graham, in Act Three.

6 Ambrose Bierce, *The Devil's Dictionary* (1911; repr., New York, 1979), 49.

7 Churchill said this in a tribute to the late prime minister, Neville Chamberlain. in a speech in the House of Commons on Nov. 12, 1940.

unforgettable characters and vivid description. There is tension and conflict. It has a plot. And we cannot forget the drama. The only difference between it and a page-turning novel is that history must be true, factual, immovably based on real people and actual events.

Historians can't make up anything. We quote only what was said or reported, and we ensure it is quoted exactly. Everything that is happening and who it is happening to in this book's collection of portraits is true, or as close as I can get to the truth from the available sources. Nothing is made up, not the weather, or a fact or a description or a word of conversation, as it is in fiction. We don't have to make anything up. Letters, newspapers, journals, memoirs, and diaries from the Civil War are humming with colorful characters, compelling dialogue, and vivid description.

In fiction, the story is pieced together from the writer's own experience, knowledge, research, skill, and imagination, his or her own internal store of source material. It gives slack for straying from truth or mixing truth with fiction. In writing history, this does not happen. Poetic writing, however, is allowed. The only difference between narrative history and fiction is the source material. The writing shouldn't be any different, nor should the reader's enjoyment. I have yet to read a novel about the Civil War that is better than the story as it really happened.

Writing fiction or history is telling a story about the people in a certain period and their circumstances. The leg up that history has over fiction is that the people are real—people who lived and died, loved, and hated, just like all of us today.

Real people, plots, places, and facts—they are the raw material of the historian. All those ingredients, together with the perspective, are in the research material. The historian's job is to find those ingredients and blend them together into a gripping, poetic work that reads like fiction. In my mind, that is what narrative history writing amounts to.

The poet Muriel Rukeyser wrote, "The universe is made of stories, not of atoms."[8] Stories, driven by its characters, are what history is all about, and what this book is all about.

This book is not a history of the Civil War. It is but a rummaging around, stumbling about in that nation-changing era by a writer-historian who has found tragedy, passion, irony, and comedy in the past. My intention with these sketches and word portraits is to rekindle that passion and hook a few non-believers onto the undeniable drama of history.

8 Muriel Rukeyser, *The Speed of Darkness* (New York, 1968). The words cited are from poem number 9 with the same title as the book.

Chapter 1

Three for the Ages

A trio of unforgettable men, Henry Clay (Kentucky), John C. Calhoun (South Carolina), and Daniel Webster (Massachusetts) came together to form a unique political trinity in the Antebellum years of American history. Together they formed a political trio, the like of which has not been seen since.

This trinity dominated American politics in the first half of the 1800s, just as the Founding Fathers dominated in the late 1700s. These three charismatic young men burst onto the stage together, burning with ambition and talent. Slavery was the central issue that consumed their political lives.

They had become known as the "Great Trio," or "The Great Triumvirate." All three were iconic political powerhouses. Each yearned to be president, but that would never happen. They were sometimes friends and allies. Sometimes they were political enemies on opposite sides of nation-warping issues. Together on the Senate floor, where they often were, they seemed larger than life: dynamic, dramatic, dominant, and magnetic.

The great theater of the nineteenth century, in their heyday, was political theater. The preeminent political stage of the time, largely because of them, was the hallowed old Senate Chamber in the capitol building in Washington. In that chamber, they were the star actors. Their voices vibrated Union-wide. Whenever one of them spoke on an explosive national issue, it was to standing room only.

The chamber and galleries teemed with witnesses to their greatness in what Henry Clay called "this noble theater."[1]

By 1850, old, tired, and dying, they came together one last time on the Senate floor to try to save the Union from the demon of slavery, to keep the Union from breaking into civil war and disunion. They tried, through a steaming Washington summer, but failed. By 1860, before the dreaded war came, all three had died.

So, who were these distinguished men? What were their likes and dislikes, their deepest thoughts and desires, their strengths, and weaknesses?

The Eloquent Gambler

Tall and slender, the tobacco-snuffing Henry Clay was arguably the greatest of the three. He was a leader, always seeking the middle ground, and reaching for compromises to save the Union. Earlier, he had successfully found a middle ground during the Missouri Compromise of 1820, and the South Carolina nullification battle in the early 1830s. But in a mighty effort, he tried, and failed, to find a similar foothold in the slavery debates on the Senate floor in the sweltering Washington summer of 1850.

There was no more beloved man in the country than Henry Clay, a Kentucky Whig, the acknowledged leader of his party. Young Abraham Lincoln looked up to him, calling him his "beau ideal of a statesman."[2] This beau ideal was so lionized that he couldn't travel normally, but as one contemporary observed, he could "only make progresses. When he left his home, the public seized him and bore him along over the land, the committee of one State passing him on to the committee of another, and the hurrahs of one town dying away as those of the next caught his ear."[3]

Clay attempted to become president five times, but he was rejected every time. One said that he "can get more men to run after him to hear him speak and fewer to vote for him than any man in America."[4]

Dressed in black with a high-standing collar reaching his ears, Clay eclipsed other stars in the political galaxy simply by showing up. When entering the House of Representatives for the first time in 1811, he was elected Speaker.

1 Thomas Hart Benton, *Thirty Years' View: or a History of the Workings of the American Government for Thirty Years, from 1820 to 1850,* 2 vols. (New York, 1968), 2:401.

2 Lincoln, *CW,* 3:39.

3 James Parton, *Famous Americans of Recent Times* (Boston, 1867), 4.

4 Holmes Alexander, *The Famous Five* (New York, 1958), 11.

Henry Clay

Library of Congress

Clay stood over six feet, "slender and loose jointed."[5] He oozed charm from every pore. He could take snuff, to which he was addicted, "more elegantly than

5 Merrill D. Peterson, *The Great Triumvirate* (New York, 1987), 10.

any man of his time."[6] He was a gambling man, dominating the gaming table much as he dominated the Senate. In 1850, age seventy-three, he could no longer gamble all night and debate all day. But he could gamble well enough still. In the heyday of his gaming years, a friend of his wife Lucretia asked her, "Don't it distress you to have Mr. Clay gamble?" "No, my dear," Lucretia said, "he almost always wins."[7]

Clay brought a compelling talent, not only to the gaming table, but to his affinity for national healing, for finding a compromise in chaos, standing on the middle ground, and pulling the country up with him. He was endowed with parliamentary finesse powered by a hypnotic personality matched by a mesmeric voice.

An admirer wrote:

> No orator's voice superior to his in quality, in compass and in management, has ever, we venture to say, been raised upon this continent. It touched every note in the whole gamut of human susceptibilities; it was sweet, and soft, and lulling as a mother's to her babe. It could be made to float into the chambers of the air, as gently as descending snow-flakes on the sea; and again it shook the Senate, stormy, brain-shaking, filling the air with its absolute thunders.[8]

A reporter from the *National Intelligencer* noted that when speaking, Clay's "whole body would become eloquent."[9] He gesticulated all over, another reporter recalled: "The nodding of his head, hung on a long neck, his arms, hands, fingers, feet, and even his spectacles, his snuff-box, and his pocket-handkerchief, aided him in debate. He stepped forward and backward, and from the right to the left, with effect. Every thought spoke; the whole body had its story to tell."[10]

His voice, one admirer said, "filled the room as the organ fills a great cathedral."[11] With this voice, "musical yet mighty," another admirer believed, he could put "an amazing weight of expression on to the backbone of a single word" and he seemed always ready to limber up and fire away, like "a sort of flying

6 Neil MacNeil, "The House Shall Chuse Their Speaker…." in *American Heritage* (Feb. 1977), 29.

7 Theodore N. Parmelee, "Recollections of an Old Stager," in *Harper's New Monthly Magazine* (Jan. 1873), 96.

8 Edward G. Parker, *The Golden Age of American Oratory* (Boston, 1857), 38.

9 Oliver Dyer, *Great Senators of the United States Forty Years Ago* (New York, 1889), 229.

10 Benjamin Perley Poore, *Perley's Reminiscences of Sixty Years in the National Metropolis*, 2 vols., (Philadelphia, 1886), 1:143.

11 Parton, *Famous Americans*, 11.

artillery."[12] Another more reluctant admirer said, "I'm damned if I can listen to Mr. Clay speak and believe him to be wrong."[13] It is difficult to believe that this brilliant orator stammered in his youth.

Clay's mixed medley of rhetoric—lullaby-soft to tempest-tossed—cascaded from a mouth "of generous width, straight when he was silent, and curving upward at the corners as he spoke or smiled." It was "a singularly graceful mouth . . . indicating more than any other feature the elastic play of his mind."[14] Clay's mouth, was in truth, cave-like. It was enormously broad-beamed as if split open "with a broad axe."[15] Someone said it "looked like the stone mouth of the great Sphinx."[16]

It was a mouth, which, when speaking, could paralyze a hooded cobra. Calhoun remarked, "I don't like Clay. He is an impostor, a creature of wicked schemes. I won't speak to him—but by God, I love him."[17] One wary newcomer to a congressional seat in 1821 was asked by a mutual friend, "May I introduce you to Henry Clay?" The newcomer said, "No, sir! I am his adversary, and choose not to subject myself to his fascination."[18]

That was the magic of Henry Clay.

Paladin of the South

John C. Calhoun is hardly less fascinating. He was South Carolina's prophet of Southern anger. His dying on the last day of March 1850, during the debates on the slavery issue in the Senate, was itself unreal. Harriet Martineau, the celebrated English writer who had visited America, seeing him in his prime, called him "the cast-iron man, who looks as if he had never been born and never could be extinguished."[19]

In 1850, during his last living months, he was haggard, frail, riddled with tuberculosis, and wracked by coughing. His long magisterial hair hung limply along the sides of his sunken face, around deep-pocketed eyes. He seemed more a

12 Parker, *The Golden Age*, 38, 43, 46.

13 Alexander, *The Famous Five*, 2.

14 Poore, *Perley's Reminiscences*, 1:34.

15 Parker, *The Golden Age*, 36.

16 Edgar Dewitt Jones, *Lords of Speech: Portraits of Fifteen American Orators* (Chicago, 1937), 20.

17 Alexander, *The Famous Five*, 2.

18 Horace Greeley, *The Autobiography of Horace Greeley, or Recollections of a Busy Life* (New York, 1872), 250.

19 Harriet Martineau, *Retrospect of Western Travel*, 3 vols. (New York, 1969), 1:243.

John Calhoun

Library of Congress

specter than a man. But this belied "the young Hercules"[20] of his younger years, six feet, two inches tall, who had served a dynamic lifetime at the altar of public service. Calhoun had been a congressman, senator, secretary of war, and vice president—a career lacking only a presidency, like the other two, desperately longed for but never realized.

Varina Davis, wife of Jefferson Davis, who saw Calhoun often in the antebellum years, described his forehead as "low, steep, and beetled squarely over the most glorious pair of yellow brown shining eyes that seemed to have a light inherent in themselves." Those brilliant eyes, Varina said, "looked steadily out from under bushy eyebrows that made the deep sockets look still more sunken." They were eyes that Varina supposed got lowered less than any eyes she ever saw, bending steadily, laser-like, on whomever he was looking. On some people, Varina believed, that stare had "an almost mesmeric power."[21]

Calhoun's impressive mane of hair could mesmerize. Long and coarse, it made a majestic statement by itself. His hair had whitened over the years, and he wore it as he always did, cascading down either side of his stern face in masses from his forehead. It was his physical beacon on the world despite himself. He said of it, "I have always endeavored to dress with a simplicity that would not attract notice, and I have succeeded, with the exception of my hair."[22]

A reporter staring at the whole Calhoun and that mane of hair saw a body "without an ounce of superfluous flesh, with a serious expression of countenance rarely brightened by a smile, and with his long . . . hair thrown back from his forehead, he looked like an arch-conspirator waiting for the time to come when he could strike the first blow."[23]

The voice that spun from this apparition was not musical, like Clay's. Varina described it rather as "the voice of a professor of mathematics," that "suited his didactic discourse admirably. He made few gestures, but those nervous gentlemanly hands seemed to point the way to empire. He always appeared to me rather as a moral and mental abstraction than a politician."[24]

Calhoun had been delivering didactic discourses on behalf of his beloved South and its "peculiar institution," slavery, for decades. As the crisis intensified and the danger to his section deepened, he changed from an ardent Unionist to "the stern

20 Peterson, *The Great Triumvirate*, 18.

21 Varina Howell Davis, *Jefferson Davis, Ex-President of the Confederate States of America: A Memoir by His Wife*, 2 vols. (1890; repr., Freeport, NY, 1971), 1:209-10.

22 "Reminiscences of Washington," in *Atlantic Monthly* (Dec. 1880), 800.

23 Poore, *Perley's Reminiscences*, 1:64.

24 Davis (Varina), *Jefferson Davis*, 1:210.

zealot,"[25] "the arch defender of the slave system," its "terse, vigorous relentless champion,"[26] its paladin, hammering for its extension into the territories, for free trade, for state sovereignty, and for political parity, without stint and without a scintilla of compromise.

Calhoun, a cotton farmer's son, never considered a wider occupation for himself, until he was eighteen years old. It was then he discovered that he possessed a mind that everyone saw as extraordinary. That landed him at Yale, where he took everything seriously, never joked, and impressed all with his bulldozing intelligence. He took his Yale education and rock-like confidence in himself directly into politics. A fellow South Carolinian remarked that Calhoun, "sprang into the arena like Minerva from the head of Jove, fully grown and clothed in armor: a man every inch himself and able to contend with any other man."[27] He entered Congress in 1811 at the age of 28, in that same extraordinary freshman class with Clay.

Over the years, they would become friends and political allies, then enemies. When he and Clay later clashed in the Senate, it was said to be "a conflict of giants." Clay was a hip-shooter, "intolerant and aggressive, delighting in gladiatorial combats." Calhoun, on the other hand, was a sniper, unequaled for careful, incisive analysis.[28]

Calhoun, one colleague recalled, was "like a college professor demonstrating to his class," a well-oiled reasoning machine with "a perceptive, comprehensive, and analytic mind."[29] Harriet Martineau believed his theories of government were "almost the only subject on which his thoughts are employed" and were "the squarest and compactest theories that ever were made."[30]

Despite their deep differences, there was love and appreciation of Clay and Calhoun for one another. When Clay retired for the first time from the Senate in 1842, they had been on the outs for half a decade. As Clay made his farewell

25 Ibid., 1:20.

26 Chaplain W. Morrison, *Democratic Politics and Sectionalism: The Wilmot Proviso Controversy* (Chapel Hill, NC, 1963), 5.

27 Richard Hofstadter, *The American Political Tradition and the Men Who Made It* (New York, 1974), 93.

28 Parmelee, "Recollections of an Old Stager" (Oct. 1863), 758-59.

29 John Wentworth, *Congressional Reminiscences: Adams, Benton, Clay, Calhoun, and Webster* (Chicago, 1882), 20-22.

30 Martineau, *Retrospect*, 1:243.

speech, Calhoun, a man who hid the trace of a gentle heart within that stern exterior, "gave way to his feelings and shed tears like a woman."[31]

That was the enigma that was John Calhoun.

America's Political Vesuvius

Daniel Webster, the third significant figure in this political trinity, was, unlike the other two, a Yankee.

He was born in New Hampshire in the late eighteenth century, two months before Calhoun was born, and five years after Clay was born. He arrived in Congress two years after Clay and Calhoun. At thirty years old, he rocketed into politics from the launch pad of a brilliant law career. He had never served in or run for any office when elected to the Thirteenth Congress from Massachusetts, bypassing all the usual lower stops. When he arrived on the House floor in 1813, the great trio came together for the first time.

Like Clay and Calhoun, Webster was one of a kind. The Washington reporter Ben Perley Poore saw him as "one of the few to whom Divinity had accorded a royal share of the Promethean fire of genius."[32] Another observer recalled, "when I first put eye upon him . . . I was as much awe-stricken as if I had been gazing upon Bunker Hill Monument."[33]

Rising on March 7, 1850, to deliver his powerful speech backing Clay for compromise and Union, his once raven black hair atop his large head had changed to a rich iron gray. It was a head that was often called leonine.

The look of him overwhelmed strangers. Jenny Lind, the renowned Swedish Nightingale who took concert halls by storm with her rich soprano of "placid sweetness," was as celebrated as any figure in her day, and not often impressed with mere mortals. Meeting Webster, she exclaimed, "I have seen a man!"[34]

Another who saw him thought him "a whole species in himself."[35] He was not tall like Clay or Calhoun. Powerfully built, with an enormous head housing that oversized brain, he appeared a giant. One writer wrote, "he must be an impostor, for

31 Parmelee, "Recollections of an Old Stager" (Oc. 1863), 759.

32 Poore, *Perley's Reminiscences*, 1:79.

33 Parton, *Famous Americans*, 57, 98.

34 Henry W. Hilliard, *Politics and Pen Pictures at Home and Abroad* (New York, 1892), 241.

35 Parton, *Famous Americans*, 98.

Daniel Webster

Library of Congress

no man can be so great as he looked"[36]—"a small cathedral," exclaimed another.[37] Thomas Hart Benton, the senator from Missouri, served with the trinity for part of the first half of the nineteenth century. He saw Webster as "the colossal figure, bearing the constitutional ark of his country safely upon his Atlantean shoulders."[38]

Webster was the ultimate patriot, America's senator. He had delivered a career of brilliant speeches on and off the Senate floor, each brimming with love of country. "The hold Clay had upon the heart of his countrymen," a friend said, "Webster had upon the American mind."[39] The great literary beacon from New England, Ralph Waldo Emerson, believed people saw Webster "as the representative of the American Continent . . . he alone of all men did not disappoint the eye and the ear, but was a fit figure in the landscape."[40]

Webster's eyes, rather like Clay's mouth, were big, deep, bottomless pools, cavernous and hypnotic, black as pitch, "living coals." Thomas Carlyle, the Scottish writer-philosopher, described them as, "sleeping furnaces . . . needing only to be blown."[41] Webster's eyes were likened by another as "great burning lamps set deep in the mouths of caves."[42]

Matching those otherworldly eyes was an otherworldly voice, deep, melodious, theatrical, and mesmeric. New York's Horatio Seymour called it "a voice of great power and depth—a voice full of magnetism, a voice such as is heard only once in a lifetime."[43] When roused, one writer wrote, his speech was akin to heavy cannonading, "Vesuvius . . . in full blast. No Gothic language has ever been pounded into more compact cannon-ball sentences."[44]

The sight of Daniel Webster taking the floor, as he did on March 7, 1850, to speak for compromise on the slavery issue, was one of the most riveting in American politics. One observer wrote: "the getting up of Daniel Webster was not a mere act; it was a process. The beholder saw the most wonderful head that his vision ever rested on reaching slowly upward; he saw a lionlike countenance, with great, deep set, luminous eyes, gazing at him with solemn majesty; in short, he saw

36 Ralph Waldo Emerson, "The Fugitive Slave Law," in *The Complete Essays and Other Writings of Ralph Waldo Emerson*, Brooks Atkinson, ed. (New York, 1940), 863.

37 Parker, *The Golden Age*, 49-50; Alexander, *The Famous Five*, 53.

38 Dyer, *Great Senators*, 297-98.

39 Parker, *The Golden Age*, 84.

40 Emerson, "The Fugitive Slave Law," 863.

41 Peterson, *The Great Triumvirate*, 223.

42 Dyer, *Great Senators*, 252.

43 Howard Carroll, *Twelve Americans: Their Lives and Times* (1883; repr., Freeport, NY, 1971), 7.

44 Parker, *The Golden Age*, 93, 113.

the godlike Daniel getting on his feet, and his heart thrilled at the thought of what might be coming."[45]

That was the mesmerism of Daniel Webster.

* * *

On the last day of March 1850, as the debate raged over compromise, Calhoun died. Within two years, Clay and Webster would follow. They had only seemed immortal.

These three prominent senators were stars in American politics for almost fifty years. Their passing closed an epic passage of American politics. They were an unrivaled trio in politics, with unmatched presence, power, and personality.

However, even with their combined political magnetism and talents, they could not stop what was coming—a house-dividing civil war. It is just as well they didn't live to see it.

45 Dyer, *Great Senators*, 288-89.

Chapter 2

Four Failed Presidents

In the twelve years between James Polk, a good president, and Abraham Lincoln, a great president, four men who were neither good nor great led the nation toward civil war.

Those years 1850 to 1861 were arguably the most critical in our history—when "the sense of imminent catastrophe was ever-present."[1] They were years that would tell if we lived or died as a republic. In 1850, Lincoln was still twelve years from the White House. The four presidents were Zachary Taylor, Millard Fillmore, Franklin Pierce, and James Buchanan.

Taylor and Fillmore, the first two, were determined but lacked time or skill for such an enormous task. The other two who followed, Pierce and Buchanan, were clear disasters. It was their failures, in particular, that hastened civil war.

The Presidential Novice

Zachary Taylor, 5'8", was not tall, as were Washington, Jefferson, and Lincoln, all over six feet. But in some other ways, he more than measured up. He was a brave general, and one of the top American commanders in the 1800s, after Andrew Jackson and Winfield Scott.

As an Indian fighter between wars, Taylor had no equal. He was a compassionate enemy, who tried to protect the rights of the Indians, even as he was fighting them. He objected when the government cheated Indians of their land for white settlers,

1 Constance McLaughlin Green, *Washington: Village and Capital, 1800-1878* (Princeton, NJ, 1962), 178.

Zachary Taylor

National Archives

as he considered them worthy opponents. Taylor had driven whites off Indian-owned land.[2] He knew greed when he saw it.

Though he didn't smoke, Taylor was a tobacco chewer of renowned aim. He was skilled at hitting a cuspidor from impressive distances, rarely missing his target.[3]

As a general in the "Mexican and American War" of the 1840s, Taylor fought and won impressive battles. He became a national hero and converted himself into the leading presidential candidate of 1848.

2 Elbert B. Smith, *The Presidencies of Zachary Taylor & Millard Fillmore* (Lawrence, KS, 1988), 33.

3 Richard M. Ketchum, "Faces from the Past: Zachary Taylor," in *American Heritage* (Oct. 1963), 53.

He would have presented a challenge to a modern-day political spin-doctor. His adoring soldiers called him "Old Rough and Ready." By the time of the campaign, he was weather-wracked, wrinkled, and wind-blown by four decades of relentless military campaigning. His personality was unriveting and his oratory unmoving. He would not have come across well on television.

Taylor's outer veneer, however, was misleading, as he was the son of wealthy, well-educated parents. He was a man of the frontier, Virginia-born and Kentucky-raised, like many other distinguished men in our early history, though not without a touch of what passed for nobility in Young America, a mid-1800s youth reform movement: Taylor and his eight siblings were second cousins to James Madison and related to the Virginia Lees. His family could trace their line to Plymouth Rock.

With Mrs. Taylor, he produced a son and five daughters. One of their daughters, Sarah Knox Taylor—"Knoxie"—married Jefferson Davis in June 1835. This was done without her father's permission, approval, or presence. Taylor didn't want his daughters marrying soldiers. He knew from experience how hard that life was. Knoxie tragically died three months after her wedding day. Malaria took her in New Orleans at the height of the fever season. Davis, her devastated bridegroom nearly died of it at the same time.

Frail to begin with, Gen. Taylor's wife, whom he called Peggy, was by 1849 a semi-invalid. Before she married Taylor, she was Margaret Mackall Smith, the daughter of a major in the Continental Army and a planter.

Taylor didn't look like presidential material, and in fact, he wasn't. He was abysmally unprepared for the role. He was a shrewd military commander, with a good head for business, not politics. A wealthy man, Taylor owned two plantations in Louisiana and Mississippi, with 145 slaves, whom he treated more like friends than servants. He never sold one or broke up their families. He also gave them Christmas bonuses.

Taylor was not a prolific speaker. There was no Clay or Webster in him. He often stammered, mispronounced words, and broke down mid-sentence. He was capable of malaprops. In his first, and what would be his only message to Congress, he opened with this gem: "We are at peace with all the nations of the world, and the rest of mankind."[4] But it more than covered the ground.

George Julian, a congressman from Indiana, said of Taylor, "I decidedly liked his kindly, honest farmer-like face, and his old-fashioned simplicity of dress and manners. His conversation was awkward and labored, and evinced a lack of self-possession; while his whole demeanor suggested his frontier life, and that he

4 "Reminiscences of Washington" (Feb. 1881), 240-41.

reached a position [president] for which he was singularly unfitted by training and experience, or by any natural aptitude."[5]

He was "a perfect novice in politics," as one later historian remembered.[6] No president before him had come so remotely removed from politics to become president. Never in his sixty-four years of life had he ever voted or held political or civic office. Like many soldiers, he deplored politics and politicians. A Congressman said of him as president, "I have never been able to converse one minute with [him] about politics without his changing the subject."[7]

Serious doubt about Taylor's competence and fitness for the job was widespread. One observer summed up the common perception, saying that Taylor was, "of all men who have filled the presidential chair by the choice of the people, the one least competent to perform his duties."[8]

The New York editor, Horace Greeley, said of him, "Old Zack is a good old soul but don't know himself from a side of sole leather in the way of statesmanship."[9] "About as fit for President of these United States as any New England Farmer that one might select out of a thousand, with his eyes shut," said another.[10] Yet another doubter believed that the president "knew no more of statesmanship or the operations of government than a Comanche Indian."[11]

Taylor himself, a staunchly honest man, agreed with those assessments. "I have frankly avowed my own distrust of my fitness for that high station," he wrote, "but having at the earnest solicitation of many countrymen taken my position as . . . a candidate."[12]

As a politician, he was the despair of both parties, but each wanted him as their presidential candidate in 1848. The Whigs, who finally snagged him, had a devil of a time getting him to think Whig—or even think President. At first, he clearly wanted nothing to do with the office. When a visitor toasted him as the next president in his tent in Mexico, Taylor told him, "Stop your nonsense and drink

5 George Washington Julian, *Political Recollections, 1840 to 1872* (Chicago, 1884), 82.

6 William O. Lynch, "Zachary Taylor as President," in *Journal of Southern History* (Aug. 1938), 282.

7 Ibid., 290-91.

8 "Reminiscences of Washington" (Feb. 1881), 234.

9 Horace Greeley to Schuyler Colfax, March 17, 1849, in Allan Nevins, *Ordeal of the Union*, 8 vols. (New York, 1970), 1:229.

10 Benjamin Brown French, *Witness to the Young Republic: A Yankee's Journal*, Donald B. Cole & John J. McDonough, eds. (Hanover, NH, 1989), 214.

11 Parmelee, "Recollections of an Old Stager" (Oct. 1873), 588.

12 Taylor to J. S. Allison, April 22, 1848, in Homer Hamilton, *Zachary Taylor, Soldier in the White House* (Indianapolis, 1951), 79-80.

your whisky."[13] About the same time, he told the New York publisher Thurlow Weed, "The idea that I should become president seems to me too visionary to require a serious answer. It has never entered my head, nor is it likely to enter the head of any sane person."[14]

But the idea of a Taylor candidacy lodged firmly in other heads. Eventually, as the clamor for him rose, he admitted he would serve, "if the good people were to be imprudent enough as to elect me."[15] The Whigs finally wrested from him the tortured admission, "I am a Whig, but not ultra Whig."[16] What that meant was that he was "a Whig in principles" and had owned up to that "on all proper occasions."[17] Whig principles basically meant being in favor of a national bank, an internal improvement system, a high protective tariff, and keeping slavery out of the territories.

Taylor's desire, if he had to be president, was to "not be the mere President of a party. I would endeavor to act independent of party domination. I should feel bound to administer the government untrammeled by party schemes."[18] For Whigs who preferred nothing but an ultra-Whig, this was hard to swallow. But in politics, parties often swallow any kind of castor oil if it is spooned up with the presidency.

Taylor's Southern background made Northerners nervous and Southerners overconfident. He turned out to be a boon to neither. The other major party, the Democrats, nominated Lewis Cass, the rather ancient U.S. senator from Michigan.

The Free Soil Party nominated a third-party candidate, former president Martin Van Buren. The Freesoilers had a campaign song, "Martin Van of Kinderhook," sung to the air of "Dandy Jim of Caroline:" Its opening four lines:

Come, ye hardy sons of toil,

And cast your ballots for Free Soil;

He who'd vote for Zacky Taylor,

Needs a keeper or a jailor.[19]

13 James Morgan, *Our Presidents* (New York, 1935), 105.

14 Thurlow Weed, *Autobiography of Thurlow Weed*, Harriet A. Weed, ed., 2 vols. (Boston, 1884), 1:573.

15 Brainard Dyer, "Zachary Taylor and the Election of 1848," in *Pacific Historical Review* (Jun. 1940), 174.

16 Taylor to J. S. Allison, April 22, 1848, in Hamilton, *Zachary Taylor*, 80.

17 Weed, *Autobiography*, 1:580-81.

18 Taylor to J. S. Allison, April 22, 1849, in Hamilton, *Zachary Taylor*, 80.

19 From the song book *Free Soil Songs for the People*, no. 19 (Boston, 1848), 21.

But Zacky was politically irresistible to a Whig party dying to get its hands on the White House. The Whigs would love to have him, and they got him. They nominated him at the Whig convention in 1848. Millard Fillmore, a leading New York politician from Buffalo, became his running mate.

After his nomination, the party leaders sent official notice of his nomination to Taylor in the mail. Six weeks passed and not a hint of acknowledgment, acceptance, refusal, thanks, or no thanks came back.

Whig leaders asked themselves, what did this mean? It meant that Taylor, finding his mail expense burdensome, had notified the postmaster in Baton Rouge he was unwilling to pay for un-prepaid mail. Mail delivery in those days was paid by the receiver, not the sender. The postmaster forwarded forty-eight letters, including the nomination announcement, to the dead-letter office. Finally, hearing through channels that he was the nominee, Taylor had the dead-letter mail sent back, dug the letter out, and accepted the nomination.[20]

Peggy Taylor abhorred the idea of her husband being president much as he did. On a steamboat headed for his plantation after the election, a passenger who didn't recognize him introduced the subject of politics. The stranger admitted he had voted for Lewis Cass, not believing the general was qualified. He asked Taylor if he was a Taylor man, and Taylor said, "Not much of a one, partly because he understood Old Zach's wife was opposed to sending him to Washington, where she would be obliged to go with him."[21] Old Zach won, despite Peggy's prayers to prevent it, and she reluctantly had to move with him to Washington.

Taylor was strongly opiniated, allied to a stubborn nature. His plan for solving the problem of slavery in the territories was two-pronged. California needed to become a free state quickly, because of the gold rush and the need for a stable government to control the greedy. He would then admit states carved from the New Mexico territory as soon as they were ready—as either free or slave—their choice.

On the table in the U.S. Senate was a more ambitious five-part plan. It would accomplish the first part of Taylor's plan, but also resolve three other fuse-lit issues threatening a North-South comprise over slavery. The three other measures would strengthen the Fugitive Slave Law, retain slavery in the District of Columbia but disallow the slave trade, and Texas would relinquish its claim to New Mexico territory and in return, the United States would cover Texas's debts. Taylor refused to support this so-called Omnibus Bill, which combined these five issues into one package.

20 Poore tells this dead-letter story in *Perley's Reminiscences*, 1:345-46.

21 Margaret Klapthor & Allida Black, *First Ladies of the United States of America* (New York, 2006), 32.

Taylor's obstinacy was partly personal. He simply didn't get along with the Whig leaders who ran the machinery in Congress. He had a dispute with Henry Clay, who wanted to be the Whig nominee for president in 1848, and was upset about being passed over, so he refused to campaign for Taylor.

The mutual animosity lingered on. "I have never before seen such an Administration," Clay grumbled. "There is very little cooperation or concord between the two ends of the avenue. There is not a prominent Whig in either House that has any confidential intercourse with the Executive." Clay was, if not happy, at least resigned to the situation. "I think it quite likely," he wrote a friend, "that . . . neither I nor my friends will find much favor at Court." Clay called his relations with the Executive "civil but cold. We have very little intercourse of any kind."[22]

Most Whig leaders were as out of grace with the president as Clay. Daniel Webster said, "But what can I do? He never consults me, nor asks my advice."[23]

Taylor had dealt himself out of a hand at the table. Never one to retire under fire, Taylor, proud and sensitive, stood his ground, no matter the consequence. He could no more surrender in politics than he could on a battlefield.

One issue on the table might lead to a battlefield. Among the five issues in the Omnibus Bill, one was what to do about Texas, a slave state. Slave-holding Texans were claiming much of New Mexico, a free territory, and threatening to take it by force.

Taylor bristled at this overt threat to New Mexico's independence. It was a bristling that would well give Texas pause, for this sort of problem was in Taylor's wheelhouse. Taylor said that he personally would lead an army to the territory if Texas tried any such thing. He meant it, and everybody knew he meant it, and everybody knew he could and would do it. Texas did not relish challenging the soldier in Zachary Taylor.

Texas annexing New Mexico would be Union-busting in Taylor's mind, and he would not stand for it. He was, above everything, a Unionist. He was not about to let one state run roughshod over another if he could help it.

During his brief presidency, Taylor attributed the national chaos over slavery to both the abolitionist Northerners and the pro-slavery Southerners. Taylor would be president for only sixteen months. Death stalked the old soldier, taking him in mid-1850, as it had taken Calhoun earlier, on the last day of March. Taylor had

22 Clay to James Harlan, March 15, 1850 and March 13, 1849, in Calvin Colton, *The Life, Correspondence, and Speeches of Henry Clay*, 6 vols. (New York, 1857), 4:604, 586, 603.

23 Daniel Webster to J. Prescott Hall, May 18, 1850, in C. H. Van Tyne, ed., *The Letters of Daniel Webster* (New York, 1902), 412.

celebrated July Fourth, sitting too long in a hot sun, bombarded by an interminable patriotic "long spread-eagle address,"[24] by Senator Henry Foote of Mississippi. Back at the White House, hot and hungry, Taylor gorged on cherries and cream, contracted acute cholera morbus—gastroenteritis—and it killed him, right in the middle of the argument with Congress over how to defuse the intense Union-shattering problem of slavery in the territories. When he unexpectedly died, just as his life was ended, so was his input for a solution to the problem.

The Tranquility President

With Taylor dead, Millard Fillmore, the vice president, now found himself in charge of the national chaos.

Fillmore was a handsome and friendly man, with white hair, a sturdy frame, blue eyes, and a rosy complexion. He was always self-composed, not in any way showy or brilliant, but plain and sensible. He was not a mesmerizing orator in the fashion of the times. But he looked like a president. It was easy to see that he looked more like one than "Old Rough and Ready" did.

Fillmore could have been the poster boy for how to stay healthy. He said, "I attribute my good health to the fact of an originally strong constitution, to an education on a farm and to life-long habits of regularity and temperance. I never smoked or chewed tobacco. I never knew intoxication. I never allowed my usual hours for sleep to be interrupted. The Sabbath I always kept as a day of rest." Throughout his days in Congress and the presidency, he was proud to say, "my labors were always onerous and even excessive, but I never suffered an hour of sickness throughout them all."[25]

His health was the more remarkable because Fillmore was a child of near-poverty. His father was a tenant farmer in New York. Fillmore taught himself to read and dragged himself up educationally with his own pulleys. He made substantial progress when he got help from a schoolteacher named Abigail Powers, two years his elder, and the daughter of a Baptist minister. Abigail was "tall, spare and graceful, with auburn hair, light blue eyes and a fair complexion."[26]

Fillmore admired her blue eyes and auburn hair as much as he admired her syntax. They fell in love and were married in Moravia, New York, Fillmore's

24 Poore, *Perley's Reminiscences*, 1:377.

25 *Publications of the Buffalo Historical Society*, Vol. 10, Millard Fillmore Papers, vol. 1, Frank H. Severance, ed. (Buffalo, NY, 1907), xxxvi.

26 "Reminiscences of Washington" (Apr. 1881), 539.

Millard Fillmore

Library of Congress

birthplace, in 1826. They had been engaged for seven years—not the kind of lovers who rushed into things.

Twenty-four years later, when Abigail became the First Lady, she, like so many other first wives, was less than thrilled. Jane Pierce, who succeeded her as First

Lady, passed out when she heard her husband Franklin had been nominated. It appeared to some wives to be a wrong turn into horror. Abigail Fillmore had rather read a book. Indeed, she may have been the most bookish of all our first ladies. Appalled to discover the White House had no library, she charged her husband to appropriate $2,000 from Congress so she could start one. That was the beginning of the splendid White House Library. She was the White House's First Librarian.

In his youth, Fillmore apprenticed to a cloth dresser, and then to a textile mill. After becoming literate, he became a lawyer and went into politics. He started his political career in the New York legislature in 1828, before he was thirty years old, rising rapidly. Elected to Congress from Buffalo in 1832, he served for a decade, much of it as chairman of the powerful House Ways and Means Committee. Ex-President John Quincy Adams, who served with him in the House, said of Fillmore, "whether to the nation or to the State no service can be or will be rendered by a more able or a more faithful servant."[27] High praise from a top source.

In 1844, the Whig party nominated Fillmore to be governor of New York. He lost the race, the first defeat of his political career. But even then, he was being talked about as a potential vice-presidential candidate on the Whig ticket.

Fillmore's political career took a hit when he opposed Thurlow Weed and William H. Seward in New York politics. Those two schemers, getting Taylor's ear, took control of patronage in New York, pick-pocketing the new vice president's perks and influence. Then Taylor died, and Fillmore became president. Overnight, it was Fillmore calling the shots, not Weed and Seward.

Fillmore secretly supported the controversial Omnibus Bill, but stayed neutral through the Senate debates. It is perhaps a measure of his even-handedness that in the North he was seen as a pro-Southerner, while the South accused him of being an abolitionist. That often happened to any leader who was moderate on the issue of slavery.

Fillmore meant to make the Constitution his rule book, regardless of any personal preferences he had. He did not intend that either the abolitionists in the North or the firebrands in the South would sink the Union on his watch.

This meant that Fillmore would be no more amenable to seeing Texas annex New Mexico by force than Taylor. He couldn't lead an army there himself, as Taylor could and would, but he was ready to send an army. Fillmore sent 750 troops, just in case. He also sent troops south when South Carolina made noises about seizing the U.S. forts in Charleston harbor. He would have nothing to do with threats to the Union any more than Andrew Jackson had in the 1830s, Taylor in the 1850s, or Lincoln in the 1860s.

27 Robert J. Scarry, *Millard Fillmore* (Jefferson, NC, 2001), 81.

The Omnibus crashed in the senate soon after Fillmore became president, though the different parts passed separately, as the Compromise of 1850, and Fillmore was delighted to sign them all.

In Fillmore's two and a half years as president, his eighty-year-old tenant-farmer father, "Squire Fillmore," came to visit once. On his way there a passenger, boasting of his knowledge of Washington and those who ran it, asked, "By the way, where does your son live in Washington? It is just possible I may have heard of him."

"Yes," said the old man, "it is possible. . . . He lives in the White House."[28]

The squire didn't like his son living there and wanted to get out himself. Urged to stay a few days longer, the squire protested, "No, no! I will go. I don't like it here; it isn't a good place to live; it isn't a good place for Millard; I wish he was home in Buffalo."[29]

Fillmore gets a bad rap in history. Only president for a little over two years, historians picture him as weak and vacillating. But Fillmore was self-confident and did what he could to keep the Union one and indivisible. His presidency was one of tranquility. The country was prosperous, quiet, and appeared united once more. He did not win re-election, even though he tried. Considering the two presidents who succeeded him when the Union got un-tranquil again, that was probably not a good thing for the country.

Bar Room Companion

The Union then got Franklin Pierce. He was the first genuine dark horse nominated and elected president in the young country's history. At forty-eight, he was also the youngest ever elected, but had experience in New Hampshire Democratic politics. He was the grandson of a militia brigadier, and son of a former governor of the state.

He was elected to the U.S. House of Representatives in 1833, serving two terms. He later spent most of one term in the U.S. Senate. When the United States went to war with Mexico in 1846, he left his Senate seat and enlisted in the army. No Senator, politics being what it was, stayed long in the army as a private. They instantly promoted him to brigadier general, in no way because of merit. Pierce knew nothing of military science. But he was an ardent Democrat. President James Polk, also an ardent Democrat, was willing to elevate him. As with most political generals, Pierce did not distinguish himself in Mexico. But neither did he do much damage to Manifest Destiny.

28 Ibid., 96-97.

29 Poore, *Perley's Reminiscences*, 1:386.

Franklin Pierce

Library of Congress

He was distinguished enough, however, for his name to be palpitating offstage when the Democratic Party deadlocked in its national convention in 1852. The convention nominated Piece after being unable to choose between James Buchanan or Stephen A. Douglas on the forty-ninth ballot. When she heard the news, his wife, Jane, fainted.

His opponent, as much a hero of the U.S.-Mexican War as Taylor, was Gen. Winfield Scott, the Whig nominee, who thought he wanted to be president. Scott was a great general, but like Taylor, a clueless politician. Magnificent on a battlefield, he was a bombastic, too-wordy, foot-in-the-mouth misfit for politics. Pierce, also a misfit but for other reasons, beat him in a landslide.

Pierce's wife, Jane, was the daughter of a president of Bowdoin College in Maine, Pierce's alma mater. It took Pierce even longer to tie the knot with this beauty than it took Fillmore to marry Abigail. The Pierces courted eight years before they were married in 1834.

Pierce, like Fillmore, looked presidential. He was personable, magnetic, and a fine orator, all ingredients for a great chief magistrate. But as is often the case with American presidents, looks deceived. One contemporary saw Pierce as "a pleasant, amiable gentleman, of moderate capacity, but with no more voice or authority in the government than his private secretary." Said that critic: "Rather by accident than design he drew about him a cabinet of uncommon ability," and among them "could have had little weight under any circumstances."[30]

Pierce (his friends called him "Purse"[31]) was a boon barroom companion. It is not surprising that he had a drinking problem, both early in his career and after it was over. He would ultimately drink himself to death. At Bowdoin College, he was better known for his social scholarship than for his academic prowess. Nathaniel Hawthorne, a close college friend and well-known American novelist, wrote Pierce's campaign biography.

Pierce's election resulted from the South's preference, not Hawthorne's promotional bio. Southerners loved Pierce, for they knew him as a "doughface": a Northerner who harbored Southern sympathies. Men like that were malleable, as flour dough is malleable. It was said that "he had never given a vote or written a sentence that the straightest southern democrat could wish to blot."[32] His pro-Southern leanings may have had something to do with taking him so long to marry Jane. She was an abolitionist. That tug-of-rope matrimonial arrangement in those days might have been grounds for divorce.

Pierce was popular in New Hampshire, but not highly respected. An innkeeper, asked for an estimate of him, said, "Waal, up here, where everybody knows Frank Pierce, and where Frank Pierce knows everybody, he's a pretty considerable fellow,

30 "Reminiscences of Washington," 590.

31 Ibid. (May 1881), 663; Poore, *Perley's Reminiscences*, 1:414.

32 "Reminiscences of Washington" (May 1881), 663.

I tell you. But come to spread him out over this whole country, I'm afraid that he'll be dreadful thin in some places."[33]

Pierce turned out thinner than the innkeeper suggested. The presidency quickly overwhelmed him. It began under the darkest and most tragic of shadows. Only days before he was to be inaugurated, he and Jane saw their only remaining child, a beautiful boy, Bennie, only 13, crushed before their eyes in a train accident. All three of their children died before reaching maturity.

That final loss devastated Pierce and virtually destroyed Jane. In the White House, she rarely left her bedroom, where she penned letters to Bennie, begging his forgiveness for not loving him enough when he lived, despite the fact that she absolutely doted on him when he was alive. Rarely seen now in public, Jane became known as the "Shadow of the White House." In 1863, she would die of tuberculosis.

Pierce's Unionism ran second place to his strong pro-Southernism, and that was not what the times demanded. In his first message to Congress, he vowed that the domestic tranquility and the Compromise of 1850 would "suffer no shock during my official term, if I have power to avert it."[34]

He had that power, and he failed to avert it. In 1854, the Stephen Douglas-sponsored Kansas-Nebraska Act passed Congress, admitting Kansas into the Union and allowing the country to focus on building a transcontinental railroad. In a sop to the South, Douglas agreed to a repeal of the Missouri Compromise to pass the new act.

Douglas's Kansas-Nebraska Act erased the Missouri Compromise line and cut slaveholders loose to take their slaves into any territory they wished, North or South. Whether a new state would then come in free or slave would be decided by what Douglas called "popular sovereignty," which others liked to call "squatter sovereignty," which meant: let the people in the territory decide.

Not a man of iron will, Pierce was strong-armed into signing the act and making it his own. Rarely in American history has a president made a greater mistake. The event caused anger in the North and led to a major political shift that eventually led to civil war and separation.

So, what can we say of Pierce's unfortunate presidency? Theodore Roosevelt, a later president himself, said of Pierce, he was "a servile tool of men worse than himself . . . ever ready to do any work the slavery leaders set him."[35]

That has been the general lasting opinion of that ill-starred president.

33 Ibid. (May 1881), 666; Poore, *Perley's Reminiscences*, 1:421.

34 Pierce, in his First Annual Message to Congress, 1853.

35 Quoted in a piece by Jay Tolson, *U.S. News and World Report*, Feb. 16, 2007, online version.

Another Doughface

Pierce might have been the worst President yet, but stiff competition was coming up next. The country was about to get James Buchanan.

Buchanan was yet another who looked presidential. He was a Pennsylvanian, its leading lawyer and politician, for over forty years. Becoming president at age sixty-five in 1857, he was handsome, white-haired, and always faultlessly dressed.

He was stalwart-framed, with a fair complexion, light blue eyes, and courtly manners. A passing English visitor thought he resembled "a British gentleman of the past generation, when the grave and dignified bearing of men in power was an essential attribute of their office."[36]

As Pierce was a drinking companion *par excellence*, Buchanan excelled at the dining table. He had a discriminating palate and a knack for holding his liquor. He was accomplished at dining out, but his convivial nature didn't include humor. If he had any, it rarely, if ever, surfaced. Nobody ever remembered hearing a witticism come out of his mouth.

Buchanan never married. He fell in love once, but his intended died mysteriously, and he never ventured into that exotic realm again. Instead, he assembled an army of thirty-five nieces and grandnieces and nephews and grandnephews, many of them orphans or half orphans. He lavished his love on them.

One, whom he made his ward, was Harriet Lane, who called him "Nunc." She became her bachelor uncle's official White House hostess in lieu of a First Lady. She had the good looks and eye-catching physical measurements to match her efficiency, and turned out to be more effective in her job than Nunc was in his. In 1861, the Union navy named a revenue cutter after her, but in 1863, the Confederates captured it. Recaptured at the end of the war, it was sold to private owners, for shipping, and was abandoned at sea in 1881. Harriet, the person, was a charming and diplomatic hostess, the social pacemaker in Washington, and a fashion-setter. She was also a high stepper, who loved to waltz, an activity the stiff-necked Nunc deplored. She loved to step to a new waltz, supposedly dedicated to her, titled "Listen to the Mockingbird."[37]

No man in American history came to the presidency looking better on paper than James Buchanan. For nearly fifty years, he had been a high-level factotum in American political life, a state legislator at 23, a five-term U.S. congressman beginning before he was 30, a U.S. senator for a decade, secretary of state under

36 "Reminiscences of Washington" (Dec. 1880), 800.

37 Robert Nowlan, *The American Presidents from Polk to Hayes: What They Did, What They Said & What Was Said About Them* (Denver, CO, 2014), 22, 224.

James Buchanan

Library of Congress

Polk, the American minister to Russia and then to Great Britain. Some called him "The Old Public Functionary," which he rather liked. He was a lawyer and known for his sharp legal mind. He was also called the "Sage of Wheatland," because of his mansion in Lancaster, Pennsylvania.

Not only was his mansion Southern in design, but so was he. Here was another rampant doughface. He was even more pro-Southern, if possible, than Franklin Pierce. Again, more than ever, that was not what the crisis called for.

In the nominating process of 1856, he was again the front-runner, and this time his lead held. He earned the nomination and won by a narrow margin against Gen. John C. Fremont, the celebrated explorer of the American West. Fremont was the first-ever Republican candidate.

Buchanan came to the presidency with the best of intentions. A determined man, he had a stubborn streak and acted decisively. He didn't want to hear any whispering around about disunion—a nasty word. He would act for union. Buchanan wanted to stop anti-slavery talk in the North and get rid of the Republican party. That a Republican might become president horrified him. He believed that abolitionists and Republicans in the North had caused the uproar over slavery. That the South might be a co-offender in this uncertain, contentious, and jarring situation made little headway with Buchanan.

He made happen just the opposite of what he said he wanted to happen—a peaceable, reunited nation. Few presidents have done more to frustrate their own objectives. That old saw, "We have met the enemy, and it is us," fits this besieged president.

He began his presidency by interfering behind the scenes in the Dred Scott Supreme Court decision that allowed slaveholders to take their slaves to any territory in the country, a right ostensibly granted in the Kansas-Nebraska Act. He vigorously backed a pro-slavery constitution illegally adopted in Lecompton, designed to make Kansas a slave state. In the process, he utterly alienated the powerful Illinois senator, Stephen Douglas, shattered his own Democrat party, and paved the way for a hated Republican, Abraham Lincoln, to be elected president in 1860. So thoroughly did he cripple his own party that it would be twenty-four years before another Democrat sat in his seat.

Worse than all of this, his policies not only did not slow the tide to disunion, they actively quickened it.

Decisive and stubborn in his own fashion, Buchanan swayed with the political breezes, and would jump on and off bandwagons as the prospects suited him. He was a man who liked to operate in a committee setting. Buchanan viewed himself not so much as a president with a cabinet to serve him, but as a first among equals. He was comfortable only with people around him who thought as he did, and he shaped his cabinet to keep in that comfort zone.

Buchanan's operating system by committee caused much of the country to believe he was a tool of his cabinet. To a degree, this was true. All bets were off as everything crashed in the last four months of his presidency. When Lincoln was elected, the southern states seceded.

Buchanan had a fatal flaw. He didn't believe that he could oppose secession under the Constitution, but he also denied the legality of it. Essentially, you have no right to secede; he told the South. But if you do, I do not know that the government can prevent it and legally force you back in again.[38]

New York Senator William Henry Seward lampooned Buchanan's strange policy, which in effect, Seward said, meant: "no state had a right to secede unless it wanted to and that the government must save the Union unless somebody objected."[39]

Buchanan was perhaps, given his long record in public service, too set in his ways to succeed in a time of such crisis. Lincoln was to say in his second message to Congress in December 1862, "The dogmas of the quiet past, are inadequate to the stormy present. The occasion is piled high with difficulty, and we must rise with the occasion. As our case is new, so we must think anew and act anew. We must disenthrall ourselves, and then we shall save our country."[40]

Lincoln could disenthrall himself. Buchanan, blind to the political realities of the time, could not. He had opportunities to act boldly in the right direction. He could have acted evenhandedly toward the North and the South. Buchanan could have worked with the men he hated, the Republicans. He didn't have to alienate Stephen Douglas and cripple his own party, or back a bogus constitution for Kansas. He could have acted for union and not only in Southern interests. Buchanan failed all those opportunities. When he left the presidency, the country he had hoped to save was drifting irreversibly into a civil war.

One biographer, Jean H. Baker, said, "He was that most dangerous of chief executives, a stubborn, mistaken ideologue whose principles held no room for compromise," who because of it "came closer to committing treason than any other president in American history."[41]

In the end, he was happy to be out of the mess he had helped create. No president had spent a more miserable last three months in office than James Buchanan.

This presidential quartet, mostly because of Buchanan and Pierce, along with Taylor and Fillmore, led to the most tragic four years in the history of the new republic. We got the bloody Civil War. Fortunately, we also got Lincoln, one who did not look presidential, but would win the war, end slavery, and save the Union.

38 James Buchanan, Fourth Annual Message to Congress on the State of the Union (Dec. 1860).

39 Jean. H. Baker, *James Buchanan* (New York, 2004), 128.

40 Lincoln, *CW*, 5:537.

41 Baker, *James Buchanan*, 141.

Chapter 3

Presidents and Their Ladies

Abraham Lincoln is the most unforgettable of all the unforgettables of the Civil War era.

His wife, Mary Lincoln, has an unforgettable elan of her own, for better or worse. Jefferson Davis was the besieged president of the Confederacy, as Lincoln was of the Union. He had at his side Varina Davis, his bluestocking wife, who had grave reservations about the war. At Varina's side, eloquently defending her friend's husband, if not the cause, was Mary Boykin Chesnut. She was the preeminent Confederate diarist of the Civil War and ardent Davis friend.

These five figures, at the top of the two warring sides in the Civil War, are preeminently unforgettable.

The Word Splitter in the White House

The earliest recorded words of a young Abraham Lincoln were written in a copybook:

Abraham Lincoln

His hands and pen

he will be good

but God knows When.[1]

1 Lincoln, *CW*, 1:1.

Abraham Lincoln

Library of Congress

In messages, speeches, documents, debates, and letters to people, politicians, editors, and generals, an adult Lincoln would write eloquently to save the Union. A political leader of the rarest order, his words would also elevate him into the front rank of American letters. No president before or since can match his consistent eloquence.

To write effectively, as Abraham Lincoln did, a writer must employ whatever makes his or her writing clear, powerful, poetic, imaginative, readable, and functional. Lincoln knew how to make writing all that and more. Repeatedly, he wielded this mastery of poetic prose as the Union's president and commander-in-chief in the Civil War, and before. Some suggest that he extracted "obedience from words,"[2] and it is not too much to believe that with those words, so obedient to him, he won the war.

When Earl Foell, a former editor of *The Christian Science Monitor*, died, a century and a half after Lincoln, the *New York Times* ran his obituary. The *Times* hailed Foell for his "romantic attachment to precision and clarity."[3] This also describes Lincoln as a writer. He had a binding attachment to the precision of words and, like Foell, was always "throwing ropes of clarity."[4]

A president needs to communicate well with the army, politicians, editors, and the people, particularly during wartime. Lincoln's mastery of words set him apart from other powerful men of his time. He understood the power of the word. The rail-splitter was also a word-splitter.

Lincoln wrote and spoke plainly. He spoke not only to the mind, but to the heart. What he wrote was inspiring and lovely to heart, mind, and ear. Roy Basler, editor of Lincoln's collected works, who knew his writing perhaps better than anybody, has said that he was "an indisputable master of language," and his language was "grandly beautiful."[5]

Lincoln had a lyric writing voice that weaved unforgettable images. Yet his prose had a wondrous, spare, precise quality. It was not enough for him simply to be plain in speech or word, however. He crafted everything with care and precision. He wrote as he led, deliberately, always searching for the right words and actions to give his thoughts power and meaning. This is difficult, and rarely achieved. Lincoln did not use words loosely. He groped, searched, discarded, experimented with words—as all influential writers must.

2 Jacques Barzun, *Lincoln the Literary Genius* (Evanston, IL, 1960), 26.

3 *New York Times* obituary, Jul. 13,1999.

4 Roderick Nordell, "The Incomparable Earl," in *The Christian Science Monitor*, Jul. 12, 1999.

5 Roy P. Basler, *A Touchstone for Greatness: Essays, Addresses, and Occasional Pieces about Abraham Lincoln* (Westport, CT, 1973), 71-72.

A city editor in the twentieth century posted a note on the message board in his newsroom for his reporters to read and live by. "You may use verbs freely," the editor warned, "but clear all adjectives with me."[6]

Lincoln was always clearing his adjectives, and every word, with his own internal writer's tuning fork. He would challenge each word and phrase, exchanging them for stronger words—for language that flew straighter to the heart of what he was trying to convey. The writer Jacques Barzun said Lincoln "undertook to frame all his public and private ideas with the care of a conveyancer, but in the language of daily life."[7]

Good writing demands to be polished and re-polished, fine-tuned, and articulated with great care. Lincoln knew—or sensed—that delivering a message properly might be as important as the message itself. It is rare for a writer to be finished after the first draft. That first coat is more than likely raggedy, unfinished, and not quite right. It likely needs mending, more work, more fine-tuning. Lincoln understood this. He would try on as many coats as needed. He polished and buffed his language within the limits of the time he had to produce it. Some say he used words as "as a mathematician uses his formulae,"[8] communicating with crystal clarity, brevity, and style.

There are words, and there are words. Words can be dull. Others can be sublime. Every talented writer knows the difference. Lincoln always reached for the sublime, particularly when the occasion and the times demanded it, which it so often did in his time.

He wrote a language that is gorgeously sublime, akin to music. The Gettysburg Address, his second inaugural, passages from his messages to Congress, and letters to politicians, editors, generals, and plain, grieving people, constituted his music. John G. Nicolay, Lincoln's primary personal secretary, remarked that the brevity of his work was one of the great strengths of his "music" and his principal trait as a writer.[9] It differed from the florid, histrionic style of most orators and writers of his time. Louis A. Warren, an early Lincoln historian, wrote, "He could compress the most profound and comprehensive ideas into the most condensed wordage of any contemporary statesman."[10]

6 This is from a notice on a newspaper city room bulletin board, which I saw early in my own newspaper career, and the origin of which I never knew.

7 Barzun, *Lincoln the Literary Genius*, 34.

8 Basler, *A Touchstone for Greatness*, 94.

9 John G. Nicolay, "Lincoln's Gettysburg Address," in *Century Magazine* 47, no. 4 (Feb. 1894), 597.

10 Louis A, Warren, *Lincoln's Gettysburg Declaration: "A New Birth of Freedom"* (Fort Wayne, IN, 1964), 128.

A fellow lawyer in Illinois said of him, "He always said things short, things shorter than anyone else."[11]

Nicolay remarked that Lincoln's usual habit was to use "great deliberation in arranging his thoughts, and molding his phrases mentally, waiting to reduce them to writing until they had taken satisfactory form."[12] Another writer said that he possessed an "extraordinary ability to see to the core of a question, and to state his convictions with a homely but logical and acutely telling force."[13] His writing was lean and taut. Gary Wills, in his excellent study of the Gettysburg Address, said words were Lincoln's weapons.[14]

He wielded those weapons with one central objective in mind: to be understood. Being understood meant everything to Lincoln. His intent was to deliver a coherent message that the people could readily grasp. Lincoln wrote to make "an obscure thought clear and a clear thought clearer."[15] Lincoln understood the importance of clearly communicating in those terrible war times. He once said that he was writing so that any boy twelve years old could comprehend what he was saying.[16]

That is why Lincoln told stories. He must have understood that a good story is the most effective way of communicating anything. He did not deal with abstractions. War is concrete. The language of war must be concrete. William B. Herndon, Lincoln's law partner in Illinois, said, "Mr. Lincoln was a very patient man generally, but if you wished to be cut off at the knee, just go at Lincoln with abstractions, glittering generalities, indefiniteness, mistiness of idea or expression."[17]

Barzun has called Lincoln a "literary artist, the maker of a style unique in English prose and doubly astonishing in the history of American literature, for nothing led up to it." Barzun said Lincoln wrote with "a lighting-like brevity," with a "fire and a control which show the master," and with "a vividness and force" that would be remarkable in any writer.[18] He shaped sentences that lingered

11 Ibid.

12 Nicolay, "Lincoln's Gettysburg Address," 597.

13 Junius. B. Remensnyder, "With Lincoln at Gettysburg," in *Magazine of History with Notes and Queries* (1926), 12.

14 Gary Wills, *Lincoln at Gettysburg: The Words that Remade America* (New York, 1992), 174.

15 Daniel Kilham Dodge, *Abraham Lincoln: The Evolution of His Literary Style*, quoted in Basler, *A Touchstone for Greatness*, 78.

16 Francis B. Carpenter, *Six Months at the White House with Abraham Lincoln: The Story of a Picture* (New York, 1867), 313.

17 Quoted in Barzun, *Lincoln the Literary Genius*, 16-17.

18 Ibid., 3, 17-18.

in the ear—like magnificent pieces of music. His words had rhythm and poetry, hallmarks of great writing.

Lincoln was one of the most underestimated men ever to assume that high office. An editor of an opposition newspaper once questioned Lincoln's ability to write, asking: "Who will write this ignorant man's state papers?"[19] That stunning lack of insight matches a comment in a news story in 1863 after Lincoln delivered the brief Gettysburg Address: "Once again the President has made an ass of himself."[20]

Lincoln seemed willing to use anything that worked in shaping the prose-poetry that he wrote. A strict obedience to proper grammar sometimes doesn't get the job done. During his first message to Congress in Special Session on July 4, 1861, after the start of the Civil War, Lincoln used the term "*sugar-coated*." The government printer, John D. Defrees, objected, believing it a term that lacked dignity. Lincoln said to Mr. Defrees, "Defrees, that word expresses precisely my idea, and I am not going to change it. The time will never come in this country when the people won't know exactly what sugar-coated means."[21] It remained in the message. Repeatedly, the quality of clarity reigned preeminent in that talented writer's style.

Roy Basler believed that Lincoln's writing was "applied art, utilitarian in purpose and held strictly to the matter in hand." But that applied art also "reached the heights of imagination." With his "deep-moving cadence," Basler said, he was able "to plumb depths hitherto rarely fathomed by oratory."[22]

One tool Lincoln used with power was repetition. Basler called him "one of the greatest repeaters in history, stating again and again some simple truths that needed repeating because, somehow, the American people were in his day, as in ours, great forgetters."[23]

It is no accident that popular songs—extraordinary modes of communication themselves—have choruses, which are often repeated. Lincoln must have understood that. He used it as a weapon in his own powerful literary arsenal.

Lincoln consistently communicated with his commanders in the field. His earliest attempt was to communicate with Gen. George B. McClellan. Lincoln

19 Warren, *Lincoln's Gettysburg Declaration*, 48.

20 I saw this stunning misinterpretation of that great speech in a frame hanging on a wall in Earl Foell's home. I do not remember in what paper or in what edition. But I have never forgotten what it said. It was obviously from a Democrat newspaper of the time. They couldn't bring themselves to see anything good coming from a Republican president.

21 This incident is recounted in Carpenter, *Six Months at the White House*, 126-27.

22 Basler, *A Touchstone for Greatness*, 93.

23 Ibid., 154.

failed with McClellan; anybody might have. But it was through no fault of his writing. He tried every manner and device to deal with McClellan, from the warm to strictly formal, communicating with grace. The fault lay not with the communicator, but with the communicatee.

For almost a year, Lincoln struggled to get McClellan to lead his well-tuned Union army against the enemy. The president, mostly without malice, would later describe McClellan and his army as "an admirable engineer" and a "stationary engine."[24]

In February 1862, the country and the Congress were nearly out of patience with McClellan. Lincoln was feeling the political heat from both. The popular cry was, "On to Richmond!" But those words were not moving the army.

Lincoln wrote McClellan on February 3, 1862: "My dear Sir: You and I have distinct, and different plans for movement of the Army of the Potomac." McClellan proposed moving down the Chesapeake, to the Rappahannock to Urbanna, running around the flank of the Confederate army facing Washington. Lincoln favored the direct overland route through Manassas. "If you will give me satisfactory answers to the following questions," Lincoln wrote McClellan, "I shall gladly yield my plan to yours":

> 1st. Does not your plan involve a greatly larger expenditure of *time*, and *money* than mine?
>
> 2nd. Wherein is a victory *more certain* by your plan than mine?
>
> 3rd. Wherein is a victory *more valuable* by your plan than mine?
>
> 4th. In fact, would it not be *less* valuable, in this, that it would break no great line of the enemies [sic] communications, while mine would?
>
> 5th. In case of disaster, would not a safe retreat be more difficult by your plan that mine?[25]

There is no fuzz in that communication. Lincoln is throwing McClellan ropes of clarity, hammering home what he wanted to say, like the repetition of a chorus in a song. How many times did he say, "by your plan than mine?"

On April 9, 1862, Lincoln answered McClellan's complaint that he was not being properly sustained on the Peninsula. He wrote the general as a father might a son: "And, once more let me tell you," Lincoln wrote McClellan, "it is indispensable to *you* that you strike a blow. I am powerless to help this . . . The country will not fail to note—is now noting—that the present hesitation to move upon an intrenched enemy, is but the story of Manassas repeated. I beg to assure

24 Isaac Newton Arnold, *The Life of Abraham Lincoln*, 6th ed. (Chicago, 1893), 300.

25 Lincoln, *CW*, 5:118-19.

you that I have never written to you, or spoken to you, in greater kindness of feeling than now, nor with a fuller purpose to sustain you, as far as my most anxious judgement, I consistently can. *But you must act*."[26]

As McClellan continued complaining of a perceived lack of support from Washington, Lincoln again wired him: "I give you all I can, and act on the presumption that you will do the best you can with what you have, while you continue, ungenerously I think, to assume that I could give you more if I would. I have omitted and shall omit no opportunity to send you reinforcements whenever I possibly can."[27]

McClellan's failure to pursue Lee's army after the battle of Antietam in September 1862 tested Lincoln's patience. When McClellan complained about his sore-tongued and fatigued horses, the patient Lincoln momentarily snapped. "Will you pardon me for asking," he wrote the general, "what the horses of your army have done since the battle of Antietam that fatigue anything?"[28]

In mid-October, Lincoln wrote a significant letter to McClellan, because he thought he was not pursuing Lee quickly enough. "You remember," Lincoln began, "my speaking to you of what I called your over-cautiousness. Are you not over-cautious when you assume that you can not do what the enemy is constantly doing? Should you not claim to be at least his equal in prowess, and act upon the claim?"

"In coming to us," Lincoln said of Lee's army, "he tenders us an advantage which we should not waive. We should not so operate as to merely drive him away. As we must beat him somewhere, or fail finally, we can do it, if at all, easier near to us, than far away. If we can not beat the enemy where he now is, we never can, he again being within the entrenchments of Richmond."[29]

Lincoln told McClellan, clearly and forcefully, that he could do this "if our troops march as well as the enemy; and it is unmanly to say they can not do it."[30] But McClellan still didn't move. When Lee managed to get between McClellan and Richmond, Lincoln fired the general. He then explained to his friend, Francis Blair, that McClellan "has got the slows."[31]

26 Ibid., 5:185.

27 Ibid., 5:286.

28 Ibid., 5:474.

29 Ibid., 5:460-61.

30 Ibid.

31 William Ernest Smith, *The Francis Preston Blair Family in Politics*, 2 vols. (New York, 1933), 2:145.

McClellan didn't comprehend Lincoln's simple messages. It is not difficult to understand what Lincoln was saying. Every line he threw out to that general was a rope of clarity.

Many of Lincoln's messages to his generals are classics. One of these is his letter to Gen. Joe Hooker, giving him command of the Army of the Potomac on January 26, 1863. Lincoln wrote:

> I have heard, in such a way as to believe it, of your recently saying that both the Army and the Government needed a Dictator. Of course it was not *for* this, but in spite of it, that I have given you the command. Only those generals who gain successes, can set up dictators. What I now ask of you is military success, and I will risk the dictatorship. The government will support you to the utmost of its ability, which is neither more nor less than it has done and will do for all commanders . . . and now, beware of rashness. Beware of rashness, but with energy, and sleepless vigilance, forward, and give us victories."[32]

Lincoln's friend, reporter Noah Brooks, later wrote that Hooker read that letter aloud to him, and that he finished it almost with tears in his eyes. As he folded it and put it back in the breast pocket of his coat, Hooker said to Brooks, "That is just such a letter as a father might write to his son. It is a beautiful letter, and, although I think he was harder on me than I deserve, I will say that I love the man who wrote it."[33]

The man who wrote it was a master of earthy metaphors. He used them with everybody, and repeatedly in his dealings with his generals. The noted Civil War historian, James M. McPherson, suggests that Lincoln "won the war with metaphors."[34] Hooker was on the receiving-end of several. "In one word," Lincoln once wired Hooker, "I would not take any risk of being entangled upon the river, like an ox jumped half over a fence, and liable to be torn by dogs, front and rear, without a fair chance to gore one way or kick the other." [35]

Another time he wired Hooker this classic: "If the head of Lee's army is at Martinsburg and the tail of it on Plank road between Fredericksburg and Chancellorsville, the animal must be slim somewhere. Could you not break him?"[36]

Lincoln was a man with a short tolerance for failure to pursue beaten enemies. He had sacked McClellan on those grounds. He vented his extreme disappointment

32 Lincoln, *CW*, 6:78-79.

33 Noah Brooks, *Washington in Lincoln's Time,* Herbert Mitgang, ed. (New York, 1958), 57.

34 James M. McPherson, "How Lincoln Won the War with Metaphors," in *Abraham Lincoln and the Second American Revolution* (New York, 1991), 93.

35 Lincoln, *CW*, 6:249.

36 Ibid., 6:273.

with Gen. George Meade when that general failed to pursue Lee following the victory at Gettysburg. Lincoln wrote Meade a letter, which he never signed or sent. But it clearly said what he felt. "Again, my dear general," he wrote, "I do not believe you appreciate the magnitude of the misfortune involved in Lee's escape. He was within your easy grasp, and to have closed upon him would, in connection with our other late successes, have ended the war. As it is, the war will be prolonged indefinitely."[37]

Lincoln tried to explain to his generals that Lee's army was the actual target, not Richmond, but they failed to understand. "If he [Lee] comes toward the Upper Potomac," he advised Hooker in a telegram in June 1863, "follow on his flank, and on the inside track, shortening your lines, whilst he lengthens his. Fight him when oppertunity [sic] offers. If he stays where he is, fret him, and fret him."[38]

Lincoln soon found a commander more in line with his way of thinking and acting, and with a proven capacity for fretting the enemy. He promoted Ulysses S. Grant to lieutenant general, naming him general-in-chief of the Union armies in March 1864. As Grant prepared to set his army in motion across the Rappahannock River in May, Lincoln wrote:

> Not expecting to see you again before the Spring campaign opens, I wish to express in this way, my entire satisfaction with what you have done up to this time, so far as I understand it. The particulars of your plans I neither know, or seek to know. You are vigilant and self-reliant; and, pleased with this, I wish not to obtrude any constraints or restraints upon you. While I am very anxious that any great disaster, or capture of our men in great numbers, shall be avoided, I know these points are less likely to escape your attention than they would be mine. If there is anything wanting that is within my power to give, do not fail to let me know it. And now with a brave Army, and a just cause, may God sustain you.[39]

None of what Lincoln wrote Grant, however, moved the President to vacate his responsibility. A message he wired to Grant in the field on August 17, 1864, said, "I have seen your despatch expressing your unwillingness to break your hold where you are. Neither am I willing. Hold on with a bulldog gripe [sic], and chew and choke, as much as possible."[40] On April 7, 1865, as the war was nearing its end, and the final Union success was only two days away, he wired Grant:

37 Ibid., 6:328.

38 Ibid., 6:257.

39 Ibid., 7:324.

40 Ibid., 7:499.

"Gen. Sheridan says 'if the thing is pressed I think that Lee will surrender.' Let the *thing* be pressed."[41]

Dealing with generals was one requirement of Lincoln's duty as commander-in-chief. Two other arenas tested his skill with words as well—politics and public speaking. Lincoln mastered both. It was in these utterances, in messages and speeches, that he was at his most eloquent. Many words he uttered have become a common heritage for all Americans of every generation since his time.

Who can deny the powerful eloquence of this appeal to an alienated South in his first inaugural:

> I am loth to close. We are not enemies, but friends. We must not be enemies. Though passion may have strained, it must not break our bonds of affection. The mystic chords of memory, stretching from every battle-field, and patriot grave, to every living heart and hearthstone, all over this broad land, will yet swell the chorus of the Union, when again touched, as surely they will be, by the better angels of our nature.[42]

Or of this from his annual message to Congress in December 1862:

> Fellow-citizens, we cannot escape history. We of this Congress and this administration, will be remembered in spite of ourselves. No personal significance, or insignificance, can spare one or another of us. The fiery trial through which we pass, will light us down, in honor or dishonor, to the latest generation. . . . In *giving* freedom to the *slave*, we *assure* freedom to the *free*—honorable alike in what we give, and what we preserve. We shall nobly save, or meanly lose, the last best, hope of earth. Other means may succeed; this could not fail. The way is plain, peaceful, generous, just—a way which, if followed, the world will forever applaud, and God must forever bless.[43]

What writer would not wish that he had written those sublime passages? Wielding words as weapons, Lincoln used them to tell the American people what was in his mind and in his heart. Fortunately, his skill with words matches both his mind and his heart.

He wrote to James C. Conkling, in Illinois, in August 1863, after Gettysburg and Vicksburg. His message was to be read publicly at a mass political meeting, to which Lincoln was invited, but unable to attend. In that letter, Lincoln reasoned with those who were dissatisfied with him:

41 Ibid., 8:392.

42 Ibid., 4:271.

43 Ibid., 5:537.

> To such I would say, you desire peace; and you blame me that we do not have it. But how can we attain it? There are but three conceivable ways. First, to suppress the rebellion by force of arms. This, I am trying to do. Are you for it? If you are, so far we are agreed. If you are not for it, a second way is, to give up the Union. I am against this. Are you for it? If you are, you should say so plainly. If you are not for force, nor yet for *dissolution*, there only remains some imaginable *compromise*. I do not believe any compromise embracing the maintenance of the Union, is now possible. All I learn, leads to a directly opposite belief.

Lincoln's letter to Conkling cogently argued for freedom, the Emancipation Proclamation, and the mobilization of black soldiers. Then he said in his eloquent way these words, now such a part of our written canon:

> The signs look better. The Father of Waters again goes unvexed to the sea. . . . And while those who have cleared the great river may well be proud, even that is not all. It is hard to say that anything has been more bravely, and well done, than at Antietam, Murfreesboro, Gettysburg, and on many fields of lesser note. Nor must Uncle Sam's Web-feet be forgotten. At all the watery margins they have been present. Not only on the deep sea, the broad bay, and the rapid river, but also up the narrow muddy bayou, and wherever the ground was a little damp, they have been, and made their tracks. Thanks to all. For the great republic—for the principle it lives by, and keeps alive—for man's vast future—thanks to all.[44]

The *London Star* later wrote of the letter: "It is a masterpiece of cogent argument, as an appeal to the spirit of the nation it is sublime in the dignified simplicity of its eloquence. It is worthy of a Cromwell or a Washington."[45]

I loop politicians in Civil War times with editors, as the differences were blurred. In his dealings with editors, who would insert themselves, uninvited, into affairs of state, Lincoln would scale the heights of eloquence and meaning. As in everything, he wrote to editors for a purpose. In August 1862, he wrote a famous letter to Horace Greeley, which helped him finalize the Emancipation Proclamation. Waiting for a victory on which to hang the Proclamation, Lincoln found it after the bruising battle at Antietam, a stand-off which he deemed victory enough.

He wrote these famous words, reasoning not only with Greeley, but the American people. He was preparing them for what was to be the most important of all his public papers. "I will save the union," he wrote Greeley:

> I would save it the shortest way under the Constitution. The sooner the national authority can be restored; the nearer the Union will be 'the Union as it was.' If there be those who

44 Ibid., 6:406-7, 409-10.

45 Quoted in Warren, *The Gettysburg Declaration*, 51.

> would not save the Union, unless they could at the same time save slavery, I do not agree with them. If there be those who would not save the Union unless they could at the same time *destroy* slavery, I do not agree with them. My paramount object in this struggle *is* to save the Union, and is *not* either to save or to destroy slavery. If I could save the Union without freeing *any* slave I would do it, and if I could save it by freeing *all* the slaves I would do it; and if I could do it by freeing some and leaving others alone I would also do that. What I do about slavery, and the colored race, I do because I believe it helps to save the Union; and what I forbear, I forbear, because I do *not* believe it would help save the Union. I shall do *less* whenever I shall believe what I am doing hurts the cause, and I shall do *more* whenever I shall believe doing more will help the cause. I shall try to correct errors when shown to be errors; and I shall adopt new views so fast as they shall appear to be true views.[46]

These are words of clarity, meaning, and power. There is magic in Lincoln's words, music that repeatedly merges with his great thoughts. This is best viewed within his Gettysburg Address and the Second Inaugural.

"Four score and seven years ago," he wrote in the Gettysburg Address, "our fathers brought forth on this continent, a new nation, conceived in Liberty, and dedicated to the proposition that all men are created equal." From that powerful beginning to its soaring ending: "[T]hat we here highly resolve that these dead shall not have died in vain—that this nation, under God, shall have a new birth of freedom—and that government of the people, by the people, for the people, shall not perish from the earth."[47] These are words of unsurpassed beauty.

When have words of healing ever carried such power and eloquence as these of the Second Inaugural? "With malice toward none; with charity for all; with firmness in the right, as God gives us to see the right, let us strive on to finish the work we are in; to bind up the nation's wounds; to care for him who shall have borne the battle, and for his widow and his orphan—to do all which may achieve and cherish a just, and a lasting peace, among ourselves, and with all nations."[48]

Together with his public speeches, Lincoln wrote personal letters to console the bereaved. These Lincoln also intended for more hearts than just those most directly grieved. He knew these would likely become public documents, and wrote them to last, from his heart to theirs. He wrote the parents of Elmer Ellsworth, his young friend, a colonel of the Zouaves, who was killed at the very start of the war: "In the hope that it may be no intrusion upon the sacredness of your sorrow, I have

46 Lincoln, *CW*, 5:388-89.

47 Ibid., 7:23.

48 Ibid., 8:333.

ventured to address you this tribute to the memory of my young friend, and your brave and early fallen child. May God give you that consolation which is beyond all earthly power."[49]

On December 23, 1862, he wrote young Fanny McCullough, who had lost her father, also a friend of Lincoln's, at a night battle near Coffeeville, Mississippi. "It is with deep grief," Lincoln wrote, "that I learn of the death of your kind and brave Father; and especially, that it is affecting your young heart beyond what is common in such cases. In this sad world of ours, sorrow comes to all; and, to the young, it comes with bitterest agony, because it takes them unawares."

"You are sure to be happy again," he wrote consolingly. "To know this, which is certainly true, will make you some less miserable now. I have had experience enough to know what I say; and you need only to believe it, to feel better at once. The memory of you dear Father, instead of an agony, will yet be a sad sweet feeling in your heart, of a purer, and holier sort than you have known before."[50]

Such powerful words, written heart-to-heart, remain another Lincoln hallmark. Both in private letters, and in public messages and speeches, Lincoln could carry strong thoughts on the wings of sublime words. He put his thoughts into words better—and to greater effect—than any other American president and commander-in-chief. What he said, and how he said it, as much as what he did, have made him immortal.

Roy Basler remarked, "The study of Lincoln's works reveals the dignity of a great mind and heart that seeks for rightness in principle, fairness in act, and beauty in utterance."[51]

Mary Lincoln's "Fiery Furnace of Affliction"

Mary Lincoln may have been a psychic. As a teenager in Kentucky, she predicted she would marry a man one day who would become the President of the United States. That she would pick Abraham Lincoln, a towering country bumpkin, seemed a long shot.

She said early in their marriage, "He is to be President of the United States one day. If I had not thought so I never would have married him, for you can

49 Ibid., 4:386.

50 Ibid., 6:16-17.

51 Basler, *A Touchstone for Greatness*, 100.

Mary Lincoln

Library of Congress

see he is not pretty. But look at him. Doesn't he look as if he would make a magnificent President?"[52]

52 John B. Roberts, *Rating the First Ladies: The Women Who Influenced the Presidency* (New York, 2004), 107.

Her nickname was "Molly"[53] and she was a flirt. Mary was a tad on the plump side, but had soft brown hair, with alluring blue eyes. Quick-witted, and highly cultured, she was also frank, spirited and candid. An accomplished dancer, and fluent in French, she was slightly frivolous, social-minded, and fond of glitter, show, partying, and pomp. She was a skilled seamstress who stitched her own gowns, using very rich cloth. She had an acute sense of style and wore flowers in her hair.

While visiting her sister, Elizabeth, and her husband, Ninian Edwards, in Springfield, Illinois, Mary ramped up her search for a husband who would also be sure to become the president of the United States. The Edwards home was the center of social life in Springfield. From this strategic headquarters, this alluring package was drawing the boys in. Her polar opposite, Lincoln, found her fascinating. Apparently, Mary saw potential greatness, despite his social awkwardness and his two left feet on the dance floor. He told her, "Miss Todd, I want to dance with you in the worst way," and when finished, she said, dryly, "And he certainly did."[54]

A pair of her biographers stated, "she could flutter a fan with the best of them."[55] A political rival of Lincoln's, and possibly a more graceful dancer, was Stephen A. Douglas. Douglas was also a rival for Mary's hand. These two young and ambitious Illinois politicians were vastly different, not only in their political affiliations and respective positions, but in their length as well. Lincoln towered a rail-thin six feet, four inches, while Douglas stood a foot shorter and was built like a stump.

Mary was shorter than Lincoln by about the same length. She finally snagged this tower of political potential in November 1842, after an up and down courtship, which was broken off once. What Lincoln had in Mary for a wife when it finally happened was a volatile mixture. She was smart, sensitive, impulsive, short-tempered, and aflame with ambition for her husband to scale political heights.

She clearly wanted no help in this project from other women, however. Anything that approached Lincoln in petticoats was, for Mary, persona non grata. She was not above throwing a hissy fit and insulting them to drive them away.[56] Lincoln's two young personal secretaries, John Nicolay, and John Hay, called her the "hellcat, who is getting more hellcattical day by day."[57] They had other

53 Justin G. Turner & Linda Levitt Turner, *Mary Todd Lincoln: Her Life and Letters* (New York, 1972), 12.

54 Quoted in Katherine Helm, *The True Story of Mary, Wife of Lincoln* (New York, 1928), 74.

55 Turner & Turner, *Mary Todd Lincoln*, 9.

56 Examples of Mary's volcanic jealousy are described in H. Donald Winkler, *The Women in Lincoln's Life* (Nashville, TN, 2001), 212-14.

57 John Hay, *At Lincoln's Side: John Hay's Civil War Correspondence and Selected Writings*, Michael Burlingame, ed. & intro. (Carbondale, IL, 2000), 20.

names for her, none complimentary: "Madame," "the Enemy," and "Her Satanic Majesty."[58] She didn't like the boys either, especially Hay.

When she got her man to the presidency, it is highly unlikely that she fainted, as Jane Pierce did. Mary was not destined to be the most popular of the First Ladies. She had relatives from Kentucky who seceded with the Confederacy, and this put her allegiance to the Union under a shadow. She was a spendthrift, going on shopping binges in New York, spending heavily and keeping Lincoln in the dark. Orville Browning, a close friend of Lincoln from Illinois, told an interviewer that Lincoln was "constantly under great apprehension lest his wife should do something that would bring him into disgrace."[59]

Willie, the couple's third son, died at 11 years old in the White House in 1862. While Lincoln grieved, it took Mary months to recover. She turned to séances in the White House to try to communicate with Willie in the other world. She spoke of her "fiery furnace of affliction."[60] When Willy died, she stopped the weekly summer performances of the Marine Band, widely popular with the Washington public.

Then she suffered the ultimate affliction. After the war ended, Lincoln was assassinated at Ford's Theater as he sat happily by her side watching a comedy. This death devastated Mary even more than it did the country, a psychological wound exacerbated by the loss of her teenage son, Tad, in 1871. Robert, the only son still living, had her committed for a time for emotional instability. Mary never forgave him.[61] Her post-White House years were sad and lonely. She died in Springfield on July 16, 1882, where, as a young woman on the make, she had shined so brightly on the courting circuit.

The Lincoln marriage was often tempestuous. Both partners were likely hard to live with. But they held together in mutual affection and sorrow, with the job of restoring a divided nation to be done.

Despite her emotional swings and sorrowful later life, Mary Lincoln's presence was essential for Lincoln to become president. For that, the country owes her gratitude, not harsh criticism.

58 Ibid., 85, 18; Allen Carden & Thomas J. Ebert, *John George Nicolay: The Man in Lincoln's Shadow* (Knoxville, TN, 2019), 194.

59 In a conversation with Nicolay in John G. Nicolay, *Oral History of Abraham Lincoln: John G. Nicolay's Interviews and Essays*, Michael Burlingame, ed. & intro. (Carbondale, IL, 1996), 3.

60 Mary Lincoln to Hannah Shearer, Nov 20, 1864, in Turner & Turner, *Mary Todd Lincoln*, 189.

61 For an account of Mary's trial and commitment, see Baker, *Mary Todd Lincoln*, 315-50.

The Planter from Brierfield

Jefferson Davis was that other president, the one south of the Potomac. He would lose the war, in a lost and dubious cause. He has therefore taken lumps for his trouble and has come out on the wrong side of history. Losing a war rarely puts anybody on the right side of postwar writing.

It was not because Davis lacked talent. He was a West Pointer, a courageous colonel in the Mexican-American War. Famously, he won national acclaim as a politician before secession. He had been a congressman and a senator in the antebellum Union, also a secretary of war, arguably the ablest in this nation's history. Davis was a Southern planter, with over 100 slaves on a 2,000-acre plantation called Brierfield. His plantation was situated at a bend of the Mississippi River, seventeen miles south of Vicksburg.

Davis was not known for light-hearted banter, and he was not a spinner of humorous stories to drive away his melancholy, as was the president north of the Potomac. Ironically, Davis began life on a note of parental humor. When Jeff was born, his mother, Jane, was almost forty-seven years old. Having already given birth to nine kids in twenty-three years, it was understandable that she felt tired. Jeff was the tenth, and if Jane had any say in it, he would be the last. To put a seal on Jane's druthers, they gave him the middle name, "Finis," the end of producing kids, by God![62] This was in June 1807 or 1808; Davis claims never to have been certain. He pleaded, "I am not a competent witness in the case."[63]

Davis grew up tall for his time, one-half inch under six feet, and was slender and well-formed. Since he was a West Pointer, he carried himself like a soldier, erect and straight-backed. His face was angular, with high cheek bones rising above hollow cheeks. His eyes were gray, but his left one clouded over and became nearly blind, a casualty of herpes and possible secondary glaucoma. The other eye, however, cast a penetrating gaze at all that came into its view. Davis was aristocratic, austere, and high-toned, with a bold, uncowed, unyielding, willful nature and a quick mind. He was gifted with a high intelligence and admirable powers of study and retention, with a ready familiarity with world literature.

He spoke in a supremely modulated baritone voice. His wife, Varina, thought it was "musical in the extreme," melodiously clear, she believed, like a "silver trumpet."[64] But he delivered speeches in a detached, unimpassioned manner,

62 Davis (Varina), *Jefferson Davis,* 1:512; Robert McElroy, *Jefferson Davis: The Unreal and the Real,* 2 vols. (New York, 1937), 1:3.

63 Davis (Varina), *Jefferson Davis,* 1:170.

64 Ibid., 2:303, 1:697.

Jefferson Davis

Library of Congress

much as he addressed life. He dressed, as president, in a plain gray suit and rode an iron-gray horse—ever true to Confederate colors.

There was a wildness in his nature that resented authority. From the beginning, he had trouble taming his spirit of independence. At West Point, Davis was a disciplinary problem. He clocked time in the Academy guard house. Sometimes he went to Benny Havens, a local tavern that was forbidden territory for cadets. Sneaking away to Benny's for grog and Benny's world class flapjacks, and getting caught could bring instant demerits, and possibly dismissal. But Davis thought it was worth it.

Davis had several near-brushes with expulsion in his four years at the Academy. Most of his demerits, however, were for minor misdemeanors such as missing drills, having untidy quarters, missing mandatory chapel, or not storing his gear properly. He loved playing pranks, which also attracted demerits. His record at West Point was a shade less than so-so, graduating twenty-third in a class of thirty-three. His conduct rating ranked even lower, in the bottom fourth in the entire corps. Those rankings, however, would not reflect his standing in life.

Davis was a cornucopia of conflicting traits. He was kind, fun-loving, gentle in private, but cold and austere in public, driven almost wholly by a sense of duty.

Many that have studied Davis have been cold, steely, and critical. He was seen in his time, with some justification, as stiff, humorless, austere, aloof, obstinate, petty, enigmatic, and vindictive. Sam Houston, his fellow senator from Texas, thought him "ambitious as Lucifer and cold as a lizard."[65] People who observed him found him frequently distracted, rude, moody, and argumentative, especially when he was unwell, which was often.

He had a temper, which could unravel the seams of friendship. When out of sorts, he remained that way for some time. He had few actual duels in life, but he had ample near duels. At Gadsby's dining establishment in Washington, he got into a physical altercation with his lifelong enemy, Henry S. Foote, who was also a senator from Mississippi. But he was not the only one who would have liked to punch out the irritating Foote.

Davis was thin-skinned and had an ego that was easily bruised. When his honor was called into question, he became a demon in his own defense. Instinctively, he reacted to any attempt to pressure him into anything. Challenged, he would not back down, and did not like making compromises. Verbally assailed, he would respond in kind, in a tone and a manner that escalated the confrontation rather than mitigating it. There was not much cheek-turning in his nature, or a soft word

65 Henry Bruce, *Life of General Houston, 1793-1863: The Portal to Texas History* (New York, 1891), 215.

to turn away wrath. His critics saw in him a micromanager who could halt all forward movement for hours. But when he came out of a stall, when he reached a position, he believed it was absolutely the right and only position, and all opposing views were wrong.

In the debates on the Compromise of 1850 on the U.S. Senate floor a Wisconsin senator said Davis spoke "with an air—I say it with no disrespect—which seems to say, 'Nothing more can be said—I know it all—it must be as I think.'"[66]

Davis recoiled from anything that smacked of seeking popularity, and that often caused him to appear unfriendly. He was not a glad-handing politician kissing babies. That was the way he was.

There is truth in these dark things his critics saw and which they deplored. But there were softer hues. There were kinder eyes assessing him. Shakespeare wrote in *Love's Labor's Lost*, "Study me how to please the eye indeed. By fixing it upon a fairer eye."[67] There were far fairer, kinder, more loving eyes that looked at Davis in his lifetime. One of them was Varina Davis, who admired him, loved him, married him, and gave birth to his children.

Varina lived with Davis for four decades. A very astute observer, she was not blind to his faults. She wrote her mother after first meeting Davis in 1843, when she was seventeen years old and he was thirty-six, that he was "erect, well-proportioned and active as a boy." He rode, she wrote, "with more grace than any man I have ever seen," giving her the impression of being incapable of being unseated or fatigued.[68]

Despite his grace in the saddle, Davis appeared to Varina at first acquaintance to be something less than a prince on a gray charger. She wrote to her mother that she didn't know whether he was young or old, since to her he looked both. But she believed he was old, only two years younger than her mother. However, he impressed Varina at their first meeting. "A remarkable kind of man, but of uncertain temper," who "has a way of taking for granted that everybody agrees with him when he expresses an opinion, which offends me; yet he is most agreeable and has a peculiarly sweet voice and a winning way of asserting himself. The fact is, he is the kind of person I should expect to rescue one from a mad dog at any risk, but to insist upon a stoical indifference to fright afterward."[69]

Varina did not think she would ever like him as much as she liked his older brother, Joseph. This daughter of an avid Whig father, wrote her mother, "Would

66 *Washington Union*, March 14, 1850.

67 Shakespeare, *Love's Labor's Lost*, act 1, scene 1, lines 80-81.

68 Davis (Varina), *Jefferson Davis*, 1:191.

69 Ibid., 1:191-92.

you believe it, he is refined and cultivated, and yet he is a Democrat!"[70] Varina married that Democrat on February 26, 1845, as he was beginning his remarkable rise in politics.

Politics was perhaps a wrong calling for a man like Davis. He was far more comfortable as a soldier. When called to become the president of the Confederacy, he would much rather have been called to command its armies. As Shakespeare has said, "Some are born great, some achieve greatness, and some have greatness thrust upon 'em,"[71] often in ways, in times, and in places they cannot predict, or desire.

In his time, Davis became a great man politically. As Varina admitted, "he did not know the arts of the politician, and would not practice them if understood. As a party manager he would not succeed."[72] Certainly he had a contempt for politicking and subterfuges, which did not endear him to the politicians and the rules of the game.

Varina wrote that her husband was a man of great inner warmth, painfully sensitive of his own feelings and of those of others. She said he was a man of "super-sensitive temperament . . . abnormally sensitive to disapprobation in particular. Even a child's disapproval discomposed him." He was, "a close observer of everything. Every shade of feeling that crossed the minds of those about him he noticed, and he could not bear anyone to be inimical to him." Varina said he made great "efforts to conciliate even his servants when he thought they were annoyed with him."[73]

If all that is true, it was a side of Davis that many never saw. As a sensitive person, it must have been hard for him to be president of a rebellion and to deal with constant hostility. If Davis wanted to be accepted, the last thing he ought to have become was president of the new and embattled Confederacy.

Varina was ardently against his taking the job. She well knew the misconceptions, the defamation of character, the hatred that went with politics and which would come in endless supply and "darken the sunlight and contract the happy sphere of home."[74] Davis was against taking the job himself. But, as a West Pointer and a soldier, he felt obliged to answer the call of duty when the call came, in whatever form.

Varina had long feared it would happen and foreseen its dreaded outcome. It is said that the year before the war Varina prophesied to a friend, "The South

70 Ibid., 1:192.

71 Shakespeare, *Twelfth Night*, act 2, scene 5, lines 141-3.

72 Davis (Varina), *Jefferson Davis*, 2:12.

73 Ibid., 1:178.

74 Ibid., 1:206.

will secede if Lincoln is made president. They will make Mr. Davis president of the Southern side. And the whole thing is bound to be a failure."[75] Varina Davis was a Cassandra.

In private among friends and family, Varina saw her husband as affectionate, witty, and utterly loyal. She said that "his distinguishing trait, after that of mercy, was filial love and duty." That he was merciful there can be no doubt. Varina wrote of "his tender consideration for the helpless or sorrowful people who came to him." "His heart," she wrote, "was so tender that he was sometimes betrayed into misplaced sympathy." He so greatly abhorred the idea of oppressing the weak, she wrote, "that it was a difficult matter to keep order with children or servants. One of his little daughters once said, "I wish I could see my father, he would let me be bad."[76]

Children were drawn to him. They did not see him as adults did, a cold, rigid, and aloof man. He treated children with warmth, love, and affection, which they reciprocated. He had a tenderness that embraced animals as well, particularly horses. At an early age, he gave up hunting altogether. In his prison cell at Fortress Monroe after the fall of the Confederacy he domesticated a mouse, "the only living thing," he said, "that I now had power to benefit."[77]

As president, his kindness extended to condemned soldiers. Like Lincoln in the North, he was loath to permit a sentenced soldier to die, reversing many capital convictions. Utterly fearless, he never quailed. Not when he commanded the Mississippi Rifles in the Mexican War, or when he came several times under fire as president of the Confederacy. Davis understood the unnerving horror of war and was compassionate of the soldier who feared it.

The warm strain of charity and humanity that ran in him sometimes surfaced through the cold veneer with which he faced his troubled world. Varina has written that there were occasions, when he was president and reading his mail, she would hear him groan and exclaim, "Poor creature, and my hands are tied."[78]

A young woman from South Carolina wrote begging that he let her betrothed soldier, Jeems, of the 5th South Carolina Regiment, come home to marry her. She promised to send him back as soon as they exchanged vows. "I'll make him go straight back when he's done got married and fight just as hard as ever."

75 Mary Boykin Chesnut, *Mary Chesnut's Civil War*, C. Vann Woodward. ed. (New Haven CT, 1981), 800.

76 These various quotes about Davis's tenderness of heart are from Davis (Varina), *Jefferson Davis*, 1:154-56.

77 Ibid., 2:677.

78 Ibid., 2:921.

"Jeems is willin'," she wrote Davis; "I is willin', his mammy says she is willin', but Jeems's capt'n, he aint willin'. Now when we are willin' 'ceptin Jeems's captain, I think you might let up and let Jeems come."

Davis was willin'. He sent the letter to his secretary of war and wrote on the back of it, "Let Jeems go."[79]

With those he loved or admired, Davis was loyal, often to a disastrous fault. During the war, he stayed loyal to his old friends, even though they were not capable of performing well, for the sake of winning the war. On the flip side of this defect was an ability to detest men who had roused his anger. Early in the war, Generals Joseph E. Johnston and P. G. T. Beauregard got on his wrong side. He never forgave or let off being annoyed by them, with some justification.

Throughout his life, sickness and tragedy challenged Davis. His life was shadowed by numerous and intense chronic illnesses. In 1831, a savage case of pneumonia ravaged his constitution and nearly killed him. He would battle sickness and discomfort for the remainder of his life. He often suffered from rheumatism and neuralgia, which caused him facial pain. At times, he ran the Confederacy, propped up on pillows, from his bed. There were times those near him feared he would not live. But an indomitable will drove him.[80] He would live to be eighty-two years old, outliving many far hardier contemporaries and critics.

But it was tragedy that took the biggest toll on Davis throughout his lifetime. Personal tragedy began early in life for him, when Polly, his favorite sister, died in 1824, followed closely by the death of his father, Samuel, later the same year. Davis was only seventeen. The most heartbreaking blow was the tragic death of his first young wife, Sarah Knox Taylor, only three months after their wedding. Malaria contracted in New Orleans, killed her and nearly killed him.

Davis's sister Matilda died in 1834 and his mother, Jane, in 1845, just as he was rising in politics and preparing to take his first seat in Congress. In 1850, when James Pemberton, his longtime black servant who became his plantation overseer and close friend, died of pneumonia, it devastated Davis. After the war, he lost his beloved older brother, Joseph, his twelve-year-old son Willie, and his sister Lucinda in the space of a year.

He and Varina together lost four sons, all dying young, multiplying his allotment of disappointment and sorrow. The loss that unhinged him more than any other was the death of his son Joe in the spring of 1864, as dark clouds of coming defeat were lowering on the Confederacy.

79 Varina tells this story in Ibid., 2:326.

80 Harris D. Riley, Jr., "Jefferson Davis and His Health," *Journal of Mississippi History* 49, 179-202, 262-287.

Early in the war at the battle of Shiloh, Gen. Albert Sydney Johnston, the friend, and fellow West Pointer he admired and cherished more than any other man, was shot in the leg, and bled to death before realizing how serious the wound was. Davis wept. He wept again when Stonewall Jackson died after Chancellorsville, a tear falling on Jackson's open casket. "I am still staggering from a dreadful blow," he said, then, "I cannot think."[81] He wept when he learned in April 1865 that another friend, Robert E. Lee, had surrendered the Army of Northern Virginia to U. S. Grant at Appomattox.

Davis was a slaveholder, with the reputation of a benign and caring one. He forbade his overseers to whip his slaves. There is no record of his ever selling one or splitting families. However, Davis's unusual kindness was a kindness that was patronizing. He viewed blacks as he viewed children and women, as his inferiors, who needed caring for, all slaves, and he the slaveholder.

When he died in 1889, several former slaves wrote Varina a letter, which they signed: "We, the old servants and tenants of our beloved master, Honorable Jefferson Davis, have cause to mingle our tears over his death, who was always so kind and thoughtful of our peace and happiness. We extend to you our humble sympathy."[82]

That he was obstinate, there is no doubt. Varina agreed, in part with his critics, on his decided "certainty of thought" and "sincerity of opinion," which surfaced as an inability to comprehend anyone differing from him on political policy after hearing his reasoning. If they did continue differing with him, he would suspect their sincerity.[83] It was perhaps his Achilles heel as a national leader.

Yet his patience under personal inconvenience was remarkable. His mind, Varina remembered, dominated his body to so great a degree that he could endure and overcome all the stalking sickness and sorrow. He called it "toughing it out."[84] He proved his ability to tough it out repeatedly in his four years leading the Confederacy.

Davis had no talent for jocular rhyme, his wife admitted. But he loved poetry, particularly the works of Robert Burns, which he memorized, a love he shared with Lincoln. Given a line in almost any part of one of Burns's poems, Davis could repeat the rest of the passage. He also loved the poet Virgil and often quoted him.[85]

He was not musically inclined, though he loved listening to songs. Among his favorites were "Had I the Leisure to Sigh and Mourn, Fannie Dearest, I'd Mourn

81 Ibid., 2:382-83.

82 Ibid., 2:933.

83 Ibid., 1:198-9.

84 Ibid., 1:177.

85 Ibid., 1:264, 2:302-4.

for Thee." And such fashionable songs of the day as "Has Sorrow Thy Young Days Shaded," "The Harp That Once in Tara's Halls," and "The Minstrel Boy." In his later years, after war was over, and he had found some peace, he often hummed and sang as he worked in his office old familiar ballads such as "Annie Laurie," "Mary's Dream," and "The Last Rose of Summer." He admired the works of Chopin and often asked Piecake, his youngest child, to play them on the piano.[86]

Varina's view of her husband, enduring perhaps the most hard and critical gaze of any leader in American history, was this: "Forty-three years of intimate companionship, from the beginning of his political career to the end, left me with the profoundest respect for his unswerving mental and moral integrity, his staunch adherence to principle, his self-immolating devotion to duty, his calm, invincible courage, his wide sympathy with mankind, and his unfeigned reverence for his Creator."[87] In her eyes, he was "one of the most patriotic, humane, and benevolent of men." She also believed that his failure owed to the predominance of some of these "noble qualities."[88]

Faced with every hardship, he had a stoic will and unmovable self-control, even as turmoil boiled within him. He never quailed at accepting a daunting challenge or defending a forlorn hope. Nobody worked harder for the cause of the Confederacy than he or kept the faith longer.

A song was written after the war. Here is one version of the first stanza:

Oh, I'm a good old rebel, that's just what I am;
And for this Yankee nation I do not give a damn!
I'm glad I fought again' her I only wish we'd won,
An I don't ask any pardon for anything I've done.[89]

It describes Davis perfectly. He went to his grave not asking pardon for anything he'd done.

86 Ibid., 304-5; *Life and Reminiscences of Jefferson Davis by Distinguished Men of His Time* (Baltimore, 1890), 55.

87 Davis (Varina), *Jefferson Davis*, 2:933.

88 Ibid., 2:2, 2:923.

89 Porter W. Heaps & Willard A. Heaps, *The Singing Sixties: The Spirit of Civil War Days Drawn from the Music of the Times* (Norman, OK, 1960), 391.

Lady Ink-Slinger

Jefferson Davis was no match for Abraham Lincoln with words. However, his wife might claim to be. Varina Davis, the spouse of the man she called "my poor old Prometheus,"[90] knew her way around the English language. Bright, clever, widely read, and literate, the First Lady of the Confederacy knew how to write.

Her talent for penning prose with a poetic sheen was most evident in the many letters she wrote in her lifetime. After the war, she wrote articles for the publishing magnate Joseph Pulitzer's *New York World*, and a two-volume memoir of her husband after his death. The prose in her letters, some smuggled to friends in the North, sparkled.[91]

Writing to Mary Chesnut on October 8, 1864, she described the letter she was writing as "a petty maze, without a plan—meandering on coarse paper with thick ink, a bad pen, and the animus only fit to offer you."[92] Of the 1864 drowning death of Rose O'Neal Greenhow, the famous Confederate spy, Varina wrote that Rose had had a "sudden summons to a higher court than those she strove to shine in."[93]

Varina wrote that her daughter Maggie was dancing "at a fearful rate of shoe leather. Her grace is undeniable, but she comes out at the toes."[94] Because of her son, Jeff's, schoolboy jargon, she predicted that "altogether he seems in a fair way to graduate in down street dialect."[95]

Writing to Mary, she confessed, "I generally let out my crazy bone to you." Something of a skeptic about state rights she wrote: "State rights, and consequently state wrongs, are rampant. Perhaps the new wine will burst the old bottles."[96] Her baby daughter, named Winnie, but called Piecake, Varina described as "christened and not old enough to develop the world's vices or to be snubbed by it."[97]

Two days before Robert E. Lee surrendered the Army of Northern Virginia in Wilmer McLean's front parlor at Appomattox Court House, she wrote, "So I am sitting down, taking account of my dead hopes."[98]

90 Varina Davis to Mary Boykin Chesnut, Apr. 7, 1965, in Chesnut, *Mary Chesnut's Civil War*, 787.

91 Joan E. Cashin, *First Lady of the Confederacy: Varina Davis's Civil War* (Cambridge, MA, 2006), 274.

92 Chesnut, *Mary Chesnut's Civil War*, 663.

93 Ibid., 664.

94 Ibid.

95 Ibid., 666.

96 Ibid., 675.

97 Ibid., 786.

98 Ibid., 786.

Varina Davis

Library of Congress

This kind of writing is the work of one who, like Lincoln, was not content to use words prosaically. One arrow in her considerable quiver, always, was her way with the well-aimed word. In that, she prevailed.

Mary Chesnut, also a wordsmith, counted Varina "among the many larger brained women a kind Providence has thrown in my way." She thought the Confederate First Lady "as witty as [her husband Jefferson] was wise . . . and that her intellect, cleverness, and wit were magnets for other bright women." Mary wrote Varina was "awfully clever—always" and that she "always had clever women around her," that they "gravitate to her." "After becoming accustomed to the spice and spirit of her conversation," Mary noted, "away from her things seemed flat and tame for a while."[99]

Varina was tall for women in her time, five feet, six inches, and of olive complexion. She was "reed thin" as a young woman, taking on heft in her seasoned years. Her speech was eloquent, and she was well-read, especially in the classics, making her a brilliant conversationalist. Both her tongue and her mind were quick. Her eyes, thought by many her most arresting feature, were "dark and expressive."[100]

In some ways, she was not the best fit as First Lady of the Confederacy. She was an unreliable rebel, entertaining doubts, from the beginning, that the Confederacy could win the war. Varina never gave up her friendship with the many northern friends she prized. During the war, she found opportunities to correspond with them *sub rosa.*[101]

Nor was she always the best fit as Jefferson's Davis's wife. She was nearly twenty years younger, still a teenager, when they married. They often disagreed, as husbands and wives will, and Varina seldom prevailed. In those days, what the husband said was law. So, it was with the Davises. "Jefferson," one of Varina's biographers noted, "did not see marriage as a partnership. Wives had many duties, he believed, and not many rights."[102] But Jefferson and Varina soldiered on together through forty years of marriage in peace and war. When he died, she wrote, "I feel like an executed person swinging in chains on a lonely road."[103]

99 The quotes in this paragraph, in order, are from Chesnut, *Mary Chesnut's Civil War*, 56, 62, 80, 91, 429, 733.

100 Cashin, *First Lady of the Confederacy*, 2, 10, 40, 111, 112.

101 Ibid., 117-18, 123, 129, 166-67, 311.

102 Ibid., 50.

103 Quoted in Ishbel I. Ross, *First Lady of the South: The Life of Mrs. Jefferson Davis* (New York, 1958), 364.

Heretic in the Family

Varina's dear friend and fellow defender of Jefferson Davis, Mary Boykin Chesnut, also knew how to hone words. Her biographer has called her diary, *Mary Chesnut's Civil War*, "in many respects the most remarkable firsthand account of the Confederacy ever written."[104]

The diary has been acclaimed by critics and dog-eared by historians for decades. I have dog-eared multiple pages of it myself. That lordly literary critic, Edmund Wilson, calls it "an extraordinary document—in its formal department, a masterpiece . . . a work of art." The "brilliant journal of Mary Chesnut," he wrote, is "so much more imaginative and revealing than most of the fiction inspired by the war."[105] Another literary critic, Daniel Aaron, agrees, claiming she "had the eye and ear of a novelist as well as the temperament."[106]

Mrs. Chesnut's majestic diary did not mask the fact that she entertained multiple heresies little tolerated in the Confederacy. She uttered them openly in her diary, and probably in her conversation, and got away with it.

The late historian, C. Vann Woodward, who had dog-eared her diary perhaps more than any historian, living or dead, is our guide to her heresies. Her father, Stephen Miller, was a leader in the nullification act of his state during the 1830s. He is also credited with originating the idea that slavery was a "positive good." Mary was the wife of one of the great slave plantation heirs of her time. She was the product and elite member of a slave-based society. She was an intimate of Jefferson Davis, a chief defender of slavery. Yet she openly derided states' rights, and detested slavery, and said so.[107]

Indeed, she embodied that ultimate no-no in the Southern catalogue of evil beings: an abolitionist. "God forgive us," she wrote of slavery, "but ours is a monstrous system, and wrong and iniquity." She recorded several times in her diary how she hated it and called it "this black incubus." She foresaw its doom from the war's start and rejoiced in its collapse at the end.[108]

Mary was also heretical about another no-no in the male-dominated Southern society, as deeply entrenched as slavery, if not more so—the heresy of militant feminism. She was the plain-speaking, sharp-tongued defender of oppressed

104 Elizabeth Muhlenfeld, *Mary Boykin Chesnut: A Biography* (Baton Rouge, LA, 1992), 191.

105 Edmund Wilson, *Patriotic Gore: Studies in the Literature of the American Civil War* (New York, 1962), ix, 279.

106 Daniel Aaron, *The Unwritten War: American Writers and the Civil War* (New York, 1973), 251, 259.

107 Chesnut, *Mary Chesnut's Civil War*, xlvi.

108 Ibid., xlvi, 29, 168, 238, 246, 718.

Mary Chesnut

National Archives

womanhood and the male dominance and female subordination that it bred. "There is no slave, after all like a wife," she railed. She believed "all married women, all children, and girls who live in their father's houses are slaves."[109]

In April 1840, Mary Boykin married James Chesnut, Jr., the heir to one of the wealthiest southern plantations. She had just turned seventeen. Her husband was a U.S. senator from South Carolina before the war, and during the war, an aide and intimate of Jefferson Davis. He and Mary moved among the elites in the antebellum South and in the Confederacy, where she was "a woman of discerning intellect and great charm, a woman of strong opinions, strong loves, strong hates."[110]

Through his embattled presidency, Davis had no kinder eye viewing him, besides Varina's, than Mary Chesnut's. Middle-aged, witty, and highly literate, Mary lives for us today as the preeminent Southern diarist. Her diary is an American classic. I have returned to it again and again to help evoke the drama of the Civil War. She is a goldmine of information and observations before and during the war.

109 Ibid., 59, 729.

110 Muhlenfeld, *Mary Boykin Chesnut*, 72.

Varina called her "my dear Mrs. C."[111] She was one of Mrs. Davis's ladies. It was said: "Mrs. Davis's ladies are not young, are not pretty." Mary, confessed, "I am one."[112]

She was also a Jefferson Davis lady. Even before Davis's new Confederate Provisional Government ordered the firing on Fort Sumter in April 1861, Mary was writing, "It seems to me already men are willing to risk an injury to our cause if they may in so doing hurt Jeff Davis."[113] She deplored this. "Mr. Davis's hands ought to be strengthened," she insisted. "He ought to be upheld. A divided house must fall . . . we all say."[114] Distressed, she found many Southerners had forgotten they were fighting the Yankees and were abusing one another. She asked herself, "Are we going to be like the Jews when Titus was thundering against their gates—quarreling?" "Quarreling among ourselves," Mary moaned into her journal, "makes me faint with fear."[115] She wrote of "the senseless abuse heaped upon Jeff Davis."[116] "Here," she complained, writing from Columbia, South Carolina, "I do not know a half-dozen men who would not gaily step into Jeff Davis's shoes, with a firm conviction that they could do better in every respect than he does. The monstrous conceit, the fatuous ignorance of these critics!"[117]

She repeatedly leaped to Davis's defense with her wit and her pen. She decried the cabals against him, holding them in uttermost disdain, refusing to join in. "Thank God I am loyal," she wrote. "I am for *our* side—come what may—for Jeff Davis! The head of the Southern Confederacy! These people 19 hundred years ago would have all been for Pontius Pilate."[118]

Davis might have been thinking of Mary Chesnut when he said, in 1864, "No wonder men were willing to fight for such a country as ours—and such women. They were enough to make heroes of any material."[119]

Yet Mary admitted to being "afraid of him, a little, too much afraid of him," she confessed, "to say very much in his presence."[120] But she was often in his

111 Chesnut, *Mary Chesnut's Civil War*, 117.

112 Ibid., 91.

113 Ibid., 12.

114 Ibid., 136.

115 Ibid., 225.

116 Ibid., 204.

117 Ibid., 305.

118 Ibid., 673.

119 Ibid., 566.

120 Ibid., 17, 549.

presence, invited to sit in his pew at St. Paul's Episcopal Church, and often at the presidential table. Davis liked having Mary sit opposite him, for he liked her style of chat. He was unfailingly kind to her, and she compared him to Moses and believed he would save the Confederacy. "He will be the last man to give up heart and hope," she predicted.[121] As indeed he was.

Mary was a tireless reader of anything that fell into her line of sight, with a special affection for novels. She would often churn her way through a book a day in any of three languages, English, French, or German. Her mother-in-law marveled that she had "a greediness of books such as I never saw in any one else. And strange to say she never buys a book—or has been known to take a magazine or Periodical. But she has them all—they gravitate toward her—flow into her room."[122]

In the late 1860s, after the war, Mary ventured into other writing disciplines, including fiction, but they were misfires compared to her magnum opus of the Civil War.[123]

For that magnificent diary alone, she is enshrined in the pantheon of American literature. There are few Civil War historians who haven't read it, and silently muttered thanks for Mary Chesnut and her keen eye and literate pen.

121 Ibid., 332.

122 Ibid., 49, 51, 53.

123 Chesnut, *Mary Chesnut's Civil War*, xxiv, xlvii.

Chapter 4

Pantheon Commanders

Three great commanders led the armies of the Civil War era. All had earned or enhanced their reputations as soldiers during the War with Mexico. The unique and eccentric Winfield Scott dominated the years leading up to the war. U. S. Grant was the leader of the Union armies that won the war. Robert E. Lee, leading the Southern armies, was the commander outgunned by Grant's massive edge in numbers and material, and lost the war.

Captain of the Age

Winfield Scott was fault-ridden, a discordant symphony of personal imperfections and irregularities. He spoke and wrote with a trouble-prone tongue and reckless pen. He was pompous, domineering, contentious, elitist, and jealous of rank. Scott was often insubordinate, quarrelsome, quick to take offense, and afire with a sleepless hunger for power and prestige. He had a very high opinion of himself and a very low opinion of many others. He feuded with contemporaries and turned friends into enemies.

This flawed man was also a gifted strategist and one of the great battlefield generals in world history. Yet this great American commander has nearly faded from American memory, eclipsed over the past century and a half by later, if not greater, men and stirring events.

During the first half of the nineteenth century, from the War of 1812 to the beginning of the Civil War, Scott was the dominant figure in the American military establishment. For much of that time, he was the most celebrated soldier

Winfield Scott

Library of Congress

in America. None have matched his excellence, either in the field or within the command structure, in war and peace, at such a high level for such a long time. He was an icon in his time, and an American original.

Scott was a big-bodied giant just under six feet, five inches tall. Ralph Waldo Emerson called him "the stateliest form in America." Edwin Stanton remarked in early 1861, in the chaotic beginning of the war, "He is, in fact, the government."[1] Lincoln, the newly inaugurated president, noted, "Scott will not let us outsiders know anything of his plans."[2]

He was as big mentally as he was physically, a constant reader, as much at home in philosophic theory, history, literature, and diplomacy as he was on a battlefield. He was a strict person with endless self-confidence, intelligence, and courage.

Not only was he the nation's most prominent and dominant soldier for half of the nineteenth century, but he was also its primary military thinker. He rewrote the tactical manuals that became standard in the army long past his lifetime. He authored regulations that professionalized the Old Army, which was previously made up of volunteer soldiers.

Scott was always on the cutting edge of the prevailing science and theory of arms and unafraid to put them into practice. He carried a portable library of military books to every battle he fought, including books on tactics and strategy, and biographies of great commanders. He called it his *bibliotheca.* Scott was an apostle of attack strategy on the battlefield, never comfortable when on the defensive. Only age and infirmity would defeat him in the end.

The Lincoln biographer-poet, Carl Sandburg, described Scott as he was in his declining years. With the Civil War approaching, Scott was seventy-five years old, older than the Capital, and well past his prime.

"Six Feet five inches tall," Sandburg wrote, "three hundred pounds of weight, in shining gold braid and buttons, in broad epaulets and a long plumed hat, when he walked he seemed almost a parade by himself. When he paused, the apparent parade halted. Small boys waited of a morning to see him come out of his house and move like six regiments toward a waiting carriage."[3] With age, dropsy, vertigo, and two British bullets in his body, he could no longer mount a horse.

Scott was born on the family plantation in Dinwiddie County, Virginia, fourteen miles from Petersburg on June 13, 1786. An orphan by age seventeen, he

1 Carlos Baker, *Emerson Among the Eccentrics: A Group Portrait* (New York, 1996), 443-44; Edwin Stanton to James Buchanan, May 16, 1861, in George Ticknor Curtis, *Life of James Buchanan Fifteenth President of the United States*, 2 vols. (New York, 1883), 2:548.

2 Don E. Fehrenbacher & Virginia Fehrenbacher, *Recollected Words of Abraham Lincoln* (Stanford, CA, 1996), 337.

3 Carl Sandburg, *Abraham Lincoln: The War Years*, 4 vols. (New York, 1939), 1:29.

aspired to the law and studied for it. But there was a drum and bugle beating and sounding within that Herculean frame. In 1807, at twenty-two, he dropped the law and joined the Virginia Militia Cavalry—as another war with Britain threatened. "Heard the bugle and the drum," Scott explained, which "was the music that awoke ambition." [4] A different career than the law suddenly dawned on him.

If a physical ruin in his going, he was a comet in his coming. As the war in 1812 crept closer, he gave in permanently to the blast of the bugle and the hammer of the drum. He joined the regular army as a captain of light artillery, ending his four-year indecision between the "bar and the sword." Scott had decided to "write my history with a sword."[5]

He quickly rose in rank in the army, becoming a major general at age twenty-seven, the youngest ever. President James Madison, who had once balked at promoting such youth to such high command, was no longer uncertain. Scott would be the highest-ranking soldier in the U.S. Army for forty years, serving as the general-in-chief during the last twenty.

War was not the usual pathway for a man who had been educated by Quakers. When he revisited his old teachers after the War of 1812, a national hero, one of them said, "Friend Winfield, I always told thee not to fight, but since thou wouldst fight, I am glad that thou was not beaten."[6]

A situation more fitting the Quaker doctrine, peace, descended after the War of 1812, somewhat to Scott's disgust. Peace wasn't a condition he much welcomed since he thirsted for distinction and promotion. What he hankered for was a battle, never having a notion that such a thing could just as easily kill as elevate him.

In the Mexican-American War of 1846–1847, Scott would shape a military masterpiece, marching his small, vastly outnumbered, and outgunned army 250 miles from Vera Cruz to Mexico City. It was one of the most astonishing and successful feats of arms in military history. As a work of intelligent strategy and tactics, it is unmatched to this day.

One of his officers marveled at the notion of 10,000 men "marching through a hostile country upon a capital containing upwards of 200,000 inhabitants defended by 30,000 troops with 100 pieces of cannon, and fortified by both nature and art."[7] But that is what happened. To do it, as another of his officers said, "in

4 Winfield Scott, *Memoirs of Lieut.-General Scott, LLD*, 2 vols. (1864; repr., Freeport, NY, 1970), 1:21.

5 Ibid., 1:30, 43.

6 Ibid., 1:7n.

7 William Montgomery Gardner, "The Memoirs of Brigadier General William Montgomery Gardner," Elizabeth McKinne Gardner, ed., typescript copy of a series of articles in the *Memphis Commercial Appeal* (1912), U.S. Military Academy Library, West Point, NY, 33.

a series of victories without check,"[8] was a military campaign for the ages. Scott was an unrelenting patriot, called in his time "The Greatest Captain of the Age."[9]

The Mexican War made him a mentor to entire generation of subalterns who later ascended to high command in the Civil War. Union Gen. George B. McClellan wrote to him in the summer of 1861: "All that I know of war I have learned from you, & in all that I have done, I have endeavored to conform to your manner of conducting a campaign. It is my ambition to merit your praise & never to deserve your censure."[10] When command did come for McClellan, he could not, or would not, campaign at all like Scott.

Confederate general-to-be Robert E. Lee, who always merited Scott's praise, wrote him about that same time: "To no one, General, have I been so much indebted as to yourself for uniform kindness and consideration, and it has always been my ardent desire to meet your approbation. I shall carry to the grave the most grateful recollections of your kind consideration, and your name and fame will always be dear to me."[11] Those two grateful commanders, schooled by Scott, went out to fight one another.

Leading armies was not Scott's sole talent. He had a surprising knack for diplomacy. Of the fourteen presidents he served, many sent him on missions of peace. He would wield a deft and delicate diplomatic touch, a talent for pacification that mirrored his talent in war. Scott used a smart combination of war and diplomacy to rule a conquered Mexico. He knew how to balance the sword with the olive branch.

As Scott thought and fought big, he also squabbled big. Despite his diplomatic capacities, he was always quick to resentment and he took pains to refute criticism. He had several towering arguments with other great men of his time. Andrew Jackson and Scott had a falling out that nearly got to the dueling ground. Eventually, however, they became close friends.

Erasmus Keyes, Scott's long-time aide-de-camp, said, "In matters of rivalry he was easily vexed, and when the thing pursued was of great distinction, he seemed to go out of his skin into that of an angry porcupine with every quill standing on end."[12]

8 Dabney H. Maury, *Recollections of a Virginian: In the Mexican, Indian, and Civil Wars* (New York, 1894), 45.

9 Nathaniel Chears Hughes & Roy P. Stonesife, Jr., *Life and Wars of Gideon J. Pillow* (Chapel Hill, NC, 1993), 109.

10 George B. McClellan, *The Civil War Papers of George B. McClellan: Selected Correspondence, 1860-1865*, Stephen W. Sears, ed. (New York, 1989), 60.

11 Robert E. Lee, Jr., *Recollections and Letters of General Robert E. Lee* (New York, 1909), 24-25.

12 Erasmus Darwin Keyes, *Fifty Years' Observation of Men and Events* (New York, 1884), 11.

Scott believed that a general of his greatness should dress the part. He loved to wear showy military uniforms, the brighter, the better. He decked himself in military finery of eye-numbing brilliance with shiny buttons, gold braid, and epaulets. This caused him to be known as "Old Fuss and Feathers."[13] He was a notable concoction of gasconade, ostentation, bluster, courage—and undeniable military talent.

One contemporary described Scott's get up from head to toe: "Cocked hat, loop, cockade, tassels, yellow swans' feathers drooping, black silk stockings, shirt, brimstone colored vest, silk undershirt, osnaburgh suspenders, blue-and-brimstone coat, epaulettes, buttons, trowsers, boots, gloves, sky-blue sash, sword-knot, belt, plate, spurs, stockings, garters, drawers, and pocket handkerchief!"[14]

Some have said that when he bought his first uniform, after becoming a captain in the regulars, he locked his bedroom door. Donning the new uniform, for two hours he strutted before the mirrors as his self-approval escalated.[15]

Scott was a larger-than-life figure with a colossal ego, helpless in holding his rampant ambition in check. He was egotistical, seeking praise and recognition, while he avoided having to admit any weaknesses. He had an enormous vocabulary, but the word "humility" was not in it. Scott, like Jefferson Davis, believed himself to be always right.

He had one of the most maladroit, self-destructive pens of any great man in American history. He wrote constantly, using a verbose, showy, old-fashioned writing style, which often led to criticism and ridicule. Scott had a unique knack with his pen, for turning friends into enemies. Some said that on one occasion he came near to "committing suicide with a goose quill."[16]

Scott coped with stress by writing long, offensive letters brimming with strange ideas. To his regret, the ink coming from his quill was often very quotable, with catch phrases that went public. He is famous for saying as he went off to fight the War with Mexico, he feared "a fire upon my rear, from Washington, and the fire, in front, from the Mexicans."[17] President Polk was unhappy about the fire at the rear remark, and it made Scott less popular with opposing political groups.

13 John S. Eisenhower, *Agent of Destiny: The Life and Times of General Winfield Scott* (New York, 1997), 184, 320; Timothy D. Johnson, *Winfield Scott: The Quest for Military Glory* (Lawrence, KS, 1998), 2.

14 Quoted in Allan Peskin, *Winfield Scott and the Profession of Arms* (Kent, OH, 2003), 114.

15 Charles Winslow Elliott, *Winfield Scott: The Soldier and The Man* (New York, 1937), 23.

16 Ibid., 417.

17 Winfield Scott to William Marcy, May 21, 1846, U.S. Congress Senate Documents, no. 378, 29th Cong, 1st sess.

From the very beginning of his military career, Scott was a bold attacker. He was, perhaps, the very first American commander to refine to full effect the art of the unexpected maneuver. Scott would turn up at unexpected places at unexpected times, with an unexpected strategy, and push the enemy relentlessly. He set an example of audacity that became the hallmark of great commanders that followed: Grant, Sherman, Sheridan, Lee, Jackson, and Forrest.

Even in his seventies, when hobbled by dropsy and vertigo or unable to walk for more than a few paces at a time, he was still a tower of strength. When secessionist elements from Maryland and Virginia threatened to disrupt Lincoln's first inaugural, Scott assured him, "I'll plant cannon at both ends of Pennsylvania Avenue and if any of the Maryland or Virginia gentlemen who have become so threatening and troublesome of late, show their heads, or even venture to raise a finger, I'll blow them to Hell."[18]

If anyone tried to stop the vote count, Scott said he would shoot them out of a window using a cannon. "I would manure the hills of Arlington with his body," Scott pledged, "were he a senator or chief magistrate of my native state. It is my duty to suppress insurrection—*my duty*."[19] He meant it, and everybody knew he would do it.

That didn't sit well with secession-minded Virginians who thought him a traitor to his state. But he could not have cared less. He loved the Union. Before retiring on November 1, 1861, to give his job up to George B. McClellan, he suggested a so-called "Anaconda Plan." The plan was to surround the Confederacy, as an anaconda, and squeeze the rebellion into submission instead of rashly attacking.

That was too slow a remedy for public opinion when the battle cry was "On to Richmond!" Scott reaped ridicule for it. But in the end, that is how the rebellion ended. The only trouble with the plan, besides lacking passion and instant gratification, was that it was premature. Its time had not yet come, just as his time had passed.

Winfield Scott died in May 1866 at West Point and was buried there. The cadets down at Benny Havens, the famed off-limits-to-cadets drinking establishment, added a new verse to their famed drinking song:

18 Douglas L. Wilson & Rodney O. Davis, eds., *Herndon's Informant: Letters, Interviews, and Statements about Abraham Lincoln* (Champaign, IL, 1997), 709. There are other variations on this typical Scott statement. But they all mean the same.

19 Elliott, *Winfield Scott*, 690-91.

Another star has faded, we miss its brilliant glow,
For the veteran Scott has ceased to be a soldier here below,
And the country which he honored now feels a heartfelt woe,
As we toast his name in reverence, at Benny Havens Oh![20]

Scott was a complex man, a military genius, the greatest captain of the age, which spanned half a century. It would be difficult to imagine a more fascinating and complex character. For half a century, it was impossible to imagine a greater soldier.

The Horse Whisperer

Ulysses S. Grant became a soldier, and the star commander of the Civil War, despite himself. He was born and raised in Ohio, the son of a tanner. He was not the military sort, and becoming a soldier never entered his young head. He said, "A military life held no charms for me."[21] Unlike Scott, he had no ambition for military glory. It is inconceivable that he would lock himself up in a room and admire himself in uniform for two hours, as Scott did.

Grant had one love in life besides his wife: horses. At West Point, which he attended under parental order and without enthusiasm, that love of horses, and his way with them, would become legendary. In horsemanship, he was noted as most proficient in the Academy.[22]

Grant's father, mindful of his own lack of education, was bent on his son having one. Grant never applied to attend West Point. His father applied for him, and the son told the father, "But I won't go." The father said he thought he would go, and the son was wise enough to know that if the father thought he would, he would have to think so too.[23]

Grant was the fallback replacement of a cadet who failed the entrance examination. He arrived at West Point in 1839. As he had an aptitude for mathematics, as well as horses, he passed the entrance exam "without difficulty, very much to my surprise."[24]

Mathematics was the horrifying engine that drove academics at antebellum West Point. The academy was an engineering school masquerading as a military

20 Ibid., 763.

21 Ulysses S. Grant, *Personal Memoirs of Ulysses S. Grant*, 2 vols. in 1 (repr., New York, 1972), 27.

22 *New York Times*, Jul. 24, 1885.

23 Grant, *Personal Memoirs*, 24.

24 Ibid., 27.

Ulysses S. Grant

Library of Congress

academy, and engineering leaned heavily on mathematics. To flunk mathematics at West Point in the 1840s was a sure way to be shown the door. It was West Point's grim reaper, scything the mathematically inept without mercy. But in Grant's case, mathematics was a stalk too tough for a grim reaper to scythe. He was too good at it.

From the start, Grant insisted, "I had not the faintest idea of staying in the army even if I should be graduated, which I did not expect." He did not take his academic studies seriously. He found them wearisome and uninteresting. "I rarely ever read over a lesson the second time during my entire cadetship." Grant never thought to aim for the top of his class.[25]

Instead of just sitting in his room, he would check books out from the academy library. He read mostly novels and great literature, instead of honing deeper into his studies. That is the way Grant trotted through the academy, and with little effort, graduated in the middle of the class of 1843. His only plan was eventually to leave the army and perhaps teach math at a small college.

In one weak moment at West Point, Grant had a premonition. It was an epiphany that proved foretelling. Winfield Scott, with his outstanding height, bulk, legendary reputation, and his military moxie, often visited West Point to review the cadets. Grant wrote later, "I thought him the finest specimen of manhood my eyes had ever beheld, and the most to be envied. I could never resemble him in appearance, but I do believe that I did have a presentment for a moment that some day I should occupy his place on review—although I had no intention of remaining in the army."[26]

It was but a fleeting vision, a fantasy without foundation. Grant graduated in 1843, and would remain in the army, but only for the required time.

Three years out of West Point, Grant was a young lieutenant when the United States declared war on Mexico in May 1846. Like most of the other West Point graduates he went to war. Grant went as a quartermaster of the Fourth Infantry Regiment. It was not a fighting assignment, but Grant had a fighter mentality, and he would find a way.

He was at Monterey when Gen. Zachary Taylor, the other great American commander in that war, stormed the Mexican stronghold in September 1846. In the intense fighting, Grant's unit began to run low on ammunition. Grant volunteered to ride back to Taylor's headquarters to ask for more.

It was a suicidal assignment, a death-dealing gallop past shot-torn crossings alive with bullets. Every alley and every street were being raked by Mexican gunners, firing at anything that moved. The ride defied the mathematics of survival. But it

25 Ibid.

26 Ibid., 29.

was just the thing for a horseman of Grant's consummate skill. He rode his horse lying along its side Indian style, holding onto the saddle and shielding himself from enemy fire. He galloped quickly past each crossing, miraculously making it through without any injuries to himself or his horse.[27]

Grant passed another test of his courage, his savvy, and his tactical awareness at the San Cosme Gate in Mexico City. While his comrades fought at the gate, he commandeered a mountain howitzer, ordered it hauled into the belfry of a nearby church, and from there, less than 300 yards from the gate, dropped fire on the startled and confounded Mexicans with striking effect and to the intense gratification of Grant's commander, Gen. William W. Worth.[28]

Grant would not last long in the army after the war with Mexico. Stationed on the western frontier, he was far away from his wife Julia, whom he deeply loved and desperately missed. Lonely and unhappy, he drank too much, and when he left the army in 1854, it was with the sullied reputation as a drunk.

Out of the army, Grant finally settled in Galena, Illinois, living a hardscrabble life marked by little accomplishment and zero promise. A failure on the frontier in the old army, he was also a failure in civilian life. But despite his youthful disavowals of the soldierly life, Grant had in fact incubated within himself the characteristics and the skills of a very good soldier. He possessed a storehouse of know-how and intuition for war. He knew West Pointers would be in demand in this new war looming darkly on the near horizon.

When war became a reality in April 1861, Grant organized a regiment in Illinois and became its colonel. By mid-summer, he was promoted to brigadier general in the U.S. volunteers, starting a steady climb upward, proving himself by military competence. He was learning things he perhaps hadn't known before, and showing a talent for applying what he was learning.

At the battle of Belmont, in Missouri, in early November 1861, he experienced his first clash with a Confederate enemy. It was there that he was visited by another moment of epiphany. With his heart in his throat, he wished to be anywhere but there. But when the enemy kept retreating as he advanced, he had his epiphany. He later wrote, "This was a view of the question I had never taken before; but it was one I never forgot afterwards. From that event to the close of the war I never experienced trepidation upon confronting the enemy, though I always felt more or less anxiety. I never forgot that he had as much reason to fear my forces as I had his."[29] It was another important turning point in Grant's learning curve.

27 This daring gallop is described by Grant in ibid., 72.

28 This story of the howitzer in the belfry is in ibid., 96-97.

29 Ibid., 149.

Shed of fear, in February 1862, he went on to conqueror Confederate Forts Henry and Donelson on the Tennessee and Cumberland Rivers. He commanded Union forces at Shiloh in early April 1862, where he pulled victory from likely defeat in that bloody battle's second day. He commanded Union forces in the Vicksburg campaign in 1863, forcing a Confederate surrender, and clearing the Mississippi of Rebels for the length of the river. "The Father of Waters," Lincoln exulted, "again goes unvexed to the sea."[30]

Grant had caught Lincoln's attention. The battle at Shiloh in April 1862 had been a near disaster on the first day, before Grant turned it around on the second. When unhappy voices urged Lincoln to remove Grant from command for the mistakes of the first day, Lincoln said, "I can't spare that man; he fights." Some still thought Grant was a drunkard. When asked if he had really been searching for where Grant bought his liquor, Lincoln said he wanted to send some of the same brand to his other generals.[31]

In the summer of 1863, after Grant captured Vicksburg and a Union army had lost the battle at Chickamauga in Georgia, Lincoln ordered Grant to take command of Union operations around Chattanooga, Tennessee. Accommodating the president, Grant pushed the Confederates out of Chattanooga back toward Atlanta, adding more gloss to his reputation.

After Chattanooga, Grant was riding a high crest of success on a string of victories no other Union commander in the war could claim. In March 1864, Congress created a new permanent rank of lieutenant general in the regular army. Lincoln immediately filled it with Grant, his winningest general. The West Point cadet who once had the fleeting fantasy of someday standing in Scott's place, stood there now. Grant was to be the first, and only, permanent lieutenant general in the army since George Washington. Scott held the rank only by brevet.

Lincoln called Grant east to Washington, putting him in command of all the Union armies, and charging him to beat Robert E. Lee, capture Richmond, and end the war.

It wouldn't happen overnight. Following a bloody summer of desperate fighting in 1864, lengthening into 1865, Grant finally cornered Lee in Petersburg and caged his army behind a thirty-mile line of parallel trenches. There, he finally wore Lee down with his unbending persistence. In early April Lee was forced to pull out of Petersburg and Richmond and make a run to the North Carolina border. The chase lasted as far as Appomattox Court House in Virginia, where Lee

30 Lincoln, *CW*, 6:409.

31 Fehrenbacher & Fehrenbacher, *Recollected Words of Abraham Lincoln*, 92-93, 315.

saw that further fighting would be futile. There, on April 9, 1865, he surrendered his tattered Army of Northern Virginia to Grant.

Grant's hammering had cost thousands of Union soldiers' lives, earning him the nickname of "The Butcher." But he had ended the war as Lincoln had told him to do.

What does this tell us about Grant as a general? It tells us he had a winner's mindset. There was that epiphany at Belmont, that the enemy was as frightened as he was. Grant appreciated one thing as perhaps no other Union commander did, the huge Union bulge of resources. Hit the enemy hard enough, without ceasing, with unlimited power and personnel, and they would hammer him into submission. That was Grant's mindset and strategy, and it worked.

This cadet, who became the greatest of the Civil war generals, based his campaigns on what he learned from observing his future opponents in the Mexican War. That war, he would later remark,

> made the officers of the old regular armies more or less acquainted, and when we knew the name of the general opposing we knew enough about him to make our plans accordingly. What determined my attack on Donelson was as much the knowledge I had gained of its commanders in Mexico as anything else. But as the war progressed, and each side kept improving its army, these experiments were not possible. Then it became a hard, earnest war, and neither side could depend upon any chance with the other. Neither side dared to make a mistake.[32]

With his knack of knowing what an opposing general might do, Grant made few mistakes. The indifferent West Pointer had become a keen learner, who would educate himself from the battlefield to the presidency in 1868, and again in 1872. Not bad for a tanner's son who never wanted to be a soldier, a general, or a president, but who loved horses, his wife, and was good at mathematics.

Granny Lee

If there was any individual in the Civil War era who might have been considered perfect or near perfect as a human being, it had to be Confederate General Robert E. Lee. If there was a smudge on that perceived perfection, few could see it.

Sure, he was a slave holder and Southern rebel against his country, a traitor, depending on what section of the divided country you lived in. Yet he lives in American memory as a military ideal.

32 John Russell Young, *Around the World with General Grant*, 2 vols. (1879; repr., Baltimore, 2002), 391.

Robert E. Lee

Museum of the Confederacy

He stood five feet, ten inches, with a physique of perfect symmetry, astride a grey warhorse also of perfect symmetry named Traveller. Many believed Traveller's rider to be the most handsome man on the planet.

At West Point, he was about as perfect as it gets. He marched through without a single demerit, which was just short of supernatural. The only minor mark on Lee's West Point years is that he finished second instead of first in his class. Charles Mason took that honor, and he retired from the army two years after graduation, becoming an eminent jurist in Iowa. The two finished virtually neck and neck with the highest two grades in West Point history. He showed throughout those four years not only a talent for avoiding demerits, but a gift for leadership. In his final year, 1829, he was made an adjutant of the corps of cadets, the most coveted of cadet honors. The future would confirm Lee's utter preeminence among his peers.

Lee had Olympian virtues to match his Olympian looks and mind. It was said he was "calm when others were frenzied, loving when they hated, and silent when they spoke with bitter tongue."[33] He was a tactful and friendly gentleman, who made people around him feel at ease.

The distinguished British Field Marshal, Viscount Wolseley, Lee's contemporary, called him "the renowned soldier, whom I believe to have been the greatest of his age . . . whom I have always considered the most perfect man I ever met." Wolseley saw in Lee a calm, self-possessed dignity that he had never seen in other men. When he first met Lee, Wolseley said, he felt he was "in the presence of a man cast in a grander mold, and made of different and a finer metal than all other men."[34]

This paragon came to be seen as the man who would save the Confederacy. It was his sword, as one hopeful Georgia wife wrote, "to which the Southern people looked for liberty and independence."[35] However, at first, the common perception of many Southerners, despite his perfect presence, was he would not measure up militarily. Many frowned on his penchant for digging in and called him the "King of Spades." Some called him "Granny Lee," because they believed he lacked audacity. It was a misconception Lee would shatter, as few commanders have been more audacious or offense-minded than he.

He built his military career on a solid foundation of a military engineering education. He went with many of his fellow West Pointers to the Mexican War, in which many excelled. Like most of these West Pointers, he fought under Winfield

33 Douglas Southall Freeman, *R. E. Lee: A Biography*, 4 vols. (New York, 1935), 4:494.

34 From an article Wolseley wrote about Lee titled "General Lee," reprinted in Gary W. Gallagher, ed., *Lee the Soldier* (Lincoln, NE, 1996), 95, 102, 108-9.

35 Laura Nesbit Boykin, *Shinplasters and Homespun: The Diary of Laura Nesbit Boykin*, Mary Wright Stock, ed. (Rockville, MD, 1975), 33.

Scott. These Academy-trained officers couldn't have had a better tutorial on how to wage war on a grand scale. From this unique vantage point, under that brilliant commander, they could see the way of a military master, to observe first-hand how he thought and fought.

Not all learned as well from Scott as did Lee. What Lee learned was to prepare him to command on a scale as enormous as the Civil War. From Scott, Lee learned the priceless value of audacity. He learned to delegate responsibility to a carefully selected and talented team of lieutenants. He learned the great value of reconnaissance, artfully executed, skillfully interpreted, and intelligently applied. Lee had been the reconnaissance star for Scott in the war with Mexico.

From Scott, Lee also learned the virtue of selectively and boldly violating accepted military practice where it served his purpose. He learned the value not only of swiftness, but surprise, and the priceless value of a successful flanking movement.

These qualities Lee saw in the way Scott fought the Mexican War, and he processed it to perfection. He learned how to apply it. Those were the acquired gifts he would bring to the Civil War, gratis Winfield Scott.

Lee was an engineer on Scott's staff in Mexico and became highly respected for his daring reconnaissance at Cerro Gordo and the battle of Contreras in Mexico City. Three times during the night, in a lashing rainstorm, and using only lightning to see by, Lee crossed the Pedregal, a rock-packed nightmare outside Mexico City. The Pedregal was a fearsome thee-mile wide outcropping of twisted lava that the soldiers called "hell with the fires out."[36] It was a satanic devilish barrier lying directly in the way General Scott was considering taking his army. He sent Lee, his premier engineer-reconnoiterer, to see if he could find a way through, which he did.

Lee was a soldier with an innate gift for reading terrain, and he found a passage. Scott saw Lee's three crossing of the Pedregal "the greatest feat of physical and moral courage performed by any individual, in my knowledge, pending the campaign."[37] He later called Lee the "very best soldier I ever saw in the field."[38]

As the Civil War approached, Scott told an acquaintance, "I tell you, that if I were on my deathbed tomorrow, and the president of the United States should tell me that a great battle was to be fought for the liberty or slavery of the country, and asked my judgment as to the ability of a Commander, I would say with my dying breath, 'Let it be Robert E. Lee.'"[39]

36 David Nevin, *The Mexican War* (Alexandria, VA, 1978), 179.

37 A. L. Long, *Memoirs of Robert E. Lee*, Marcus J Wright, ed. (1886; repr., Secaucus, NJ, 1983), 58.

38 Quoted in William Jones, *Life and Letters of Robert Edward Lee, Soldier and Man* (New York, 1906), 127-28.

39 Long, *Memoirs of Robert E. Lee*, 482.

Though not yet on his deathbed, but old, overweight, and at the end of his spectacular military career, Scott did tell a president that. He told Abraham Lincoln that Lee was his first choice to command the Union armies in the East, and the command was offered. But Lee could not lift his sword against his own state of Virginia, and defected to the Confederacy instead, taking all his military and leadership skills with him.

Lee was not only a student of strategy and tactics, but a student of men. He knew his enemy thoroughly. He knew his enemy commanders, knew how each was likely to act or react. Like Grant, he had observed most of them during the Mexican War and remembered. He knew when to ante-up and when to fold. Lee divided his army in the face of overwhelming Union might, first against George B. McClellan on the Peninsula, against John Pope at Second Manassas, and again against Joe Hooker at Chancellorsville. He engineered stunning flanking maneuvers that defied conventional warfare.

This paragon made mistakes on the battlefield, and he had his critics. Sent to western Virginia, before he became commander of the Army of Northern Virginia, to hold it for the Confederacy, he failed. At Gettysburg, he didn't follow his chief lieutenant's advice to defend, and instead, attacked the Union lines in a calamitous frontal assault known to history as Pickett's Charge. It was a disaster.

When she first saw Lee in July 1861, Mary Chesnut, with just a hint of sarcasm, said, "[the] man and horse and everything about him, was so fine looking. Perfection—no fault could be found if you hunted for one. He looks so cold and quiet and grand."[40]

Mary's opinion of Lee turned dark after his poor performance in western Virginia, and the loss of Port Royal to the Union. "Preux chevalier," she huffed, "Booted and bridled and gallant rade [rider] he. So far, his bonnie face has only brought us ill luck."[41] When Lee began winning battles in emphatic style, from the Peninsula to Chancellorsville, Mary's criticism tailed off.

Others found fault in his strategies, such as not defeating McClellan's army, overextending his own army, and underestimating the Federals. Additional critiques included risking himself too much in battle and sacrificing too many soldiers.

Few, however, criticized Lee's character. And there was only one vital criterion of a great general he failed to fulfill: while he won battles, he did not win the war. It was Grant who won the war. But even in losing, it was not because he did not fulfill the essential criteria of a great general. He did not lose for lack of knowledge of his opponent or of a lack of audacity. He lost the war, as he believed

40 Chesnut, *Mary Chesnut's Civil War*, 116.

41 Ibid., 230. By the word "rade," she likely means "marvel" or "wonder."

and said in his General Orders No. 9, the farewell to his army, "to overwhelming [enemy] numbers and resources."[42] Unfortunately, he fought in defense of an overwhelmingly bad cause: slavery.

That might have been the one smudge of imperfection someone might find in Lee. Fighting for a bad cause and losing a war muddies perfection.

42 Lee's farewell to his army is reprinted in Freeman, *R. E. Lee*, 4:154-55.

Chapter 5

Twin Terrors

Thomas Jonathan Jackson and Nathan Bedford Forrest were two of the Confederacy's most fearsome commanders. Neither side produced another two generals quite like that unique pair.

They were so different, and so alike. While their personalities were different, they were eerily similar on the battlefield. It is that striking similarity that pairs "Stonewall" with the "Wizard of the Saddle."[1]

Jackson's sister–in–law, the Southern poet Margaret Junkin Preston, said he was "a man *sui generis*; and none who came into close enough contact with him to see into his inner nature were willing to own that they had ever known just such another man."[2] She could have said the same of Bedford Forrest.

There was an abyss of personal differences between these two renowned soldiers. Jackson was a West Pointer, well acquainted with the theory and practice of war. Forrest was wholly unacquainted with the military arts. Jackson was a religious zealot, giving credit for his victories to Providence. While reverent and respectful, Forrest wouldn't go that far. He was a pragmatist who instead put his

1 "Stonewall" was the nickname widely applied to Jackson after his "standing like a stonewall" at the first battle of Manassas early in the war. "Wizard of the Saddle" was the well-used nickname for Forrest, for the fact that he was a cavalry commander of apparently wizardly skill.

2 Margaret Junkin Preston, "Personal Reminiscences of Stonewall Jackson," *Century Magazine* (Oct. 1886), 927.

faith, as he said, in "getting there first with the most men, never letting the other fellow make the fight for me."[3]

Jackson was devoutly religious, opposed to writing, reading, even mailing or receiving a letter on Sunday, and opposed to fighting on the Sabbath. However, when duty called, Jackson would fight on the Lord's Day like Satan incarnate. Unencumbered by religious piety, Forrest was ready to "mix it with 'em," as he said, any day of the week, Sundays included.[4]

Jackson had many ailments, real and imaginary, for which he was always concocting theories and unique remedies. But that didn't stop him from inviting death on the battlefield. He figured Providence was taking care of that detail. Forrest never paid attention to protecting his physical well–being. He seemed gratified to throw himself into danger's path on any day.

Forrest was reasonably gregarious, while Jackson preferred privacy. There are other character differences, but that is not the subject of this sketch. Instead, it is a study of their similarities as fighters.

On a battlefield, they were twin terrors. Their "hit 'em with everything you have and pursue 'em to death" styles were consistent. Jackson on a confused battlefield, some said, is where his perceptions were sharper, and he saw the situation clearer.

I believe that describes what happened with Stonewall Jackson and Bedford Forrest on battlefields. Their cool deepened in chaos and confusion. They saw everything clearly, leaving no doubt about what must occur next.[5] Not every general is so gifted. As with Jackson and Forrest, such commanders are in the pantheon of military greatness with Scott, Grant, and Lee.

Being What He Resolved to Be

One might rather liken Stonewall Jackson to a country schoolmaster than a soldier. He was awkward in the saddle despite the many long hours he spent there. He frequently became distracted, as if he was engaged in a difficult mathematical problem or pondering the truth about Providence and life. In polite company, he

3 Quoted by Rambaut, "Forrest at Shiloh," in Robert Selph Henry, ed., *As They Saw Forrest: Some Recollections and Comments of Contemporaries* (Wilmington, NC, 1987), 57. For background on Forrest's famous modus operandi—"getting there first with the most men"—see Robert Selph Henry, *"First With the Most" Forrest* (1959; repr., Westport, CT, 1974), 19-20.

4 Richard Taylor, *Destruction and Reconstruction: Personal Experiences of the Late War* (New York, 1883), 244.

5 I call this the Joe Montana syndrome, from something the great San Francisco 49ers quarterback reportedly said. During the last two minutes of a game, everything became clear to him as he led the 49ers downfield for a game-winning comeback. He understood with stunning clarity everything happening on the field. This was a peculiar cool that deepened in the fourth quarter.

Stonewall Jackson

Library of Congress

was diffident, clinging to the background. His wife, Anna, however, swore that in the privacy of their Lexington parlor, he danced the polka.[6]

6 John Esten Cooke, *Stonewall Jackson and the Old Stonewall Brigade*, Richard Barksdale Harwell, ed. (Charlottesville, VA, 1954), 152; Mary Anna Jackson, *Memoirs of Stonewall Jackson* (1895; repr., Dayton, OH, 1985), 47.

One Confederate officer gave up trying to figure him out. "There is a magnetism in Jackson," that officer admitted, "but it is not personal. All admire his genius and great deeds; no one could love the man for himself"—Anna excepted. "He seems to be cut off from his fellow men," the officer continued, "and to commune with his own spirit only, or with spirits of which we know not."[7]

Jackson was stiff, but not unfriendly, with a sweet, winning smile. He was considerate and honest in his dealings. If he was slightly eccentric, it was because he followed his own inner drum, and sense of duty, with Providence in charge. Away from a battle, nothing about Jackson hinted at the inner warrior. He appeared "unprepossessing"—as one West Point classmate described him.[8]

In battle, when the cannon thundered, musket fire rattled, and bayonets flashed, Jackson became another being. Gone was the contemplative, tentative schoolmaster, replaced by the unrelenting fighter. Out went tranquility and abstraction, in came devouring excitement. Stonewall was Jekyll and Hyde, fire, and ice. On the battlefield, he was fearless. One soldier spoke of his "war-look," as he rode about like an avenging angel. He would pay no attention to the explosions and chaos, looking as if nothing was going on but the work of the Lord.[9]

An Irish rebel saw him on the field in the summer of 1862, during the Shenandoah Valley campaign, and exclaimed, "B' jabers, have your eye on auld Jack. I'll wager you he thinks them blatherin' bangs are singin' birds."[10]

Jackson was not only a man of courage; he was a man of axioms. His most famous saying was, "You can be whatever you resolve to be."[11] Another Jacksonism, recited on the battlefield, was, "Take no counsel of [your] fears." He lived by that axiom, preaching it to his generals and soldiers alike.[12]

He was secretive, saying he would not tell even the buttons on his coat where he was going, the direction, or his intentions upon arrival. He once remarked, "If my coat knew what I intended to do, I'd take it off and throw it away."[13] Jackson always knew where he was going, but rarely did his lieutenants and soldiers know

7 Quoted in Foote, *The Civil War*, 1:429.

8 Gardner, "Memoirs," 9.

9 Cooke, *Stonewall Jackson and the Old Stonewall Brigade*, 152.

10 Henry Kyd Douglas, *I Rode with Stonewall* (1940; repr., Chapel Hill, NC, 1968), 58.

11 Jackson, *Memoirs of Stonewall Jackson*, 35. As a West Point cadet, Jackson compiled a private blank book listing a set of rules and maxims for living his life. They can be found in full in Mrs. Jackson's *Memoirs of Stonewall Jackson*, 35-38.

12 William Allan, *History of the Campaign of Gen. T. J. (Stonewall) Jackson* (1880; repr., Dayton, OH, 1987), 123n; Jedediah Hotchkiss, *Virginia*, Vol.4 of *Confederate Military History, Extended Edition*, Clement A. Evans, ed. (1899; repr., Wilmington, NC, 1987), 249-250.

13 Douglas, *I Rode with Stonewall*, 235.

until they were in the middle of his plan. Even Anna, whom he dearly loved and called his "little esposita," didn't have a clue.[14] Certainly, the enemy didn't.

Jackson showered the utmost tenderness and love on Anna, calling her "my little one," "my little somebody," and "my little darling." In her memoir, she constantly spoke of his tenderness, which nobody, either in the army, or his personal life, seemed to notice.[15]

Whatever Jackson had in his mind under that little faded kepi he wore, it was bound to start early. It was early to rise and late to bed with Jackson, sometimes never to bed at all. He liked to move his army at daybreak or start the night before. One soldier described him as a "second day man," beginning early and fighting late and beginning again early the next day. His basic work ethic was to advance, fight, and to go on advancing and pursuing until the enemy was whipped.[16]

He earned the nickname, "Stonewall," at First Manassas, standing resolutely in the path of Union soldiers assaulting Henry Hill. In resolve, he was seen as a stone wall before they christened him that in fire and blood at Manassas. Fifty-eight West Point classmates had learned that about him years before. They saw many times how he marched resolute and unmoving to his own drum. When he was moving his army in war time, however—when not standing as a bulwark—he was alacrity personified. West Point professor Dennis Hart Mahan could have pointed to Jackson as an example of the importance of common sense and celerity on the battlefield.

While not a big talker, Jackson would occasionally speak about tactics. He once told John Imboden, a cavalry officer, that there were two rules a general must never fail to follow:

> "Always mystify," Jackson said, "mislead and surprise the enemy, if possible; and when you strike and overcome him, never let up in the pursuit so long as your men have strength to follow; for an army routed, if hotly pursued, becomes panic-stricken, and can then be destroyed by half their number."

The other rule, Jackson continued, is "never fight against heavy odds, if by any possible manoeuvering you can hurl your own force on only a part, and that the weakest part, of your enemy and crush it. Such tactics will win every time and a

14 Jackson, *Memoirs of Stonewall Jackson*, 122n, 126.

15 Ibid., 135, 129.

16 Cooke, *Stonewall Jackson and the Old Stonewall Brigade*, 42-43.

small army may thus destroy a large one in detail, and repeated victory will make it invincible."[17]

Jackson's doctor, Hunter McGuire, in his months of close contact with Jackson, often sharing a tent, heard him say at various times: "War means fighting; to fight is the duty of a soldier; march swiftly, strike the foe with all your strength and take away from him everything you can. Injure him in every possible way, and do it quickly. Don't wait for the adversary to become fully prepared, but strike him the first blow. We must do more than defeat their armies; we must destroy them."[18]

What he didn't say of his own genius, many others have shared. Even his enemies spoke admiringly of his "peculiar strategic ability."[19] One Northerner wrote: "The pomp and glitter of war were not for him. His banners grew old and faded and shot-torn. His legions grew ragged and foot-sore and weary. No matter who hesitated, Jackson advanced. Fierce in the heat of battle, because it was his duty to kill."[20]

John Tidball, another Northerner, and West Point cadet with Jackson, said: "His chief characteristics as a military leader were his quick perception of the weak points of his enemy, his ever readiness, the astounding rapidity of his movements, his sudden and unexpected onslaughts, and the persistency with which he followed them up. Naturally taciturn and by habit the keeper of his own designs, it was as difficult for his friends to penetrate them, as it was easy for him to deceive his enemy." In any other person, Tidball said, this would have been taken as cunning and deceit; but with Jackson it was "the voice of the Lord piloting him to the tents of the Midianites."[21]

Henry Kyd Douglas, who rode with Jackson as one of his young staff officers, called him a bold leader, "probably the boldest the war produced. But he mingled with his boldness, great prudence and judgment. If he played war as poker, he knew exactly when to bluff, and against whom; consequently he was never beaten."

17 John D. Imboden, "Stonewall Jackson in the Shenandoah," in vol. 2 of *B&L* (1887; repr., Secaucus, NJ, n.d.), 297.

18 Hunter H. McGuire & George L. Christian, *The Confederate Cause and Conduct in the War Between the States* (Scotts Valley, CA, 2014), 208, 212-13.

19 Nathan Kimball, "Fighting Jackson at Kernstown," in vol. 2 of *B&L* (1887; repr., Secaucus, NJ, n.d.), 310.

20 M. Quad, "Notes and Queries: A Federal Soldier's Opinion of Stonewall Jackson," *SHSP*, vol. 10 (Jul. 1882), 334.

21 John C. Tidball, "Getting through West Point by One Who Did," typed manuscript, John C. Tidball Papers, U.S. Military Academy Library, West Point, NY.

Douglas believed Jackson's opinion of opposing generals was "wonderfully correct." But, most important in Douglas's mind, "he dared and won."[22]

Jackson's Shenandoah Valley campaign in the spring and early summer of 1862 was a tactical masterpiece. It was an impressive use of strategy, speed, and organization to defeat an enemy. One of Jackson's cavalrymen, borrowing a quote from Abraham Lincoln, said, "He always ploughed around the log."[23] A reporter recalled he was "everywhere when unexpected and nowhere when sought."[24] Another soldier said that if the enemy had a rear, Jackson would find it.[25]

As Jackson approached that enemy's rear, he was, as his brother-in-law, Gen. Daniel Harvey Hill, described it, "as still as the breeze;" but when he struck, it was "as dreadful as the storm."[26]

That was the battlefield way of Stonewall Jackson.

"Nature's Soldier"

That other battlefield terror, Nathan Bedford Forrest, was, like Jackson, an American original. That he should be a general was both obvious and hard to believe.

British Field Marshall, Viscount Wolseley, believed "this gallant, though low-born and uneducated General" to be a military genius, a "general by intuition. The *art* of war was an instinct in him." He was "most verily, nature's soldier." Wolseley recorded, "He was essentially a practical man of action, with a dauntless, fiery soul, and a heart that knew no fear . . . [a] heaven-born leader of men."[27]

Forrest knew absolutely nothing of accepted military tactics, and likely knew an equal amount about Napoleon, who most West Point soldiers sought to copy. Virtually uneducated and something of a social pariah, Forrest fought by instinct, his own rules, and in his own way, as Jackson did. Much like Jackson, his way was horrifying to his enemies.

One soldier shared, "I don't think General Forrest ever mastered Hardee's tactics (a tactical handbook for the times) any further or had any use for it, than the single command, 'Charge!'" "Forrest," the soldier continued, "never did anything

22 Douglas, *I Rode with Stonewall*, 62, 93.

23 John Newton Opie, *A Rebel Cavalryman with Lee, Stuart, and Jackson* (Chicago, 1899), 139.

24 George Townsend, *Rustics in Rebellion: A Yankee Reporter on the Road to Richmond 1861-1865* (1866; repr., Chapel Hill, NC, 1950), 216.

25 John O. Casler, *Four Years in the Stonewall Brigade* (1893; repr., Dayton, OH, 1982), 154.

26 Daniel Harvey Hill, "The Real Stonewall Jackson," in *Century Magazine* (Feb. 1894), 628.

27 Garnet Wolseley, "General Viscount Wolseley on Forrest," in *As They Saw Forrest*, Robert Selph Henry, ed. (Wilmington, NC, 1987), 33, 38, 50, 51.

Nathan Bedford Forrest

Library of Congress

as anyone else would have done, or even thought of doing, in regard to a fight. He was all alone, none ever came near to him or his like, but Stonewall Jackson."[28]

His soldiers saw Forrest as "a man of powerful mind, active and energetic, great will-power, keen perception, quick to act, full of strategy, with cool, daring

28 William Witherspoon, "Tishomingo Creek or Bryce's Cross Roads," in *As They Saw Forrest*, Robert Selph Henry, ed. (Wilmington, NC, 1987), 37, 113, 120.

bravery, his whole soul in the cause, his tactics common sense."[29] With those assets, he won fight after fight.

Forrest's capacity for war amazed many. "He knew what he wanted to accomplish," Wolseley said, "and he went for that object with all the cunning of an Indian, all the common sense of a business man."[30] And, Wolseley might have added, all the ferocity of a killer. "War means fighting," Forrest said, echoing Jackson, "and fighting means killing."[31] He appeared to have little regard for the Sixth Commandment.

Forrest's language was as rough-hewn as he was. He misfired often when spelling. His chief of staff, Major Charles W. Anderson, said he was "governed by sound and his spelling, like his fighting, was the shortest way to the end."[32] A contemporary Southern editor, trying to elevate it, called it "eccentric eloquence."[33]

This short description illustrates both Forrest's syntax and his fighting style: "I had a small brush with the Anamy on yesterday I suceded in gaining thir entrenchments 8 miles from hamburg and 5 behind farmington and Burned a portion of thir camp at that place they wair not looking for me I taken them by Surprise they run like Suns of Biches."[34]

Crippled syntax aside, when one Confederate staff officer first saw Forrest at Chickamauga, he exclaimed, "Did you ever see such an eye? He is a born general."[35] That is the way Forrest struck virtually all who met him. Every Yankee who fought against him, and survived, firmly believed it. "The very name of Forrest is a host in himself," a Confederate infantryman noted in his diary.[36] Another said, "As a cavalry officer, we are not prepared to name his defect."[37]

The son of a backwoods blacksmith, Forrest was physically the sort of man you wouldn't want to upset. He stood six feet, two inches tall, and on horseback, standing in his stirrups, he seemed like a skyscraper. He was lithe, powerful, hard-bodied, strong, broad-shouldered, full-chested, and of a riveting presence. His eyes

29 Rambaut, "Forrest at Shiloh," 57.

30 Wolseley, "General Viscount Wolseley on Forrest," 31.

31 Ibid., 33.

32 Quoted in John Allan Wyeth, *That Devil Forrest: Life of General N. B. Forrest* (1899; repr., Baton Rouge, LA, 1989), 554.

33 Paul Ashdown & Edward Caudill, *The Myth of Nathan Bedford Forrest* (Lanham, MD, 2005), 74.

34 Henry, *As They Saw Forrest*, 288.

35 W. H. Brand, "Lieutenant-General N. B. Forrest," in *The Land We Love* (Aug. 1866), 275.

36 Henry, *"First with the Most" Forrest*, 273.

37 Brand, "Lieutenant-General N. B. Forrest," 269.

were dark gray, bright, and searching. His hair was iron-gray, and he sported an ink-black moustache and goatee.

Forrest was kind, polite, and didn't have any ungodly habits like smoking, drinking, or womanizing. He was respectful to women. But he had a hair-trigger temper, and when aroused, he erupted into a volcano of cuss words. He was a social hybrid, composed of gentleness and violence in extreme measure. One biographer believed him to be two men at once, "a soft-spoken gentleman of marked placidity and an over-bearing bully of homicidal wrath."[38] Another Jekyll and Hyde.

His dark side was very dark. He was a racist. He joined the Confederate service in 1861, as a millionaire whose fortune was made as a slave trader. For a time, after the war, he was involved with the early Ku Klux Klan. However, when they started terrorizing whites and hanging blacks, he pulled out. Forrest did not believe that was the intent of the Klan, which he saw as opposition to Northern radical reconstruction of the South.

The darkest taint on Forrest's reputation in the war was his capture of Fort Pillow on the east bank of the Mississippi River in Tennessee in July 1864. Half the garrison at Fort Pillow, more than 250 men, were free blacks, soldiers enlisted after the Emancipation Proclamation. Instead of taking them prisoner, Forrest's soldiers, with malice, began shooting them down in cold blood. Forrest was not present at the scene, but did he order it? That is a controversial question to this day among historians.

"If we ain't fightin' to keep slavery," Forrest asked, "then what the hell are we fightin' for?"

It was Forrest who asked that blunt question. He kept forty-five slaves himself. But buoying his reputation was the fact that he never separated his slave families. He also would not sell a slave to a man with a reputation for cruelty. When he went to war, he told them then, if they acted faithfully, he would free them after the war. "Eighteen months before the war closed," he said, "I was satisfied that we were going to be defeated, and I gave those forty-five men, or forty-four of them, their free papers, for fear I might get killed."[39] One remained with him by choice.

On the battlefield, Forrest was a madman, a cold-blooded killer. He was at the head of his soldiers when ordering a charge, which was his preferred strategy. That order was like a "brassy clangor so unlike his quiet and low speech at other

38 Quoted in Ashdown & Caudill, *The Myth of Nathan Bedford Forrest*, 9.

39 U.S. Congress, Forrest testimony in the "Ku Klux Report" of 1872, 2nd sess. 42nd cong., Senate Document no. 41, vol. 13, p. 24.

times."[40] On a battlefield, his roar was answered with the blood-freezing rebel yell from his soldiers as they sprang toward the enemy to "mix it with 'em."

Forrest killed thirty officers and men in hand-to-hand fighting, sustaining four wounds himself. No other general in the Civil War matched his appalling numbers. His recruiting pitch was "Come on boys if you want a heap of fun and to kill some Yankees."[41]

When fighting, Forrest appeared deranged, a maniac, terrifying to look upon. He was even more terrifying to encounter, savage and profane. Forrest was the Four Horsemen of the Apocalypse on a single steed. He lost twenty-nine horses under him in the war. The historian and Forrest specialist, Robert Selph Henry, surmised, "it would seem that nothing was quite as unsafe as a horse carrying Old Bedford."[42]

A fellow officer who saw him in battle, near the end of 1861, was stunned:

> It was the first time I had ever seen the colonel in the face of the enemy, and when he rode up to me in the thick of the action, I could scarcely believe him to be the man I had known for several months. His face flushed till it bore a striking resemblance to a painted Indian warrior's, and his eyes, usually mild in their expression, were blazing with the intense glare of a panther's springing upon its prey. In fact, he looked as little like the Forrest of our mess-table as the storm of December resembles the quiet of June.[43]

One of Forrest's soldiers, J. P. Young, a sergeant from Tennessee, said, "It cost something to ride with Forrest:"[44]

> It meant days and nights of sleepless toil and motion. It meant countless miles under a burning sun in the choking dust. It meant limitless leagues across icy wastes, with a blanket of snow at night for a covering. It meant to run down and destroy miles of freighted supply trains, to burn depots of stores, to scale the parapets of redoubts, and to plunge, mounted, into the seeming vortex of hell, lighted with the fires of myriad rifles and scores of belching guns. It meant to meet death face to face like a drillmaster, to look into his dread eyes, to toy with the horrid trappings of his trade, to scorn the deadly chill of his breath, and to turn away unscathed or sink into the oblivion of his eternal embrace.[45]

40 Henry, *"First with the Most" Forrest*, 18.

41 Ibid., 82.

42 Ibid., 55.

43 Henry, *As They Saw Forrest*, 34-35.

44 J. P. Young, "Monument to General N. B. Forrest" in *Confederate Veteran*, vol. 13 (Sep. 1905), 389.

45 *Confederate Veteran*, 13:389.

Another soldier said, "He ruled them so that they feared him more than the enemy."[46] Yet another soldier remarked, "He rode the lines, the light of battle in his eye and the thunderous 'Charge!' upon his lips." That same soldier, thirty-five years later, wrote, "he rode into my heart as well . . . and rides there still."[47]

Forrest was gifted, as Wolseley said, with a military instinct approaching genius. "Truly a diamond of the first water," one admirer wrote of him, "rough, unpolished, just from its native quarry."[48] Confederate Gen. Dabney Herndon Maury, a West Pointer who knew and admired Forrest, said his "natural qualifications as a soldier were phenomenal," that he had an "extraordinary capacity for war."[49]

The oldest of twelve children, Forrest, was born on July 13, 1821, twin to a sister, Fanny, in Chapel Hill in Middle Tennessee. He grew up poor in Tennessee and Mississippi, supporting his mother and siblings from age fifteen, when his father and twin sister died of scarlet fever.

Forrest only had six months of formal schooling and could scarcely read before adulthood. Some have called him "unlettered."[50] He could have been called poor white trash. But his force and drive were frightening. He became a Mississippi gambler, horse trader, slave trader, speculator, planter, and a Memphis alderman before the war. Forrest was strikingly able and successful at all his callings. He was a self-made everything.

Forrest married in September 1845, following a courtship so brief it defies belief. His wooing was waged in his unique style. Mary Ann Montgomery, nineteen, was with her mother in a carriage, stuck in the mud, near Hernando, Tennessee. The driver was vainly trying to dislodge the carriage as two gallants sat on a bank nearby, watching, but not offering help.

Along rode Forrest. Although dressed in his Sunday best, he dismounted, and waded into the mud. He carried both women to the creek bank, then waded back to heave the carriage out. He chased away the two idlers with threats of bodily violence. Mud-splattered, he introduced himself to the ladies, asking if he might call. Permission granted, he called virtually without waiting, again chasing off the two same gallants present now on the porch, and immediately asked Mary Ann to marry him.

46 Lafcadio Hearn, *Occidental Gleanings*, 2 vols., Albert Mordell, ed. (New York, 1925), 149.

47 Walter A. Clark, *Under the Stars and Bars: Memories of Four Years of Service with the Oglethorpes of Augusta, Georgia* (Augusta, GA, 1900), 157, 161.

48 Brand, "Lieutenant-General N. B. Forrest," 270.

49 Maury, *Recollections of a Virginian*, 204, 205.

50 Henry, *As They Saw Forrest*, 297.

Rightly thinking this was far too premature, she turned him down. The next time, he again proposed, and she refused. But on his third assault, Mary Ann gave in and said yes. He was a hard man to say no to.

When Forrest asked permission of her guardian, a noted clergyman, to marry her, he was appalled. "Why, Bedford," the minister objected, "I couldn't consent. You cuss and gamble and Mary Ann is a Christian girl." "I know it," Forrest replied. "That's just why I want her."

His persistence could wear down granite. Within the month, the minister relented, and Bedford and Mary Ann were married by the minister-guardian himself.[51] It was a happy marriage, producing two children and lasting until Forrest's death in 1877. Mary Ann, who became to Forrest the "best friend I have on earth,"[52] was said to be a "gentle lady, to whom he was careful in his deference."[53] His last words before dying in October 1877 were, "Call my wife."[54]

When war came, Forrest enlisted in the Confederate cavalry a month before his fortieth birthday, as a private. The Tennessee governor, who knew him by reputation, sent him to raise a battalion of mounted rangers for the Confederacy. Overnight, Pvt. Forrest became Lt. Col. Forrest. As the war thundered on, he was soon a colonel, then a brigadier, then a major general, and by the war's end, a lieutenant general. One soldier recounted, "His commission was signed not only by Mr. Jefferson Davis, but by the Almighty as well."[55]

"He seemed to go by his horse's leaps from promotion to promotion," marveled another soldier.[56] By war's end, he was thought, by friend and enemies, as perhaps the most brilliant cavalry commander the war had produced, a "Wizard of the Saddle."

Union Gen. William Tecumseh Sherman, the Western commander, broke his lance repeatedly trying to be rid of him, calling him "that Devil Forrest," that

51 The story of this short, but utterly unique courtship and wedding, comes from Sarah Hall, Mary Ann's bridesmaid and schoolmate, later Mrs. Joel Jones of Nashville, in the *Nashville Banner*, Jul. 7, 1935.

52 Charles W. Anderson, "My Last Meeting with Gen. Forrest," in *Confederate Veteran*, vol. 4 (Nov. 1896), 387.

53 Maury, *Recollections of a Virginian*, 215.

54 Noted by his friend, Minor Meriwether, in the Meriwether Family Papers, Southern Historical Collection at the Louis Round Wilson Special Collections Library, University of North Carolina, Chapel Hill, NC.

55 Sergeant Frank T. Reid, in *Military Annals of Tennessee Confederate*, 1st ser., John Berrien Lindsley, ed. (Nashville, 1886), 851.

56 Arlin Turner, ed., "George W. Cable's Recollections of General Forrest," *JSH* (May 1955), 226.

"Hell-hound."[57] After the war, Sherman remarked, "I think Forrest was the most remarkable man our Civil War produced on either side. In the first place, he was uneducated, while Jackson and Sheridan and other brilliant leaders were soldiers by profession. He had never read a military book in his life, knew nothing about tactics, could not even drill a company, but he had a genius for strategy which was original, and to me incomprehensible."[58]

Forrest wore Sherman ragged, raiding his supply lines, destroying rail lines, and cutting communications. Sherman was convinced, correctly, that Forrest had "got some of our troops under cower." Believing "there never will be peace in Tennessee until Forrest is dead,"[59] Sherman trotted out generals four times with orders to corner and kill or capture the pest. None could until the war's end.

With Forrest, some said, "his doggedness of resolution was proverbial. It was like the grasp of death."[60] His fear of death was non-existent, and nothing was impossible. He seemed to possess an eerie ubiquity, his whereabouts the subject of inquiry, no one knowing when he would turn up.

In August 1862, Forrest unexpectedly raided the Union headquarters of the District of West Tennessee in Memphis in the middle of the night. Its commander, Gen. Cadwallader C. Washburn, narrowly escaped capture. Leaving his uniform and accouterments behind in his room, he hit the road in his "nocturnal habiliments."[61] Union Gen. Stephen Hurlbut, whom Washburn replaced, famously said, "They removed me from command because I couldn't keep Forrest out of West Tennessee, and now Washburn can't keep him out of his own bedroom!"[62]

A soldier recounted, "his immediate presence seemed to inspire every one with his terrible energy, more like that of a piece of powerful steam machinery than of a human being."[63] It wasn't in Forrest's nature to await an attack. He believed that no victory had ever been won without bringing on a fight. If a fight was brewing,

57 U.S. War Department, *War of the Rebellion: Official Records of the Union and Confederate Armies*, 128 vols. (Washington, D.C., 1880-1901), ser. 1 vol. 39, pt. 3, 659, in Sherman dispatch to Grant, Nov. 6, 1864. Henceforth, this source will be cited as *OR*; Witherspoon, "Tishomingo Creek or Bryce's Cross Roads," 123.

58 Wyeth, *That Devil Forrest*, 635.

59 *OR*, ser. 1, vol. 38, pt. 4, 480. Sherman dispatch to Stanton, Jun 15, 1864.

60 Brand, "Lieutenant-General N. B. Forrest," 270.

61 Henry, *"First With the Most" Forrest*, 338; *OR* ser. 1, vol. 39, pt 1, pp. 469, 484. The Official Record's report on the Memphis raid is in Ibid., 468-87.

62 Quoted in Henry, *"First with the Most" Forrest*, 338.

63 John Preston Young, *The Seventh Tennessee Cavalry (Confederate) History* (1890; repr., Dayton, OH, 1976), 77.

Forrest more than met it halfway with a charge, or a countercharge, no matter the disproportionate numbers.

Someone recorded, "he struck as the lightning strikes."[64] "He was an electric storm," another soldier declared, "a Mississippi hurricane embodied." Yet, when the hurricane subsided, he expressed "the kindliest feelings toward prisoners and wounded."[65]

Forrest stated he would give more for fifteen minutes of "bulge" on the enemy than for a week of tactics. He often said he could whip any man if he could get there first with the most men and deliver the first blow. Forrest often got there first, but rarely with the most men. He whipped the enemy, including West Pointers. "Whenever I met one of them fellers that fit by note," he stated, "I generally whipped [hell] out of him before he got his tune pitched."[66]

Forrest fought all his battles by ear, holding nothing back. Reserves did not seem to be in his vocabulary. When he fought, everybody fought, even those without guns. "He acted upon the principle," one private wrote, "that an unarmed man was better for the occasion than no man at all, for, if a recruit had nothing but the 'rebel yell,' he could at least help to intimidate an adversary."[67]

Forrest's standard tactic was to attack the front, both flanks, and the enemy's rear, if possible, simultaneously. When leading a charge, he shouted "Forward, Men, and mix with 'em."[68] "Like a ruthless besom of destruction," his young artillery captain, John Morton, said, he "charged the air with electric energy as he hurled himself upon the foe."[69]

The powerful embodiment of a close-quarters fighter, Forrest could not keep from hurling himself upon the foe. Naturally left-handed, he was ambidextrous by training, swinging a sabre or firing a six-shooter accurately from either side.

Striking first with all his force and ferocity, he would pursue relentlessly, like a demon unhinged. The Battle of Brice's Cross Roads in Mississippi in June 1864 was perhaps his finest hour. He rode, one soldier recalled, "[m]ounted on his big sorrel horse, sabre in hand, sleeves rolled up, his coat lying on the pommel of his saddle,

64 John W. Morton, "A Soldier Sums Up," in *As They Saw Forrest*, Robert Selph Henry, ed. (Wilmington, NC, 1987), 276.

65 Lewis Montgomery Hosea, *Some Sidelights on the War for the Union: Paper Read Before the Ohio Commandery of the Loyal Legion of the United States at Cleveland, Ohio* (Oct. 9, 1912), 11.

66 "Bulge" in Henry, *"First With The Most" Forrest*, 17. The rest is from Morton, "A Soldier Sums Up," 272.

67 John Milton Hubbard, "Private Hubbard's Notes," in *As They Saw Forrest*, Robert Selph Henry, ed. (Wilmington, NC, 1987), 149.

68 Taylor, *Destruction and Reconstruction*, 244.

69 Morton, "A Soldier Sums Up," 275.

looking the very God of War."[70] After winning the battle against Federal numbers two or three times his own, Forrest, in his mind, did not believe it was over.

There was still the pursuit, and to Forrest, pursuing the enemy was important. As he explained to John Morton, the idea was to "get 'em skeered, and then keep the skeer on 'em."[71] He had the enemy beaten and skeered at Brice's Cross Roads, and he intended to keep it that way. Forrest relentlessly chased the Union army for seventy-five miles, until they reached Memphis.

One Union officer called it a "regular stampede."[72] The defeated Union commander, Gen. Samuel Davis Sturgis, a West Pointer, said, "my whole army became literally an uncontrollable mob."[73] Fleeing, Sturgis declared, "For God's sake, if Mr. Forrest will let me alone I will let him alone."[74]

Forrest had a streak of insubordination that would have gotten any other man in serious trouble. He was, John Morton wrote, "the most insubordinate of men."[75] He followed sensible orders willingly but didn't tolerate abuse or incompetence from his superiors. True to his nature, Forrest did not back down from saying so, to the offending superior's face.

Perhaps the most damning moment of insubordination was when Forrest fired point blank anger against his superior, Gen. Braxton Bragg. Bragg was inept, and Forrest had come to distrust and despise him. Raging against yet another command that Bragg had issued, Forrest rushed to his tent, passed the sentry, and exploded into the general's quarters. Failing to salute, or shake hands, he bellowed:

> I have stood your meanness as long as I intend to. You have played the part of a damned scoundrel, and if you were any part of a man I would slap your jaws and force you to resent it. You may as well not issue any orders to me, for I will not obey them, and I will hold you personally responsible for any further indignities you endeavor to inflict upon me. . . . [I]f you ever again try to interfere with me or cross my path it will be at the peril of your life.[76]

70 Hubbard, "Private Hubbard's Notes,"163.

71 John W. Morton Papers, Spring of 1861 to November 5, 1864, in Special Collections, Jean and Alexander Heard Library, Vanderbilt University, Nashville, TN, 181, 198; Henry, *"First With the Most" Forrest*, 535.

72 *OR*, ser. 1, vol. 39, pt. 1, p. 170.

73 Ibid., 218.

74 Ibid., 214.

75 Morton, "A Soldier Sums Up," 272.

76 Quoted in Wyeth, *That Devil Forrest*, 264-66.

Forrest stomped out, leaving Bragg shaken. Nothing further came of it. Bragg inflicted no further indignities, interfered with, or crossed Forrest's path again. Perhaps he took at face value the phrase "at the peril of your life."

When the luck of the Confederacy played out in the spring of 1865, it forced Forrest to surrender. Some of his solders wanted to fight on, but Forrest would have none of it. Ferocious in war, he was gentlemanly in peace. In his final message to his solders he said, "I have never on the field of battle sent you where I was unwilling to go myself, nor would I now advise you to a course which I felt myself unwilling to pursue. You *have been* good soldiers, you *can be* good citizens. Obey the laws, preserve your honor, and the Government to which you have surrendered can afford to be, and will be, magnanimous."[77]

I am convinced that had Jackson lived, he would have echoed this sentiment. In the final act, he and Forrest, twins in how they waged war, would have been twins in waging peace.

77 From Forrest's farewell address to his solders at their surrender on May 9, 1865, in Henry, *As They Saw Forrest*, 299.

Chapter 6

The Equality Seekers

There were two voices, in particular, that resonated loudly against slavery. They were black voices. Frederick Douglass was one of those voices, a celebrated orator, newspaper publisher, and former slave. Sojourner Truth was the other, an illiterate talker and singer, whose powerful voice thundered for justice. They were seeking equality for their race, a thankless task in the face of widespread white supremacy.

The President's Friend

Frederick Douglass, a black man, raised himself from a lowly slave into one of the great men of the nineteenth century. Command and distinction radiated from him. To hear him speak was to hear one of the greatest orators of his time. A slave in Maryland for the first twenty years of his life, Douglass was a powerful presence. When he and President Lincoln first met in 1863, it was a study in equality without a taint of prejudice. The relationship between the two is one of the most dramatic and moving friendships in American history.

When Lincoln ran against Stephen Douglas (one "s") for the U.S. Senate seat in Illinois in 1858, Douglass (two "s's") saw something to praise; Lincoln viewed Blacks as people, not property, and talked about equal rights and equal opportunity. When Lincoln became president in 1861, and faced increasing pressures to compromise, Douglass would demand the president honor his first principles. With Civil War breaking out, nobody was harder on Lincoln than Douglass. Lincoln's caution in doing something about freeing the slaves enraged

Frederick Douglass

National Archives

Douglass. He spoke of Lincoln's "slothful deliberation."[1] Something Lincoln said or did would hearten Douglass, then something done or not done next would

1 "Douglass' Monthly," October 1862. University of Rochester Frederick Douglass Project.

enrage him. This kept Douglass on a roller coaster of hope and despair. Lincoln was deliberate, operating at his own speed, and didn't allow himself to be rushed.

Powerful and effective, Douglass threw verbal daggers. He blasted Lincoln over the proposal to repatriate Blacks back to Africa, a notion Lincoln finally abandoned as unworkable. Douglass criticized Lincoln for telling two of his generals, John Charles Fremont and David Hunter, to cancel their orders freeing the slaves in their areas of command. Lincoln saw it as premature. Besides, it was not a general's job to free slaves; it was a president's.

Douglass was more than unhappy with Lincoln and the Republican party for upholding the Fugitive Slave Law. He called Lincoln the abolitionists' worst enemy. He deplored Lincoln's first inaugural address, especially the ending about not wanting to be enemies with the slave-holding South.[2]

Finally, in September 1862, after the battle of Antietam, Lincoln did what Douglass and the abolitionists had long wanted. He issued an Emancipation Proclamation, freeing all slaves in the South, to take effect on January 1, 1863. Douglass was ecstatic, and full of hope. The proclamation also opened the gate to enlisting Black soldiers into the Union armies, a move Douglass had long pushed.

"Colored" units began forming in the North. Douglass stopped being just an orator and newspaper publisher to become a recruiting agent. He helped set up two regiments in Massachusetts and Pennsylvania. Around 180,000 Black soldiers would become Union soldiers during the war.

In the summer of 1863, a serious turn of events shook Douglass. The Confederate states announced they intended to treat African American troops, if captured, as insurgents, not prisoners of war. This meant execution or enslavement. They were not to be exchanged, as White soldiers were. A worried Douglass went to see Lincoln in person. He was looking for assurances on the treatment of captured soldiers of color, and to see if Lincoln would retaliate.

Lincoln and Douglass had never met or spoken to one another. Douglass was not sure Lincoln would even receive him and didn't know how to proceed. In Washington, senators and other distinguished men walked freely about the city. Meeting one of them on the street was not uncommon. On his way to the White House, Douglass ran into Senator Samuel C. Pomeroy of Kansas, who offered to introduce him to the president.

2 John Stauffer, *Giants: The Parallel Lives of Frederick Douglass and Abraham Lincoln* (New York & Boston, 2008), 391n, 23.

At the White House, many were waiting to see the president. Lincoln called such scenes the "Beggars' Opera."[3] Douglass believed it would take half a day for Lincoln to get to him. But within two minutes after sending up his card, he and Pomeroy were called to the president's office. When he entered, Douglass later wrote, Lincoln was:

> Seated in a low chair, surrounded by a multitude of books and papers, his feet and legs were extended in front of his chair. On my approach he slowly drew his feet in from the different parts of the room into which they had strayed, and he began to rise, and continued to rise until he looked down upon me, and extended his hand and gave me a welcome. I began, with some hesitation, to tell him who I was and what I had been doing, but he soon stopped me, saying in a sharp, cordial voice: 'You need not tell me who you are I know who you are, Mr. Douglass, I know who you are.'[4]

Douglass immediately stated his business. "Mr. Lincoln," he said, "if you wish to make this branch of the service successful you must do four things." He ticked them off—compel the Confederates to treat Black soldiers as prisoners of war, retaliate in kind for any of them hanged, give Black soldiers the same pay as Whites, and when any Black soldier excels in the field he is to be promoted as White soldiers are promoted.[5]

To all but one demand Lincoln assented, assuring Douglass he was working on them. However, he balked at retaliating in kind. "Once begun," he said, "I do not know where such a measure would stop." He said he couldn't have men killed in cold blood for what others did. Lincoln could not kill the innocent for the guilty.[6]

Throughout the interview, there was an unexpected undertone. Both seemed to feel comfortable. Often with his White abolitionist friends, Douglass endured awkward moments. Not with Lincoln. Douglass recalled, "He was the first man that I talked with in the United States freely, who in no single instance reminded me of the difference between himself and myself, of the difference of color."[7]

3 Edward D. Neill, "Reminiscences of the Last Year of President Lincoln's Life," in vol.1, *A Series of Papers Read before the Minnesota Commandery of the Military Order of the Loyal Legion of the United States* (1887; repr., Wilmington, NC, 1992), 37.

4 Allen Thorndike Rice, ed. *Reminiscences of Abraham Lincoln by Distinguished Men of His Time* (New York, 1885), 186.

5 Ibid., 186-87.

6 Ibid., 188-89.

7 Ibid., 193.

In his visit, the astonished ex-slave, Douglass, realized he had become friends with the president of the United States, whom he had so often criticized.[8] They would have other meetings during the war and the friendship cemented.

This did not mean that Douglass stopped protesting many of Lincoln's policies. The frustrations still happened. Douglass disagreed with Lincoln's Reconstruction plan and was upset with how he responded to the Fort Pillow massacre in 1864. Neither was Douglass thrilled by Lincoln's letter to Horace Greeley before the Emancipation Proclamation. In that letter Lincoln famously said he was indifferent to slavery, and that reunion was the central purpose of the war.[9]

When Lincoln delivered his short, famous Second Inaugural Address, Douglass was there. He was also at the reception following the inauguration. Douglass supposed it was "the first time in any colored man's life" to even try such a thing. As he approached the White House's entrance, he was seized by two policemen. He protested, saying if Lincoln "knew I was at the door he would order my admission." Then he bolted past the two policemen.

Inside, he was taken into custody by two other policemen. Instead of being conducted to the president, he was being pushed out a window on a plank. "Oh," Douglass said, "this will not do, gentlemen," and called out to a passer-by, "Just say to Mr. Lincoln that Fred. Douglass is at the door. The passing gentleman ran inside and almost in less than half a minute I was invited into the East Room of the White House." There, he later recalled, he found himself in wholly uncharted territory:

> A perfect sea of beauty and elegance, too, it was. The ladies were in very fine attire, and Mrs. Lincoln was standing there. I could not have been more than ten feet from him when Mr. Lincoln saw me; his countenance lighted up, he said in a voice which was heard all around: "Here comes my friend Douglass." As I approached him he reached out his hand, gave me a cordial shake, and said: "Douglass, I saw you in the crowd today listening to my inaugural address. There is no man's opinion that I value more than yours: what do you think of it?" Douglas replied: "Mr. Lincoln, it was a sacred effort."[10]

A little over a month later, Lincoln was assassinated at Ford's Theatre in Washington. Douglass was devastated. The nation had lost a president. He had lost a friend.

8 Douglass's description of his first meeting with Lincoln is in Rice, *Reminiscences of Abraham Lincoln*, 185-89.

9 Stauffer, *Giants*, 285.

10 Douglass's account of Inaugural Day events is in Rice, *Reminiscences of Abraham Lincoln*, 190-93.

The grieving Mary Lincoln, with the help of her assistant, Elizabeth Keckley, sent mementoes to special people. To Douglass, she sent Lincoln's favorite walking staff. This gesture moved Douglass. In his thank you note to Mrs. Lincoln, he wrote:

> I assure you, that this inestimable memento of his Excellency will be retained in my possession while I live—an object of sacred interest—a token not merely of the kind consideration in which I have reason to know that the President was pleased to hold me personally, but as an indication of his humane interest [in the] welfare of my whole race.[11]

Together, these two distinguished men, black and white, president and his critic, had shown their country how to eradicate racism: strike up a friendship.

War'n't She a Woman?

Sojourner Truth, the ex-slave and "tongue of fire"[12] was an itinerant preacher, speaker, and singer for the rights of Blacks and women.

She was nearly six feet tall and gaunt in her gray dress and white turban. Her voice was like a trumpet, deep-toned, with "a pitch like rolling thunder," not seeming to be that of a woman. Some, therefore, thought her a man. To disprove that assumption, she would bare her naked breasts to audiences.[13]

She claimed though she was a woman, she had "as much muscle as any man, and can do as much work as any man. I have plowed and reaped and husked and chopped and mowed, and can any man do more than that? I can carry as much as any man, and can eat as much too, if I can get it. I am as strong as any man that is now."[14] She was probably ready to prove that, too, with some heavy lifting.

The litany that she is best known for, best remembered for, to this day, is "Ar'n't I a woman?" They were powerful identifying words, which have been a rallying cry in women's rights movements ever since. But they are words she never spoke, pure folklore, insist her biographers, tacked on to her by a contemporary,

11 Douglass, "Your Late Lamented Husband: An Unpublished Letter of Frederick Douglass to Mary Todd Lincoln" manuscript (New York, 2000), 5, 10.

12 Sojourner Truth, *The Narrative of Sojourner Truth: By Sojourner Truth-Illustrated* (1850; repr., Mineola, NY, 1997), 117.

13 Ibid., 5, 90, 92, 94-95; Carlton Mabee, "Sojourner Truth and President Lincoln," in *New England Quarterly*, Vol. 61 (Dec. 1998), 223.

14 Quoted in Erlene Stetson & Linda David, *Glorying in Tribulation: The Life Work of Sojourner Truth* (East Lansing, MI, 1994), 114.

Sojourner Truth

Library of Congress

Frances Dana Gage.[15] If she never said those words, she might just as well have, as they have stuck to her like glue.

Sojourner Truth, a name she gave herself, meant a traveler spreading the truth. She was a slave for thirty years in New York, before it was outlawed there in 1827. She was born in New York's Hudson River Valley, in sight of the Catskill Mountains, about 1797. No one is certain of the exact year. She was first called Isabella, but renamed herself Sojourner Truth after what she called her rebirth in June 1843. Her first language was Dutch. She became fluent in English, but never learned to read or write in either language.[16]

"I tell you, I can't read a book," but "I can read de people." She spoke extemporaneously, she said, not knowing what the Lord would put into her mouth next. She said, "I go to hear myself as much as anyone else comes to hear me."[17] When what she spoke thrilled her, she would say, "I felt so *tall within*—I felt as if the *power of a nation* was with me."[18]

She preferred to keep her speech homely and rich with humor. Sojourner would deliver her talks in an Afro-Dutch accent, accompanied with a lightning wit. She found audiences liked it that way. It was more picturesque, bewitching, and memorable. She molded her public image around her illiteracy.[19]

Sojourner Truth is considered an "invented great," like Jesus and Joan of Arc, according to her biographer, Nell Irvin Painter. Most of what we know about Sojourner Truth comes from educated white women, such as Harriet Beecher Stowe.[20]

The author of *Uncle Tom's Cabin* called Sojourner the "Libyan Sibyl," and said, "I do not recollect to have been conversant with any one who had more of that silent and subtle power which we call personal presence." Stowe wrote of Sojourner's "great, gloomy eyes . . . wonderful physical vigor, her great heaving sea of emotion, her power of spiritual conception, her quick penetration, and her boundless energy."[21]

Sojourner's powerful singing voice awed many, and she sang whenever she spoke. It would not be far wrong to call her the Marian Anderson of the Civil War era.

15 Nell Irvin Painter, *Sojourner Truth: A Life, A Symbol* (New York, 1996), 171, 281-87; Mabee, *Sojourner Truth*, 76-78, 80-81.

16 Truth, *Narrative*, viii, xv, 9, 24n, 248; Painter, *Sojourner Truth*, 4, 5-6, 11, 73-74.

17 Mabee, *Sojourner Truth*, 64, 65.

18 Truth, *Narrative*, 30.

19 Mabee, *Sojourner Truth*, 65.

20 Painter, *Sojourner Truth*, 174, 285.

21 Quoted in Truth, *Narrative*, 103, 104, 115.

Much of what Sojourner Truth sang, she composed herself, but of course, never wrote down. A stanza from one of these compositions, celebrating the Black soldier in the Union army and set to the tune of "Battle Hymn of the Republic" went like this:

We are done with hoeing cotton, are done with hoeing corn,
We are colored Yankee soldiers as sure as you are born
When Massa hears us shouting, he will think 'tis Gabriel's Horn
As we go marching on.
Glory, glory, hallelujah! Glory, glory, hallelujah!
Glory, glory, hallelujah, as we go marching on.[22]

One can imagine that great voice singing this one, which rather summarizes what she was about, tuned to "Auld Lang Syne:"

I am pleading for my people,
A poor, downtrodden race,
Who dwell in freedom's boasted land,
With no abiding place.
I am pleading for the mothers
Who gaze in wild despair
Upon the hated auction block,
And see their children there.[23]

Sojourner, like Douglass, went to see Lincoln, near the end of his first term, on October 29, 1864. She survived a long round-about journey from Battle Creek, Michigan, where she lived, to Washington. When Lincoln got to her at the "Beggars Opera," she said:

> Mr. President, when you first took your seat I feared you would be torn to pieces, for I likened you unto Daniel, who was thrown into the lions' den; and if the lions did not tear you into pieces, I know that it would be God that had saved you; and I said if He spared me I would see you before the four years expired, and He has done so, and now I am here to see you for myself.

22 Ibid., 86.

23 Mabee, *Sojourner Truth*, 222.

When the conversation got around to Lincoln's proclamation freeing the slaves in the South, he named several of his predecessors and said, "They were all just as good, and would have done just as I have done if the time had come." He pointed toward the Potomac and said, "If the people over the river had behaved themselves, I could not have done what I have, but they did not, and I was compelled to do these things." Sojourner replied, "I thank God that you were the instrument selected by Him and the people to do it."

Sojourner handed Lincoln a little book, and he took it and wrote, "For Aunty Sojourner Truth, October 29, 1864," and signed it, "A. Lincoln." As she rose to leave, Lincoln took her hand and said he would be pleased to have her call again. She discovered with Lincoln the same color-blindness that had so moved Douglass. She was "never treated with more kindness and cordiality than I was by that good and great man," Sojourner Truth recalled later. [24] Lincoln had acquired another Black friend.

24 Benjamin Quarles, *Lincoln and the Negroes* (New York, 1962), 206.

Chapter 7

Lincoln's "Political Little Ones"

When the Republican party nominated Lincoln as its presidential candidate in May 1860, he soon had a mail problem. He mentioned it to his friend, Orias M. Hatch, the Republican secretary of state, in Illinois. "I wish," Lincoln said, "I could find some young man to help me with my correspondence. It is getting so heavy I can't handle it. I can't afford to pay much, but the practice is worth something."[1]

Hatch unselfishly recommended his own able chief clerk, twenty-eight-year-old John George Nicolay, and Lincoln hired him. Soon, Nicolay himself was swamped, recommending to Lincoln that they bring on Nicolay's twenty-two-year-old friend, John Hay.

These two young men worked for Lincoln through the canvass, and when Lincoln was elected, they went with him to the White House. The two young men shared a bedroom and performed secretarial duties for the president of the United States. Smart and quick, they impressed Lincoln. They would do fine as his personal secretaries.

There was a small problem bringing both with him. The president was allotted only one paid secretary, Nicolay. So, Lincoln had Hay appointed a clerk in the Department of the Interior, assigned to the White House.

Hay tells us what their duties were:

1 Augustus S. Chapman, "The Boyhood of John Hay," *Century Magazine* 46 (Jul. 1909), 452; Nicolay, *An Oral History*, xii.

> Nicolay received members of Congress, & other visitors who had business with the Executive Office, communicated to the Senate and House the messages of the President, & exercised general supervision over the business.
>
> I opened and read the letters, answered them, looked over the newspapers, supervised the clerks who kept the records and in Nicolay's absence did his work also. When the President had any rather delicate matter to manage at a distance from Washington, he very rarely wrote, but sent Nicolay or me.[2]

Both young men idolized the president for whom they worked. Hay called him "the Cincinnatus of the prairie,"[3] saying "Lincoln, with all his faults, is the greatest character since Christ."[4] He continued, "His great character and example went abroad on the wings of every wind that blew."[5]

The two secretaries called Lincoln "the Tycoon," "the Ancient," and occasionally "the Premier" or "the American."[6] One Lincoln critic saw these two young men, not yet out of their twenties, as the president's "political little ones."[7] It was not a compliment.

The Bavarian in the White House

It seems reasonable to assume that any personal secretary to a president of the United States ought to be a genuine 100 percent American, a citizen from birth. No alien need apply.

It is an important, sensitive position. Congress might see a foreigner so close to the president's side as a threat to national security. Today there would likely be angry televised congressional hearings in both Houses.

Lincoln's leading personal secretary for his entire first term as president was John George Nicolay. He was not an American citizen. John G. Nicolay was an

2 Hay, *At Lincoln's Side*, 110.

3 Ibid., 5.

4 Ibid., 111.

5 Ibid., 130.

6 John Hay, *Inside Lincoln's White House: The Complete Civil War Diary of John Hay*, Michael Burlingame & John R. Turner Ettlinger, eds. & intro (Carbondale, IL, 1997.) These Nicolay and Hay nicknames for Lincoln are sprinkled throughout Hay's two books—*Inside Lincoln's White House*, his diary, and *At Lincoln's Side*, his Civil War correspondence, and selected writings. Both were edited by Michael Burlingame, a noted Lincoln scholar. They are invaluable contributions to the Lincoln canon.

7 Adam Gurowski, *Diary*, 3 vols. 1862-1866 (New York, 1968), 3:80.

John George Nicolay

National Archives

immigrant, a foreigner, an alien, a Bavarian, subject to the King of Bavaria. A citizen of Germany![8]

Nobody was aware of this but Nicolay, and he never mentioned it. Everybody from Lincoln on down just assumed he was a citizen. Nicolay acted like one. He voted in elections, swore loyalty oaths, got admitted to the bar in Illinois, and signed as a citizen for a patent (he had five patents, four more than Lincoln). He

8 Allen Carden & Thomas J. Ebert, *John George Nicolay: The Man in Lincoln's Shadow* (Knoxville, TN, 2019), 91.

would not become a naturalized citizen until October 1870, five years after he had finished serving the martyred president.[9]

Yet nobody, not even the most purely conceived American citizen from birth, could have served Lincoln so devotedly or so well as this immigrant German.

The association between Lincoln and Nicolay began in Springfield, Illinois, in the late 1850s. Nicolay was chief clerk in the office of the Illinois secretary of state Hatch. Lincoln frequently visited Hatch's office, which served as the Republican Party's unofficial headquarters in Springfield.

Nicolay was self-educated, intelligent, well read, and spoke three languages—English, German, and French. Occasionally, when Lincoln dropped in, he and Nicolay would talk and play chess.

Nicolay was born in Esslingen, in the kingdom of Bavaria, on February 26, 1832, the son of a maker of wine casks. In 1837, when he was five, young Nicolay migrated to America with his parents, settling in Cincinnati. In 1842, the family moved to Pittsfield, Illinois, a town in Pike County between the Mississippi and Illinois Rivers.

Nicolay was then ten years old, a physically frail "freckle-faced red-headed boy in bed-ticking trousers and straw hat."[10] Fully grown, he would stand just a shade over five feet ten inches tall. But "never in his lifetime," his daughter Helen confided, "would he weigh more than one hundred and twenty pounds."[11] Nicolay was built like a human pencil.

Zachariah N. Garbutt, editor of the *Pike County Free Press* in Pittsfield, liked Nicolay so much that he basically adopted him, plugging him into the newspaper business. In the next eight years, starting as an apprentice, then as a reporter, Nicolay eventually became the paper's editor and publisher. In the same eight years he educated himself, leaning heavily on Shakespeare, *The Bible*, and Blackstone's *Commentaries on the Laws of England*, a legal handbook for American and British lawyers. This was much the same way Lincoln had educated himself.

Nicolay possessed a sky-high intelligence and a tireless work ethic. However, as a young man, he was "always a modest, perhaps even diffident person, very, very painfully shy." A friend remembered Nicolay as so shy he would "shun the streets where the elite of the village were most likely to be passing."[12]

9 Ibid.

10 James Thompson, "Nicolay was a German Citizen," unidentified newspaper clipping, Carl Sandburg Collection, at Rare Book & Manuscript Library, University of Illinois, Urbana; Nicolay, *An Oral History*, xi.

11 Helen Nicolay, *Lincoln's Secretary: A Biography of John G. Nicolay* (New York, 1949), 84.

12 Thomas Hall Shastid, *My Second Life* (1944, repr., London, 2018), 72n; Nicolay, *An Oral History*, xi.

When Nicolay reached Washington with Lincoln, however, none of that shyness remained. Lincoln's first official act after his inauguration in 1861 had been to appoint Nicolay as his private secretary. In effect, Nicolay became Lincoln's hard-nosed chief of staff, sitting at his desk in a room next to Lincoln's office. There, he mercilessly blocked the way to the busy president of many Civil War elites. He was Dr. Jekyll, transformed into Mr. Hyde. Noah Brooks, the reporter covering Washington for a newspaper in California, pictured him as a Cerberus, the mythical three-headed hound guarding Hades to keep the dead from escaping.[13]

Nicolay was "the bulldog in the anteroom." William O. Stoddard, a second assistant secretary brought in out of necessity, called him that. Stoddard thought people who did not like Nicolay considered him "sour and crusty." The personality change was necessary. "It is a good thing, then, that he is," Stoddard wrote. "If you will sit in that chair a month or so, you will see what has become of any good-nature you sat down with."[14] Stoddard knew this from experience, having filled in briefly when both Nicolay and Hay were out on missions for Lincoln. He survived but was thankful it wasn't his regular day job.

When Nicolay was not Cerberus, he was his genial, good-natured self, invited often to social events. He had no standing in Washington society. But he was quick-witted, had a gift for languages, and carried an impressive knowledge of politics, music, and literature.

But somebody in the White House had to say "no" when necessary to protect the time and interests of the president. That was Nicolay's job. He had to say "no" often, frequently to some of the most powerful figures in the country. The flood of petitioners wanting something from the president rolled in, while Lincoln was busy conducting a war. The president compared the situation to being "so busy renting out rooms at one end of his house that he could not stop to put out the fire that was burning the other end."[15]

Nicolay could also say "yes" when he thought it warranted, needed, or requested by Lincoln. He was then a bulldog getting the petitioner's wishes courteously and speedily fulfilled. In all things, Nicolay was discreet, trustworthy, efficient, and dedicated to Lincoln's best interests.

Nicolay compared the daily stampeding of people to his office with the swarming insects that came through the White House windows. He wrote about them to his fiancé, Therena Bates, in Pittsfield:

13 Carden and Ebert, *John George Nicolay*, 291.

14 William O. Stoddard, *Inside the White House in War Times* (New York, 1892), 104; Nicolay, *An Oral History*, xiii, 124n.

15 Brooks, *Washington in Lincoln's Time*, 254.

> The gas lights over my desk are burning brightly and the windows of the room are open, and all bugdom outside seems to have organized a storming party to take the gas light. The air is swarming with them. They are on the ceiling, the walls and the furniture in countless numbers, they are buzzing about the room, and butting their heads against the window panes, they are on my clothes, in my hair, and on the sheet I am writing on. They are all here, the plebian masses, as well as the great and distinguished members of the oldest and largest patrician families—the Millers, the Roaches, the Whites, the Blacks, yea even the wary and diplomatic foreigners from the Musquito Kingdom. They hold a high carnival, or rather a perfect Saturnalia. Intoxicated and maddened and blinded by the bright gas-light, they dance and rush about in wild gyrations, until they are drawn into the dazzling but fatal heat of the gas-flame when they all fall to the floor, burned and maimed and mangled to death, to be swept out into the dust and rubbish by the servant in the morning.

This nightly summer's swarming of insects brought to Nicolay's mind all the "big bugs, buzzing and gyrating round the great central sun and light and source of power of the government."[16]

Another species buzzing constantly around were the job seekers. Hay wrote his friend, William Leete Stone, "The throng of office-seekers, is something absolutely fearful. They come at daybreak and still are coming at midnight."[17] Lincoln estimated that 30,000 office seekers came looking for government jobs in the war years. But this onslaught was softened by another number, the "some 30,000,000 who ask for no offices."[18]

Many, however, had something to say about Nicolay's *modus operandi.* Of the negative voices, a critic from New York advised Lincoln that "if the stories I hear about Nicolay . . . are true, you ought to dismiss him. People say he is very disagreeable and uncivil."[19] Lincoln's friend Alexander K. McClure, who disagreed occasionally with Nicolay, disdained him as "a good mechanical clerk," but his "removal was earnestly pressed upon Lincoln on more than one occasion because of his want of tact and fitness for his trust." McClure believed, "Only the proverbial kindness of Lincoln saved him from dismissal."[20]

John Russell Young, a newspaper correspondent, wrote that Nicolay had "great powers of application" and "the close methodical, silent German way about

16 The long-indented quote and the short one following are in John Nicolay to Therena Bates, Jul. 20, 1864, Nicolay Papers, Manuscript Division, Library of Congress.

17 Hay, *At Lincoln's Side*, 5.

18 Ibid., 125.

19 Robert Colby to Lincoln, May 18,1861, Lincoln Papers, Library of Congress; Nicolay, *An Oral History*, xiii.

20 "The Defeat of Hamlin," *Washington Post*, Jul. 9, 1891; Nicolay, *An Oral History*, xiii.

him." Contrary to the bulldog image, Russell thought Nicolay "scrupulous, polite, calm, obliging, with the gift of hearing other people talk." In the Capitol, Nicolay came and went "like a shadow."[21] Young saw him as a "man without excitements or emotions, never saying anything worth quoting, and in that regard invaluable as a private secretary; absorbed in the President, and seeing that the Executive business was well done."[22]

As the war ended, Lincoln's second term began. Exhausted, both Nicolay and Hay wanted out. Both men had snagged jobs independently in the U.S. embassy in Paris, Nicolay as the consul, Hay as secretary of legation. Before they left for Paris, Lincoln was assassinated at Ford's Theater. His two secretaries left for Paris with broken hearts.

Nicolay got into serious trouble about Paris with Therena Bates, his unofficial fiancé. He wrote on May 5 saying he was "sorry to say that I think that I will not be able to take you to Paris with me this time." She was having none of it. Therena told him if he was going without her, the romance was over. She had selflessly waited for him for four years while he was in Washington. She did not intend to see him now go off to Paris and leave her again. Urged by friends to think again, Nicolay proposed. She accepted instantly, and they set about preparing to get married and leave for Paris together.[23]

The two lovers had met in Pittsfield. Nicolay had learned to play the organ and performed regularly in church. While he played, he would sneak looks at the very diverting Therena, with her "olive cheek and knot of blue-black hair."[24] Nicolay called her Maggie.[25] They lived, and he worked, in Paris, still not a U. S. citizen, for four years, until 1869. There, Maggie delivered a daughter they called Helen.

Back in the United States, in 1872, Nicolay landed the choice position of marshal of the United States Supreme Court, holding it for the next fifteen years. Since the job was not demanding, he began writing a definitive biography of Abraham Lincoln, to be co-authored by John Hay. It would be Nicolay's passion for the next two decades.

Robert Lincoln made his father's papers available to them, and from 1872 to 1890, the two former secretaries wrote as time allowed. Nicolay did most of the research, and they produced a majestic biography that first ran serially in *Century*

21 Young, "Lincoln as He Was," *Pittsburgh Dispatch*, Aug. 23, 1891; Nicolay, *An Oral History*, xiii.

22 Ibid.; see also Ward Hill Lamon, *Recollections of Abraham Lincoln, 1847-1865*, Dorothy Lamon Teillard, ed. (1895; repr., Lincoln, NE, 1994), 482.

23 This lover's argument is in Carden and Ebert, *John George Nicolay*, 205.

24 Nicolay, *Lincoln's Secretary*, 11.

25 Carden and Ebert, *John George Nicolay*, 36.

Magazine. It was reproduced by Century as a ten-volume work, titled *Abraham Lincoln: A History*.

Sadly, Maggie, the love of Nicolay's life, who had been helping him with the biography, would never read it in its finished form. She died in November 1885. She was only forty-nine years old. When she died, their daughter, Helen, then twenty years old, and who was to become an acclaimed writer in her own right, helped Nicolay to finish his work. She would later write a biography of her father. Nicolay had devoted nearly three decades of his life to Abraham Lincoln

"Every task ever asked of him by Lincoln," two Nicolay biographers have written, "was accomplished to the complete satisfaction of the president. There is no record of Nicolay ever violating a confidence, failing an assignment, or otherwise disappointing the expectations and trust Lincoln placed in him."[26]

Nobody was closer to Lincoln and knew him better than Nicolay and Hay. "During more than four years," Nicolay said, "[I] had opportunities almost daily and nightly to witness his bearing under most trying conditions and circumstances."[27] When the twentieth century was not yet two years old, Nicolay was sixty-nine years old and dying. Six days before he died, John Hay came to visit his old and dear friend. Nicolay's daughter, Helen, described Hay as he "mounted the stairs slowly" to go to Nicolay's bedside. She watched as he descended the stairs later "more slowly still, his face stricken with grief."[28]

The next day, Hay wrote to his other close friend, Henry Adams, "N----- is dying. I went to see him yesterday and he did not know me."[29] On September 26, 1901, Nicolay died. Theirs had been a friendship around great events, a forever friendship. The day Nicolay died, the other intimate friend of his life, Lincoln, was being buried for the last time in Oak Ridge Cemetery in Springfield., Illinois. At Nicolay's death, Richard Gilder, the editor at *Century* who had worked closely with Nicolay and Hay on their magisterial biography of Lincoln, wrote a poem for Helen Nicolay about her father. The first line read, "This man loved Lincoln, him did Lincoln love."[30]

26 Carden and Ebert, *John George Nicolay*, 298.

27 Nicolay, *An Oral History*, 103.

28 Nicolay, *Lincoln's Secretary*, 342.

29 Hay to Adams, Sep. 19, 1901, quoted in Carden and Ebert, *John George Nicolay*, 302.

30 Gilder, *The Poems of Richard Watson Gilder* (Boston & New York, 1908), 310.

The Secretary with the Golden Tongue

As Nicolay shined as Lincoln's primary secretary, so did Hay as the assistant secretary. These two lifelong friends aced their jobs. They were interchangeable, and Lincoln prized them equally. He trusted them, not just as secretaries, but as trouble shooters, to take on assignments for the president outside Washington.

Lincoln needed support for his Reconstruction Plan in Florida. He commissioned Hay a major in the Union Army, so he could deal with the generals. Hay roamed about Florida for a long while. Nicolay wrote, "I infer that you are living in metaphorical clover while we poor devils are eating husks of hard work in the national pig sty."[31]

In every level of society, young Hay, like Nicolay, excelled and felt comfortable. Hay, who was barely old enough to vote, could easily socialize with high-ranking officials, including the president. Hay socialized with Nicolay, or alone in the homes of famous people such as Henry Seward, Salmon Chase, and various Union generals. Hay was intelligent, a good mixer, and knew how to talk about almost any subject. Hannah Angell, his girlfriend at Brown University, found him "very attractive as a talker" given to "abrupt, swift phrases."[32]

President Abraham Lincoln and John Hay

Library of Congress

Hay was born in Salem, Indiana, in 1838, and raised in Warsaw, Illinois, on the bank of the Mississippi River at the state's westernmost edge. He graduated from Brown University in Providence, Rhode Island, in 1858. Returning to Illinois, he began studying law in his uncle's office in Pittsfield, when Nicolay lured him to come and help carry the mail overload for Lincoln. After Lincoln

31 Quoted in Carden and Ebert, *John George Nicolay*, 174.

32 Hannah Angell, interview with William R. Thayer, John Hay Papers, Brown University, Providence, RI.

John Hay

Library of Congress

was elected, he took both secretaries to Washington. Impressed, Lincoln thought they would work well as a duo.

There developed a legacy of opinion about Hay, this too-young upstart, in his four years with Lincoln. Thomas Wentworth Higginson, a prominent Unitarian minister, abolitionist, and soldier, said Hay was "a nice young fellow, who unfortunately looks about seventeen and is oppressed with the necessity of behaving like seventy."[33]

33 Higginson, ed., *Letters and Journals of Thomas Wentworth Higginson*, 201; Hay, *Inside Lincoln's White House*, xxiv.

John Russell Young, the reporter, friend of Nicolay and Hay, often visited their offices. He thought Hay "exceedingly handsome—a slight, graceful, boyish figure—'girl in boy's clothes,' as I heard in a sniff from some angry politician." Russell thought Hay "brilliant, chivalrous," and "independent, with opinions on most questions" and not shy expressing them. Russell saw his friend as "a comely young man with a peach blossom face," as "honest as sunshine, as strong and brave as the seas," and "well suited for his place in the president's family."[34]

A gentleman who often dined in the same club with Hay from 1863 to 1865, said he was "always the same witty, genial, agreeable, effervescent and fascinating fellow," who possessed "decided genius and literary culture." He pegged Hay correctly as "a trusted friend of Lincoln's," and "probably lived nearer to that good man's heart during the years of the Civil War, than any other man."[35]

William Leete Stone, Hay's roommate at Brown, recalled "a singularly modest and retiring disposition," but with "so winning a manner that no one could be in his presence, even for a few moments, without falling under the spell which his conversation and companionship invariably cast upon all who came within his influence."[36]

There was dissent to this praise. One journalist said, "Hay was such a damned intellectual snob . . . so superior to everybody, including Jehovah, that you wanted to puke as you read him."[37] Jesse K. Dubois, a friend of Lincoln from Illinois, thought Nicolay and Hay were "too big for their breeches." Hay jokingly told Nicolay this was "a fault for which it seems to me either Nature or our tailors are to blame."[38]

Perhaps Hay's premier contribution to Lincoln was his duty as the manager of the mail. Not only was Hay a good talker, but an excellent writer. He not only opened Lincoln's mail, but he answered most of it. "He wrote very few letters," Hay said of Lincoln. "He did not read one in fifty that he received. At first we tried to bring them to his notice, but at last he gave the whole thing over to me, and

34 John Russell Young, in *Philadelphia Evening Star*, Aug. 22, 1891; Young quoted in Evans, "Personal Reminiscences of John Hay," *Chattanooga* (TN) *Sunday Times*, Jul. 30, 1905. These two sources are in turn quoted in the introduction of Burlingame & Ettlinger, *Inside Lincoln's White House*, xii-xiii.

35 *Sedalia* (Missouri) *Times*, May 11, 1871, quoted in Burlingame. & Ettlinger, introduction, *Inside Lincoln's White House*, xv.

36 William Leete Stone, "John Hay, 1858," in *Memories of Brown*, 153-54; Burlingame & Ettlinger, in introduction, *At Lincoln's Side*, xx.

37 Barbee to Gilchrist, Apr 2, 1933, in Lauriston Manuscripts, Boston University; Burlingame introduction to Hay, *Inside Lincoln's White House*, xvi.

38 Hay, *At Lincoln's Side*, 91.

signed without reading the letters I wrote in his name. He wrote perhaps half-a-dozen a week himself—not more."[39]

Hay is suspected of writing for Lincoln the famed letter to Mrs. Lydia Parker Bixby, in November 1864, consoling her on the assumed loss of five sons in the war. It said:

> Dear Madam, I have been shown in the files of the War Department a statement of the Adjutant General of Massachusetts that you are the mother of five sons who have died gloriously on the field of battle. I feel how weak and fruitless must be any words of mine which should attempt to beguile you from the grief of a loss so overwhelming. But I cannot refrain from tendering to you the consolation that may be found in the thanks of the Republic they died to save. I pray that our Heavenly Father may assuage the anguish of your bereavement, and leave you only the cherished memory of the loved and lost, and the solemn pride that must be yours, to have laid so costly a sacrifice upon the altar of Freedom.
>
> Yours, very sincerely and respectively,
>
> A. Lincoln[40]

This eloquent gem rests on the same lofty plane of excellence as Lincoln's Gettysburg Address and The Second Inaugural. It is widely seen as the third leg of one of the most elegant trifectas in the English language.[41]

Not only were Hay and Nicolay interacting personally with Lincoln in daytime, but often late at night. The president loved to read aloud from books that moved or tickled him. Hay tells of an evening after a visit to the observatory, that he accompanied Lincoln to the cottage at the Soldiers Home that the Lincolns occupied in the warm Washington summers. Lincoln "read Shakespeare to me, the end of Henry VI and the beginning of Richard III till my heavy eyelids caught his considerate notice & he sent me to bed."[42]

At another time, Hay wrote, "I would be awakened by someone seating himself on the side of my bed, and Lincoln's voice would say, "Lie still; don't get up. Would

39 Ibid., 110.

40 Lincoln, *CW*, 8:116-17.

41 There is another side to this Bixby story. This is found in Stone, "Authorship of the Bixby Letter." The Boston Constabulary would not have been surprised to learn that Mrs. Bixby lied about her sons. In fact, she had lost only two, not five in the war. Of the three survivors, one had defected to the enemy, another may have done the same, and the third was honorably discharged. Additionally, Mrs. Bixby was originally a Virginian. Her granddaughter believed her to be "secretly in sympathy with the Southern cause" and had "little good to say of Lincoln." Mrs. Bixby supposedly destroyed the letter in anger. So much for golden words, whoever wrote them.

42 Hay, *Inside Lincoln's White House*, 262n.

you mind if I read to you a little while? Then he would begin a humorous poem by [English poet] Thomas Hood, a passage from Shakespeare, or a portion of the Bible. After perhaps twenty minutes or half an hour . . . the tall gaunt figure would rise from the edge of my bed and start for the door and on down the dark corridor. The candle high in his hand would light the disheveled hair as the President in flapping night-shirt his feet padding along in carpet slippers, would disappear into the darkness."[43]

In yet another visit, a little after midnight, "the President came into the office laughing, with a volume of Hood's works to show Nicolay and me . . . seeming utterly unconscious that he with his short shirt hanging about his long legs & setting out behind like the tail feathers of an enormous ostrich was infinitely funnier than anything in the book he was laughing at."[44]

On April 14, 1865, Hay and Lincoln's son, Robert, were in the White House talking. Nicolay was out of town. Abruptly, a crowd broke into their conversation, shouting that the president had been shot at Ford's Theater. The two young men sprinted down the stairs, commandeered a carriage, and raced to the house across from the theater, where Lincoln was lying. An agonized Hay stood by the dying president's bedside all night until 7:55 a.m., when Lincoln died.

Since Lincoln's Second Inaugural, both Hay and Nicolay had been planning to leave. Four years had taken their toll. Nicolay had landed a job as American consul in Paris, though he was still a Bavarian citizen. Hay, recommended by Secretary of State Seward, would also go to Paris as secretary to the legation. In 1867 Hay would move to the same duty in Vienna, and in 1869 to Madrid. He hated them all. He did not care for Europe.

Back in the United States, Hay's reputation as a gifted writer put him on the editorial staff of the *New York Tribune*. Among the events he covered for the *Tribune* was the Great Chicago Fire in 1871, started by a lamp kicked over by Mrs. Catherine O'Leary's cow.

Hay wrote, from the scene of "one squalid little hovel," a "warped and weather-beaten shanty . . . made sacred by the curse that rested on it. For out of that house, last Saturday night, came a woman with a lamp to the barn behind the house, to milk the cow with the crumpled temper, that kicked over the lamp that spilled the kerosene, that fired the straw that burned Chicago."[45]

43 Ibid., 345-46n.

44 Hay, *At Lincoln's Side*, 263n.

45 *New York Tribune*, Oct. 17, 1871.

That is prose poetry any writer would have been proud to write. Indeed, Hay thought of himself as a poet, and during this period in his life, he wrote and published poetry.

Theodore Roosevelt, who as president would come to know Hay intimately, called him "the most delightful man to talk to I ever met, for in his conversation he continually made out of hand those delightful epigrammatic remarks we would all like to make and which in books many people appear to be making, but which in actual life hardly anybody ever does."[46] Hay had a tongue of gold.

He also had a way with women. His college roommate, Stone, said Hay "was always a great favorite with the ladies."[47] Caroline Owsley Brown of Springfield could second that. To her, Hay was "a handsome young fellow, rather short, but slender and well formed, with bright, dark eyes that wrought havoc in the hearts of susceptible maidens, and a tongue that could have talked the traditional bird off the bush." Hay "flitted from flower to flower, with a sonnet to this one's sweet eyes, and to that damsel's rosy lips, with no worse result than a fleeting pang."[48]

Hannah Angell, Hay's sweetheart at Brown, who undoubtedly gazed into those eyes, said they were "wonderful" and "hazel," and into which "you could look . . . a mile, & he looked a mile into yours."[49] But the susceptible maiden who would stare into those eyes longer than any other, for three decades as his wife, would be Clara Louise Stone.

Clara lived in Cleveland and was twenty-four years old when they met in the early 1870s. She was eleven years younger than Hay. She loved literature, as he did. Her father was Amasa Stone, a very prominent and very rich Ohio industrialist.

Clara was "a reserved and pious young woman whose robust figure, dark complexion, deep-brown eyes, and abundant dark hair gave her the air of a Roman empress."[50] Hay described Clara variously as "large, handsome and good" and "large, handsome and comfortable."[51] He loved her, whatever her size. As lovers will, Hay rather went over the top telling her so. "My mind and spirit are yours as well as my heart and life," he pledged. "I love you, your soul and body, your goodness and

46 Theodore Roosevelt to Henry Cabot Lodge, Jan 28, 1909, in *The Letters of Theodore Roosevelt*, Elting E. Morison, et. al., eds., 8 vols. (Cambridge, 1954), 6:1489-90.

47 Stone, "John Hay, 1858," 152.

48 Brown, "Springfield Society before the Civil War," in the *Journal of the Illinois State Historical Society*, vol.15 (Apr-Jul 1922), 498.

49 Angell interview with William R. Thayer, Hay Papers, Brown University, Providence, RI.

50 Patricia O'Toole, *The Five of Hearts: An Intimate Portrait of Henry Adams and His Friends, 1880-1918* (New York, 1990), 49.

51 Ibid., 53, 53n.

your beauty. You *are* my inspiration and reward. I worship you."[52] Hay told her he thought he was getting the best of the bargain. "You are crazy to give yourself to me—everything for nothing," he told her, "You are wastefully generous."[53]

They married in her parents' parlor in Cleveland on February 4, 1874, and would remain married for thirty years, until Hay died in 1905. However, later in their marriage, Hay also fell in love with someone else. Nannie Lodge was the wife of U.S. senate powerhouse, Henry Cabot Lodge. Both clandestine lovers realized how difficult and futile it was slipping around. But they stayed in love until Hay died. Neither left their spouses.

Hay's years with Lincoln and his multiple talents had not been lost. In 1881, President-elect James Garfield asked him to be his personal secretary. Hay turned him down. "The contact with the greed and selfishness of office-seekers and the bulldozing Congressmen is unspeakably repulsive," Hay wrote Garfield. "The constant contact with envy, meanness, ignorance and the swinish selfishness which ignorance breeds needs a stronger heart and more obedient nervous system than I can boast."[54]

Hay, however, continued to mix in important political and social places. Until he died, he maintained a close friendship with Henry Adams, who was a famous writer-historian and the grandson and son of two presidents.

Inspired by an anonymous and successful work that Adams wrote titled *Democracy*, Hay wrote an anonymous novel about the conflict between capital and labor. It was centered on the wave of railroad strikes in 1877. It was titled *The Bread-Winners* and was heartlessly bludgeoned by the critics as anti-labor with no hint of corporate wrong-doing.[55]

Hay's magnum opus as a writer would be *Abraham Lincoln: A History*, the 10-volume biography co-authored with Nicolay. Running a close second are Hay's Civil War diary, his published correspondence, and other selected writings. This outpouring of his observations and thoughts is a particular favorite of grateful Civil War and Lincoln scholars. It has sweetened countless books about Lincoln and his times.[56]

52 John Hay to Clara Stone, no date, John Hay Papers, Brown University, Providence, RI; O'Toole, *Five of Hearts*, 49.

53 Ibid., (both sources), May 4, 1873.

54 John Hay to James Garfield, Feb. 16, 1881, John Hay Papers, Brown University, Providence, RI.

55 O'Toole, *The Five of Hearts*, 127.

56 Great thanks are owed to Michael Burlingame, the Lincoln scholar who has edited Hay's diary, letters, and selected writings most recently in two volumes, *Inside Lincoln's White House* (with John R. Turner Ettlinger) and *At Lincoln's Side*. His introductions in both books are splendidly informative.

Hay would have close relationships with three other presidents. He knew intimately all three chief executives killed in office in the nineteenth century. Lincoln, shot by the actor, John Wilkes Booth; Garfield, gunned down by an outraged and mad politician, Charles J. Guiteau, who thought Garfield owed him; and William McKinley, killed by an unhappy anarchist, Leon Czolgosz.

Garfield had sought Hay as his personal secretary. McKinley appointed Hay ambassador to the Court of St. James, and in 1898, made him his secretary of state. When McKinley fell to Czolgosz's bullet, Theodore Roosevelt kept Hay on as his secretary of state.

In his lifetime, Hay had worked his way up from secretary to a president to third in line to the presidency itself. As Roosevelt's secretary of state, Hay crafted the American Open Door Policy in China, and the treaty confirming America's right to build the Panama Canal. As secretary of state, he helped to build the United States into a world power. Roosevelt had said that in diplomacy, "Speak softly and carry a big stick." One might assume that it was Hay who spoke softly and Roosevelt who carried the big stick.

Five years into the new century, Hay fell sick. He was dying and looking back on what his life had amounted to. He rather thought his career was a series of accidents. "I say to myself," he wrote, "that I should not rebel at the thought of my life ending at this time. I lived to be old; something I never expected in my youth. I have had many blessings, domestic happiness being the greatest of all. I have lived my life. I have had success beyond all the dreams of my boyhood. My name is printed in the journals of the world without descriptive qualifications, which may, I suppose, be called fame."[57]

Roosevelt wrote to Hay, "I wonder if you have any idea what your strength and wisdom and sympathy, what the guidance you have given me and the mere delight in your companionship, have meant to me in these three and a half years?"[58]

Hay died in Newbury-Mt. Sunapee in the mountains of New Hampshire, on July 1, 1905. He was sixty-six. Roosevelt brought his entire cabinet from Washington for Hay's funeral. It was a fitting sendoff for a man who had become a jewel of nineteenth century America. Everybody in Lincoln's time knew he was extraordinary. But nobody suspected he was as extraordinary as he became.

57 O'Toole, *The Five of Hearts*, 384.

58 Ibid., 383.

Chapter 8

Lincoln Stacks the Deck

When Abraham Lincoln was elected to the presidency in 1860, he appointed his three main rivals for the Republican Party nomination to his cabinet, causing concern among his supporters.

William Henry Seward of New York, who had been the clear frontrunner for the nomination for months, was one. Lincoln made him his secretary of state. Salmon Portland Chase of Ohio was another, who believed his party had made a monumental mistake of nominating Lincoln instead of himself. Lincoln made him his secretary of the treasury. Edward Bates of Missouri, whose name had been prominent in the speculation, was the third. Lincoln made him his Attorney General. It looked to be Lincoln's strategy to turn the trio into friendly enemies, holding them close.

Some of Lincoln's supporters thought it madness. The three politicos assumed the tall bumpkin from the West, with no executive experience, would be an easy man to turn into a puppet. Most observers believed that Seward, not Lincoln, would run the show. Seward rather thought so himself.

But he soon got a contrary message. Lincoln subtly conveyed his intention to be both the *de facto* and *de jure* president. Seward was later to say, not without affection, for these two men were to become close friends: "There is but one vote in the cabinet and that is cast by the President."[1]

1 Frederick William Seward, *Seward at Washington, as Senator and Secretary of State: A Memoir of His Life, with Selections from His Letters, 1846-1861* (New York, 1891), 528.

What were these three rivals bested by Lincoln for the nomination and then put into his cabinet like? How did they take to having this bumpkin for a boss?

A Friendship for the Ages

William Henry Seward had every right to resent Abraham Lincoln. That countrified political imposter from Illinois had snatched the Republican Party nomination for president, which Seward thought would surely be his, from his waiting hands. Lincoln was elected, became president, and now wanted to make Seward his secretary of state.

Seward would take it, with the idea in his mind that he would be the power behind the throne. What did that clodhopper know about running anything? He had never held an executive position in his life. That this man could be president was ludicrous.

That Seward should be the president *de facto* if not *de jure* looked to be a reasonable assumption. He had been the power behind the throne before. President Zachary Taylor had leaned heavily on him for advice. But it didn't work out that way with Lincoln. The frontier interloper made it clear from the start that he was going to be the president, both *de jure* and *de facto*. That was further grounds to stir up Seward's animosity.

But Seward was not into animosity. He was a friendly, outgoing man who loved to host parties and tell stories. Mary Lincoln, far more into animosity than Seward, didn't like him, calling him "that abolition sneak."[2]

Seward was a slightly built five feet, six inches tall with sloping shoulders. One English visitor believed his height was not nearly as long as his diplomatic messages, which were "a mass of diplomatic correspondence which no living man will read through in ten years."[3]

Seward's thatch of straw-colored hair was tinged with red. It sat mostly tousled, in bird-nest disarray, much like Lincoln's. His eyes were blue gray. His most salient feature was a beak of a nose. It was said that as he sat in a room with his ever-present cigar and silver snuffbox, the beak rivaled everything. Perhaps sitting there, he would read a novel by Charles Dickens or Sir Walter Scott, for both of whom he nourished the passion of a groupie. Seward had a quick mind and an acute political sagacity that had taken him to the governorship of New York and the United States Senate.[4]

2 Rice, *Reminiscences of Abraham Lincoln*, 431.

3 *New York Herald*, Dec. 1, 1863.

4 Burlton J. Hendrick, *Lincoln's War Cabinet* (Boston, 1946), 8-9.

William Henry Seward

Library of Congress

When Seward spoke, it was with dramatic pauses to dip into his snuffbox and blow his large nose with an outsized yellow silk handkerchief. Seward's voice was slow, and metallic sounding. He took no pleasure in music. He confessed he could not distinguish a chant from a jig. When responding to a serenade, he threw out words "like clanging oracles into the night."[5]

5 John Russell Young, *Men and Memories: Personal Reminiscences*, May D. Russell Young, ed., 2nd edition (New York, 1901), 60.

Instead of nursing his lost presidency, Seward soon came to admire the towering bumpkin president. In the end, Seward viewed him as "the best and wisest man he had ever known,"[6] appreciating him for his original mind and keen wit. "The President is the best of us," he told his wife.[7]

Seward became Lincoln's closest friend and ally in the cabinet. Lincoln often turned to him for his opinion, and they became companions, talking and swapping stories and mutually teasing one another.

Once, they rode together to attend a troop review across the Potomac. The road on the Virginia side was rough, seriously rutted by artillery caissons and army wagons. The unsuccessful effort to keep the wheels from dropping into ruts jarred loose a tirade of profanity from the driver, heightening with each rut. At last, Lincoln leaned over and asked the driver, "My friend, are you an Episcopalian?" "No, Mr. President," the driver confessed, "I ain't much of anything, but when I go to church at all, I go to the Methodist Church." "Oh," Lincoln said, "I thought you must be an Episcopalian for you swear just like Secretary Seward."[8]

Two days after Lincoln's reelection in 1864, Seward told a group of supporters, "Henceforth all men will come to see him, as you and I have come to see him. Abraham Lincoln will take his place with Washington, and Franklin, and Jefferson, and Adams, and Jackson, among the benefactors of the country and of the human race."[9]

John Hay, Lincoln's assistant personal secretary, was later to sum up the unique relationship between these two great men:

> The history of governments affords few instances of an official connection hallowed by a friendship so absolute and sincere as that which existed between these two magnanimous spirits. Lincoln had snatched away from Seward at Chicago the prize of a laborious lifetime, when it seemed within his grasp. Yet Seward was the first man named in his Cabinet and the first who acknowledged [Lincoln's] personal preeminence. . . . [N]o shadow of jealousy or doubt ever disturbed their mutual confidence and regard.[10]

6 George Templeton Strong, *The Diary of George Templeton Strong: The Civil War 1860-1865*, Allan Nevins & Milton Halsey Thomas, eds. (New York, 1952), 92.

7 Seward, *Seward in Washington*, 575.

8 Rufus Rockwell Wilson, *Intimate Memories of Lincoln* (Elmira, NY, 1945), 422.

9 Quoted in Seward, *Seward in Washington*, 250.

10 Hay, *At Lincoln's Side*, 128-29.

Fourth Person in the Trinity

It might not be all that far-fetched to think a relentless passion to be president gestated within Salmon Portland Chase in his mother's womb. It would never happen in three decades of hoping and assuming it would.

When the western explorer, John C. Fremont, won nomination by the young Republican Party in 1856, Chase complained that the party had "committed an act of positive injustice" in failing to take as their nominee men "who truly personified the great real issue before the country."[11] When Abraham Lincoln was nominated in 1860, he believed another act of positive injustice had been committed.

It happened yet again in 1864, when Chase, Lincoln's secretary of the treasury, not-so-covertly ran against his boss. But his campaign foundered early, and Lincoln was nominated again. As one Republican said, Chase "never forgave Lincoln for the crime of having been preferred for President over him."[12]

Lincoln's personal secretaries, John Nicolay and John Hay, believed Chase held so poor an opinion of Lincoln's intellect and character "that he could not believe the people so blind as deliberately to prefer the President to himself," that "he could not bring himself to feel that the universal demonstrations in favor of the reelection of Mr. Lincoln were genuine. He regarded himself all the while as the serious candidate, and the opposition to him as knavish and insincere."[13]

Chase likely possessed the presidential timbre to match what everybody could see, his unsleeping ambition. Lincoln knew all about it, but said if Chase became president, "I hope we may never have a worse man."[14] Chase looked presidential. He stood six feet, two inches tall, carried wide shoulders and a deep chest, and bore himself with obvious dignity, "one of the finest specimens of a perfect man that we have ever seen," a reporter who had seen him said; "a large, well-formed head, set upon a frame of herculean proportions," with "an eye of unrivaled splendor and brilliancy."[15] He looked, the politician, Gen. Carl Schurz, said, "as you would wish a statesman to look . . . a picture of intelligence, strength, courage, and dignity."[16]

11 Salmon P. Chase, *Inside Lincoln's Cabinet: The Civil War Diaries of Salmon P. Chase*, David H. Donald, ed. (New York, 1954), 3.

12 Alexander K. McClure, *Abraham Lincoln and Men of War Times: Some Personal Recollections of War and Politics during the Lincoln Administration* (Philadelphia, 1892), 119.

13 John G. Nicolay & John Hay, *Abraham Lincoln: A History*, 10 vols. (New York, 1890), 8:311, 313.

14 John Hay, *Lincoln and the Civil War: In the Diaries and Letters of John Hay*, Tyler Dennett, ed. (New York, 1939), 100-101.

15 Albert Bushnell Hart, *Salmon Portland Chase* (Boston, 1899), 415; Burton J. Hendrick, *Lincoln's War Cabinet* (Boston, 1946), 32

16 Carl Schurz, *Reminiscences of Carl Schurz*, 3 vols. (New York, 1907-1908), 2:34.

Salmon Portland Chase

Library of Congress

The reporter, Noah Brooks, believed, "If he should be the next president of these United States the Executive chair would be filled with more dignity than it has known since the days of Washington."[17] The New York editor, Horace Greeley, told him, "I know no man in our country who is in my view better qualified for president than yourself."[18]

Like his good friend, Massachusetts Senator Charles Sumner, Chase dressed presidentially, with meticulous care, considering it unthinkable to be caught without a waistcoat. He was a man of commanding presence and courtly manners, impressing Lincoln. "Chase," the president said, "is about one and a half times bigger than any other man that I ever knew."[19]

Chase was big on leading a strictly ordered life. The only form of slavery he believed in was the kind that held him in bondage to routine. Because of that, and his devotion to religion, no day began that he didn't muster his two daughters and household staff for a scripture reading. Nor would he end it without communing directly with the Supreme Being. Senator Ben Wade of Ohio, a man not without wit, retorted, "Chase is a good man, but his theology is unsound. He thinks there is a fourth Person in the Trinity."[20]

Lincoln's cabinet, not known necessarily for communing with God, had its critics. One wag said, "it had the appearance of being selected from a grab-bag."[21] "A violent mixing . . . of inimical and repulsive forces," snorted Adam Gurowski, the insufferable gadfly of Washington.[22] A bunch of "poor sticks," thought the irascible, cross-eyed James Gordon Bennett, editor of the *New York Herald*.[23] Chase agreed with these assessments—except for himself. He thought his cabinet colleagues, and Lincoln, too, were all incompetent. Noah Brooks observed that Chase's ability "is only a trifle below [his] dignity, or [he] is greatly deceived."[24]

Which brings us to Chase's drawbacks. Like all politicians, he had a few. He wasn't much of an orator. He did not have platform grace, and his speeches, although powerful, lacked passion. They were ponderous and imposing, delivered

17 Noah Brooks, *Mr. Lincoln's Washington: Selections from the Writings of Noah Brooks, Civil War Correspondent*, P. J. Staudenraus, ed. (South Brunswick, N.J., 1967), 177.

18 Harry J. Carman & Reinhard H. Luthin, *Lincoln and the Patronage* (New York, 1943), 244.

19 Hart, *Salmon Portland Chase*, 435.

20 Hay, *Lincoln and the Civil War*, 53.

21 Francis Fisher Browne, *The Everyday Life of Abraham Lincoln: A Narrative and Descriptive Biography with Pen-Pictures and Personal Recollections by Those Who Knew Him* (Chicago, 1913), 363.

22 Gurowski, *Diary*, 1:16.

23 *New York Herald*, Oct. 9, 1863.

24 Brooks, *Mr. Lincoln's Washington*, 177.

with a slight lisp. Listeners often left before a speech ended. He admitted, "I am not a rousing speaker at best."[25]

Chase wasn't a good audience for Lincoln's stories or humorists' readings either, since he lacked humor. He was unlikely to launch a funny story of his own. Nor had he a politician's talent for mixing with the people, his stately demeanor often appearing pompous. Unlike most successful politicians, he harbored an aversion to mingling with the people.

In part, Chase's pomposity had to do with his vision. He was nearsighted. The faces Chase saw approaching didn't come into focus until close by. His learning was dependent almost exclusively on the two thousand volumes lining the bookshelves in his study, including thirty dictionaries. Therefore, a reporter said, he knew "little of human nature."[26] Indeed, there was a saying: "Mr. Chase is nearsighted and does not see men."[27] He had no problem seeing and appreciating himself in a mirror. Each morning, as he viewed himself in the glass, dressed to the nines, he said, welcomingly, "Good morning, Mr. President."[28]

Chase held slavery and slaveholders in a very dim light. Slavery was "a curse, a reproach, a blight, an evil, a wrong, a sin," and slaveholding "grossly inconsistent with Democratic principles."[29] As a lawyer in Ohio before becoming nationally prominent, he had the reputation as "the attorney for the runaway slave."[30] Nor did he hold any love for secession. He looked at the Union "as we look upon the arch of heaven, without a thought that it can ever decay or fall."[31]

In a distinguished career, Chase was a governor of Ohio, U.S. senator, Lincoln's treasury secretary, and chief justice of the U.S. Supreme Court. However, he would never fulfill his dream from birth of becoming president.

Quarried from the Silurian Age

Edward Bates was the cabinet's Methuselah. He was the third of Lincoln's politically powerful rivals for the Republican nomination in 1860. When Lincoln

25 This confession is in a letter to Stanley Matthews, May 5, 1850, Salmon P. Chase Papers, Library of Congress, Washington, D.C.

26 Demarest Lloyd, "Home-life of Salmon Portland Chase," in *Atlantic Monthly* 32 (Nov. 1873), 534.

27 Robert B. Warden, *An Account of the Private Life and Public Services of Salmon Portland Chase* (Cincinnati, 1874), 582.

28 Thomas Graham Belden & Marva Robins Belden, *So Fell the Angels* (New York, 1956), 64.

29 Jacob W. Schuckers, *The Life and Public Services of Salmon Portland Chase* (New York, 1874), 110.

30 Ibid., 52.

31 Ibid., 116.

appointed him attorney general, Bates was sixty-six, a decade and a half older than the president. When he was born in September 1793, George Washington was still president.

Bates's first patriotic act for his country was against his religion. He enlisted in the Virginia militia in the War of 1812, when he was a Quaker and James Madison was president. He went to war, a violation of Quaker canon, carrying the old flintlock musket his father Thomas, also an offending Quaker, had carried in the Revolutionary War. When Edward came home, he was kicked out of his Quaker meeting house for his apostasy. It was the only tenant of Quakerism that he violated.

When Bates returned from the War of 1812 at age twenty-one, he moved to St. Louis. He became a lawyer, and one of the best loved, and oddest citizens of the town. He dressed every day as he had since his youth, in old-fashioned Quaker attire. The portrait artist, Jasper Conant, seeing him in Washington in 1861-62, thought him "the quaintest looking character that walked the streets."[32] Another quaint practice, worthy of the attire, was the bath he took every morning in cold water.

Bates kept a daily diary, entries scrawled in a "crabbed pen" and notable for their disregard of correct spelling.[33] Contemporary critics liked to call him "Granny Bates." Joseph Medill, the critical editor of the *Chicago Tribune*, called him "a fossil of the Silurian era—red sandstone at least—who should not have been quarried out of the rocks in which he was embedded."[34]

Bates stood five feet, seven inches tall, an average height for men of Civil War times. He was thin, with a striking face, a straight nose, dark eyebrows, and the questioning eyes of a lawyer. He had brownish-red hair with a pure white beard. The contrast was stunning. Lincoln teasingly explained that was "because Bates uses his chin more than his head."[35]

Bates was more Whig than Republican. He spoke of himself as a "garrulous old man,"[36] who had never been dis-embedded from the collapsed Whig Party. He became Missouri's most prominent Whig and was still admittedly an "old fogey" Whig at heart.[37] Bates continued mourning his old party's demise and never joined another party, not even the Republicans who wanted to nominate him for

32 Jasper Conant, "A Visit to Washington in 1861-62," in *Metropolitan Magazine* 33 (Jun. 1910), 313.

33 Hendrick, *Lincoln's War Cabinet*, 47.

34 Quoted in Ibid., 46.

35 Ibid.

36 Charles M. Segal, *Conversations with Lincoln* (New York, 1961), 228.

37 Hendrick, *Lincoln's War Cabinet*, 43.

Edward Bates

Library of Congress

president. "When the Whig party committed suicide in 1856, and thereby left the nation without a bodyguard," he explained, "I died with it."[38]

He was still alive enough to become Lincoln's chief legal adviser. "I know very little," he admitted, "of what is going on in politics and electioneering. . . . Nobody approaches me, to make interest, nor thinks it worth while (or perhaps safe) to tell me what he is aiming at. But in my own quiet way—by letters to friends, and by the inculcation of principles, in my opinions and other public documents—I give Mr. Lincoln the best support I can; and I believe that in some quarters it is not without effect."[39]

One thing Bates did with impressive effect was to sire offspring. As the youngest of twelve children, Bates took after his father, then passed to an even higher fertility level by five, producing seventeen children, eight who lived to adulthood. His wife Julia spent virtually all her childbearing years suffering through one pregnancy to the next.

So much did Bates favor the process that even a brief absence from her pained him, if not her. "Oh! How I long to see and press you to my bosom," he wrote when away in Congress in 1826, "if it were but for a moment."[40] Julia knew better than anybody where those presses to Edward's bosom led.

Bates was first drawn into politics in Missouri's bid for statehood that led to the Compromise of 1820. He was one of the principal architects of the new state's constitution. He was a slaveholder from a border state, and the first cabinet member from west of the Mississippi. Like most Southerners, he believed in the inferiority of the black race. But he also agreed with Lincoln and his party that slavery ought not to spread to where it did not yet exist—into the territories.

He also believed in and admired the president who made Bates his attorney general. Bates confessed, "Mr. Lincoln comes very near being a perfect man, according to my ideal of manhood."[41] Bates appreciated the president's ever "affable and kind" manner.[42] Like Seward and unlike Chase, Bates saw men, and recognized greatness when he saw it.

38 Edward Bates, *Diary of Edward Bates*, 1859-1866, in *Annual Report of the American Historical Association for 1830*, vol. 4 (Washington, D.C., 1933), 390.

39 Ibid., 350.

40 Quoted in Doris Kearns Goodwin, *Team of Rivals: The Political Genius of Abraham Lincoln* (New York, 2005), 65.

41 Quoted in Carpenter, *Six Months at the White House*, 68-69.

42 Bates, *Diary*, 429.

Chapter 9

Three From the Fiery Furnace

Not all the pests in Abraham Lincoln's life flew in on wings through the White House's open windows or crawled through its cracks. Some of the most pestilent were called Radicals. They were the abolition wing of his own Republican party, impatient and intolerant.

From the day Lincoln entered the White House, until he issued his Emancipation Proclamation, the Radicals hounded him with an incessant cry to make the war one to end slavery, not just put down rebellion.

As he viewed so many things, pests and all, Lincoln viewed these Radicals with compassion. He told John Hay, "They are nearer to me than the other side, in thought and sentiment, though bitterly hostile personally. They are utterly lawless—the unhandiest devils in the world to deal with—but after all their faces are set Zionwards."[1] Lincoln was describing the Missouri Radicals, but the Radicals everywhere were unhandy.

Too often their faces turned toward the executive mansion instead of Zion, with hard-sell lobbying and emancipation in their heads. As a trio of them approached the White House, Lincoln would share a story about a young Sunday schooler reading about Shadrach, Meshach, and Abednego. Pronouncing their names was beyond the perplexed lad's semantic powers. So, when his eye lit on their unpronounceable names coming up, he blurted out in his pain and anguish, "Look! Look there! Here come them same three damn fellers again!"[2]

1 Hay, *Lincoln and the Civil War*, 108.

2 Benjamin T. Thomas, *Abraham Lincoln: A Biography* (New York, 1952), 343.

It is likely that the trio of same damn fellers who came to bludgeon Lincoln into freeing the slaves were three of the most powerful Radicals in Congress. They were Senator Charles Sumner (Massachusetts), Senator Ben Wade (Ohio), and Representative Thaddeus Stevens (Pennsylvania).

Cannoneer for Humanity

Charles Sumner could have been born an Englishman. A visiting Brit described him as "that great sturdy English-looking figure, with the broad massive forehead, over which the rich mass of nut-brown hair, streaked here and there with a line of grey, hangs loosely, with the deep blue eyes, and strangely winning smile, half bright, half full of sadness. He is a man whom you would notice amongst other men, and whom not knowing him you would turn round to look at as he passed by. A child would ask him the time in the streets, and a woman, I think, would come to him unbidden for protection."[3]

Many mothers named their children after Sumner, a practice he discouraged, believing no child should be named for a living man. What if in the end that man fell short, or turned aside to false gods? Where did this leave the child?[4]

Lincoln liked the senator personally. He would take his feet off his desk when Sumner came to visit, viewing him as "just my idea of a bishop."[5] However, Sumner did not dress in the prevailing mode of either a bishop or a senator. He had his own fashion style, wearing a brown coat, light waistcoat, lavender or checked trousers, and shoes with English gaiters.[6]

In the Senate he sat with an unbending dignity worthy of his unbending opinions. Not even in the privacy of his own chambers would he allow himself to fall into a position he would not assume at his desk on the Senate floor. "Habit," he said, "is everything."[7] Senator James W. Nesmith of Oregon speculated, "I wonder how Sumner would look in his night-shirt?"[8] No one seemed to know.

Whether he was in a nightshirt or not, Sumner was committed to the immediate emancipation of the slaves and was impatient with any delay. "He stands six feet

3 "Washington during the War," *MacMillan's Magazine* 6 (May 1862), 25.

4 Edward L. Pierce, *Memoir and Letters of Charles Sumner*, 4 vols. (Boston, 1878), 4:96.

5 Thomas, *Abraham Lincoln*, 502; *The Diary of a Public Man: And a Page of Political Correspondence-Stanton to Buchanan* (New Brunswick, NJ, 1946), 63.

6 Brooks, *Washington in Lincoln's Time*, 33.

7 Ibid.

8 Ibid.

Charles Sumner

Library of Congress

two in his stockings," his friend, the poet Henry Wadsworth Longfellow said, "a colossus holding his burning heart in his hand to light up the sea of life."[9]

9 Quoted in Sandburg, *Abraham Lincoln, The War Years,* 1:100.

Slavery, Sumner believed, was "an intolerable, Heaven-defying iniquity." There have been crimes in human history, he believed, "but I know of none blacker than this. There have been acts of baseness; but I know of none more utterly vile."[10]

When he said as much publicly, it stirred up serious trouble. He seemed unable to speak without delivering crushing, insulting, name-calling screeds against slavery and slaveholding. That invariably inflamed the passion of Southerners. In 1856, as he sat at his desk on the Senate floor, he was caned, nearly to death, by South Carolina Representative Preston Brooks, who had taken serious exception to one of his anti-slavery speeches.

His speeches were full of poisonous invective and seeded with quotations from the classics, poetry, and history. Sumner delivered them cannonball style, in a deep sonorous voice "like the roar of a lion, or the bay of a St. Bernard."[11] Longfellow said, "Sumner stands like a cannoneer and gesticulates as if he were ramming down cartridges."[12]

Supposedly, he practiced these thunderbolts in front of a mirror before launching them from the Senate floor in what John Hay called "that high-priced style of his."[13]

Secretary of Navy Gideon Welles believed Sumner's knowledge of men was "imperfect, nearsighted, and unreliable."[14] The poet Julia Ward Howe asked him one day if he had yet seen the celebrated actor, Edwin Booth. "Why, n-no madam," Sumner replied, "l long since ceased to take any interest in individuals."[15]

Henry Wilson, Sumner's fellow senator from Massachusetts, said, "Sumner thought anything that did not originate in his own brain or the Almighty's, was not worthy of consideration."[16]

He believed delivering point blank those things originating in his brain was his obligation to humanity. The consequences could be a caning or worse. The equally incendiary *New York Herald* editor, James Gordon Bennett, called him the "John

10 Charles Sumner, "Our Domestic Relations," in Making of America digital library of primary sources, at Internet address quod.lib.umich.edu, 528.

11 Hamilton Gay Howard, *Civil War Echoes: Character Echoes and State Secrets* (Washington, D.C., 1907), 39.

12 Quoted in Sandburg, *Abraham Lincoln: The War Years*, 1:100.

13 Brooks, *Washington in Lincoln's Time*, 33-34; Hay, *Lincoln and the Civil War*, 250.

14 Gideon Welles, *Diary of Gideon Welles, Secretary of the Navy under Lincoln and Johnson*, 3 vols. (Boston, 1911), 1:502-3.

15 Donald, *Charles Sumner and the Rights of Man*, 147.

16 Howard, *Civil War Echoes*, 11.

Brown of politics," who "runs ahead of the radicals, strikes the first blow for them, and is always hung up for his pains."[17]

This Shadrach often went to the White House to do his duty to humanity.

The World Class Cusser

They called Ben Wade, the angry Radical senator from Ohio, "Bluff Ben." He was a fire-breathing abolitionist and very bluff about it, meaning blunt.

Wade had a body to match his bluntness, a block of anatomy not quite five feet, nine inches tall and weighing 185 pounds. He was seven inches shorter than Lincoln and five pounds heavier. Locked within that compact package was a manly, courageous, violent disposition, with a passion hell-bent to end slavery. Reporter Noah Brooks said he had a bulldog tenacity that was "truly masterful."[18]

Another characterized Wade as "stamped all over with honesty and fearlessness."[19] He was an angry and radical person, well-armed for his crusade against slavery. His voice was "deep and powerful," laced with "passionate invective and irony," that "quivered in all the octaves of eloquence."[20] He was a world-class cusser. "Damn it," he said, "I can't be emphatic without swearing. I don't mean any disrespect to the Deity or to my hearers."[21]

As he warmed to his anti-slavery theme, his hair, perhaps alarmed by what his mouth was saying, became ruffled and stood on end. As his rhetoric grew, he would unbutton his vest, shove up his shirtsleeves, tear off his cravat, and yank off his collar. At the apex of his argument, he would rise on his toes, hold aloft his hands at arm's length, and as he brought them down, jump onto his heels.[22]

Secretary of Navy Gideon Welles believed Wade a man with "a good deal of patriotic feeling, common sense and a strong, though coarse and vulgar, mind."[23]

Wade, dressed in black, wore a shrewd, nervous look, punctuated with dark melancholy eyes that burned with a passionate abolitionist fire. One observer called him "grim-visaged."[24] He could be a fast friend or an even faster enemy.

17 *New York Herald*, Oct. 17, 1863.

18 Brooks, *Washington in Lincoln's Time*, 225.

19 Howard, *Civil War Echoes*, 22.

20 Ibid.

21 Ibid.

22 Ibid., 23.

23 Welles, *Diary*, 2:95.

24 Howard, *Civil War Echoes*, 22.

Ben Wade

Library of Congress

Within his rough-hewn exterior dwelt something of a bleeding heart. He was gracious, even lovable, in private. But in public, he was a hater. Nobody burned hotter to destroy slavery and remake the South than Ben Wade. No Radical was more put out with Abraham Lincoln than Wade, impatient that the president would not move faster. He hated Lincoln's apparently merciful approach to Southern reconstruction at war's end. Wade insisted that was Congress's job, not the kindly president's.

One day, on one of his pilgrimages to the White House, Wade shouted at Lincoln, "You are on the road to Hell with this government, and you are not a mile off this minute." This rather struck Lincoln as amusing. "A mile from Hell, Senator?" he asked. "That is just about the distance from here to the Capitol, is it not?"[25]

Often, from the Capitol to the White House, this angry Meshach came with Shadrach and Abednego to prod this president to destroy slavery.

The Human Blowtorch

They called the third missionary from the fiery furnace, "Old Thad." Thaddeus Stevens was the oldest man in the House of Representatives, born in Vermont only ten years after the Revolutionary War ended.[26]

Now, nearly fifty years later, he was a tall and brooding presence, with bushy overhanging brows and limping on a foot clubbed from birth. He had a sallow complexion and a defiant and protruding underlip. An attack of "brain fever" left him bald early in life. He would wear an ill-fitting, usually askew, reddish-brown wig. His eyes were said to shoot rhetorical minie balls at the slave power, slicing, blasting, poisoning, and consuming.

Stevens was the dominator of the House, its "despotic ruler," chairman of the powerful Ways and Means Committee. He was considered the ablest parliamentarian in Congress. When he rose on the floor, he rose by degrees, "as a telescope is pulled out." On his feet, he was a column of iron, thundering anathemas and "dropping his sentences as though each one weighed a ton."[27]

"He cannot be said to debate," one observer remarked. "With him it is but assault. His fellow Pennsylvanian, Alexander McClure, described him as

25 Donald V. Smith, *Chase and Civil War Politics* (Columbus, OH, 1931), 68-69.

26 J. W. Binckley, "The Leader of the House," *Galaxy* 1 (Jul. 1866), 494.

27 Poore, *Perley's Reminiscences*, 2:101; Binkley, "The Leader of the House," 494; Brooks, *Washington in Lincoln's Time*, 27; Brooks, *Mr. Lincoln's Washington*, 104.

Thaddeus Stevens

Library of Congress

"the master-spirit of every aggressive movement in Congress to overthrow the rebellion and slavery."[28]

28 Binkley, "The Leader of the House," 496; John D. Ellis, *Sights and Secrets of the National Capital* (Chicago, 1869), 155; McClure, *Lincoln and Men of War Times*, 265.

He was a gambling man, an often-seen presence in one of the hundred gaming establishments in wartime Washington. Stevens gambled to unwind. He frequently hobbled onto the House floor from a night at the faro tables and throughout the day "frightened and coaxed and bullied and controlled members . . . along the path of humanity."[29]

It was not his way to please and persuade. Another of his nicknames was "Old Sarcastic" and his sarcasm was venomous. It bit and withered and defamed. At an earlier time when he was a legislator in the Pennsylvania Assembly, a fellow lawmaker spoke sharply against one of his measures. Nailing his critic with a baleful stare, Stevens addressed the chair: "Mr. Speaker, it will not be expected of me to notice the thing which has crawled into this House and adheres to one of the seats by its own slime." Later in the U.S. House he said, "I yield to the gentleman for a few feeble remarks."[30]

His own remarks were never feeble, delivered in a hollow voice devoid of music. But they often had crescendo effect. They "made play upon men and things," the politician-general Carl Schurz noted, "like lurid freaks of lightning."[31]

"He is never tender, winning and conciliatory," Noah Brooks wrote, "but always argumentative, harsh, ironical, grim, and resolute."[32] Out of his mouth came unending gall and denunciation dripping with acid. He upheld a principle with unsmiling intolerance. For the chief victims of his intolerance, the rebellious South, and its leaders, he had not a shred of compassion. He saw them as traitors, and there was to be no compromise or forgiveness. They were to be crushed with force and then subjugated with an iron grip.[33]

"Let no Slave State flatter itself," he roared, "that it can dissolve the Union and then reconstruct it upon better terms."[34] He was impatient with anyone who would be lenient, particularly Abraham Lincoln. He said, "Let the cursed rebels lie on the bed they have made."[35]

Paradoxically, this human blowtorch was also known as the "Great Commoner." Though he wasted no compassion on enemies, he lavished utter and unending

29 Ellis, *Sights and Secrets of the National Capital*, 156.

30 Thomas Frederick Woodley, *The Great Leveler: The Life of Thaddeus Stevens* (New York, 1937), 10; Fawn M. Brodie, *Thaddeus Stevens: Scourge of the South* (New York, 1959), 145.

31 Schurz, *The Reminiscences of Carl Schurz*, 3:214.

32 Brooks, *Mr. Lincoln's Washington*, 104.

33 James Albert Woodburn, *Life of Thaddeus Stevens* (Indianapolis, 1913), 165.

34 Ibid.

35 Robert Dale Owen, "Political Results from the Varioloid: A Leaf of History," *Atlantic Monthly* 35 (Jun. 1875), 662, 664.

compassion on the sickly, the outcast, and the drown-trodden. In Pennsylvania, he had the reputation as the most accomplished all-round lawyer in the state and an avowed foe of special privilege. He never married, but this lifelong bachelor had a mulatto housekeeper, Lydia Smith. Many believed she was more than just his housekeeper.

Southerners returned his malice. One outraged Rebel called him "this demon . . . this malicious, pitiless, pauseless enemy . . . this misanthrope . . . this viperous, heartless, adulterous beast . . . this hideous sepulcher of all hideous things . . . this lonely, friendless and unfriendly man." The same observer spoke of Stevens's clubfoot as "hell's seal of deformity . . . fixed in his mother's womb."[36]

Also fixed many years ago was the antislavery passion that Abednego brought often with Shadrach and Meshach to lay on Abraham Lincoln.

36 George M. Drake in the *Union Springs* (Alabama) *Times*, Jul. 24, 1867, reprinted in Brodie, *Thaddeus Stevens*, 18-19.

Chapter 10

The Georgia Boys

Interesting things often come in pairs. Often, those pairs can be odd, as history shows. The Civil War era produced at least one such pair for our entertainment.

It would be a stretch to find an odder or more important pair than two Georgia politicians. They were inseparable as friends, devoted as cohorts, and acted on most issues in tandem. Alexander Stephens and Robert Toombs, both famous Confederates, were extremely different from each other. Somehow, they meshed perfectly, and people compared them to Damon and Pythias, the celebrated friends of Greek legend.[1]

Hannibal Hamlin, Lincoln's first term vice president, described them as the two "high priests in the inner councils of the slave power."[2] The two Georgians had been Union-loving, but after their state seceded, they became vocal defenders of the South, vigorously supporting slavery and the right of slaveholders to take their slaves into new territories. Those beliefs Stephens defended with a shrill piping, and Toombs, with the voice of a bear.

Both believed strongly in state sovereignty, and that a state had a right to secede, if the cause justified it. When Georgia voted to secede in January 1861, Toombs voted for it, believing all other recourse for preventing Northern oppression of the South and its slavery was futile. Stephens voted against secession, not believing the fact of Abraham Lincoln's election to the presidency was a justifiable cause. When

1 Ulrich B. Phillips, *The Life of Robert Toombs* (New York, 1913), 17.

2 Thurlow Weed Barnes, *Memoir of Thurlow Weed* (Boston, 1884), 176.

Lincoln was elected, despite not being on the ballot in ten Southern states, seven of those states bolted.

Notwithstanding their split on that vote, the two Georgians agreed on almost everything else. Stephens became a reluctant vice president of the Confederacy. Toombs sat in its congress, became its first secretary of state, and later a brigadier general. One Confederate general, seeing that last progression, said "the 'lace and buttons of cavalry' were scarcely able to conceal the 'politician and demagogue that he was'."[3] Both Georgia boys soon became chief among critics of their own new government and the president they served, Jefferson Davis.[4]

The Brilliant Pile of Bones

They called him "Little Aleck" and it did not overstate the case. He was also often called "Sonny," which he hated. The *New York Times* called him the "Mephistopheles of Southern politics."[5]

That was Alexander Stephens, five feet, seven inches tall, but never in his life topping 100 pounds. Typically, on a heavy day, he might weigh between seventy and eighty. He was as close to being alive without an acceptable support system as anybody had ever seen, "practically a brain without a body," one biographer believed.[6] Many of his dogs, which he loved, outweighed him.[7] Abraham Lincoln, who met and liked him when they served together in Congress in 1847-1848, watched him remove his heavy coat one day and thought, from "the biggest shuck" emerged "the littlest ear" he ever saw.[8]

Stephens was a congressman from antebellum Georgia and very much pro-slavery, calling it the "corner-stone" of the Confederacy. However, he claimed to be "no defender of slavery in the abstract," but clinging to it only out of "stern necessity."[9] He was a slaveholder himself but reputed to be an exceedingly benevolent one.

3 Joseph Howard Parks, *General Edmund Kirby Smith, CSA* (Baton Rouge, LA, 1954), 147.

4 For examples of their criticisms see Rudolph Von Abele, *Alexander H. Stephens: A Biography* (New York, 1946), 207-8, 215, 219-220, 225.

5 Thomas E. Schott, *Alexander H. Stephens of Georgia: A Biography* (Baton Rouge, LA, 1988), 20; Von Abele, *Alexander H. Stephens*, 72; *New York Times*, Aug. 24, 1858.

6 Louis Pendleton, *Alexander H. Stephens* (Philadelphia, 1907), 33.

7 Schott, *Alexander H. Stephens of Georgia*, 19-21; Henry Cleveland, *Alexander H. Stephens, in Public and Private* (Philadelphia, 1866), 236.

8 Grant, *Personal Memoirs*, 591.

9 Von Abele, *Alexander H. Stephens*, 90.

Alexander Stephens

Library of Congress

"Yas suh," one of his slaves was reported to have said, "I knows Mars' Aleck—I knows him mighty well; he's kinder to dawgs 'n other mens is to people." Another of his slaves said after he died, "Ef he ain't in heaven, 'tain't no use for anybody else to try to git dere."[10]

Sickly from youth, Stephens was pain-wracked throughout his lifetime by a battalion of ailments. Rheumatoid arthritis kept his hands, arms, and legs in constant pain. Remorseless pain hammered his face, neck, teeth, and abdomen. He had piercing migraine headaches, pruritus, colitis, and bladder stones. He was easily mistaken for a boy and had about him the pallor of a corpse.

His head was small, his ears oversized and out-jutting, his black eyes incendiary, his nose thin and tapered, his lips pale and down-slopping at the corners. His fingers were long and bony. He described himself as "a malformed ill-shaped half-finished thing."[11] He was, also, like his friend and enemy Abraham Lincoln, burdened by melancholy.[12] Shakespeare could have cast him as Richard III. He had the perfect deformed body for it.

But within this wrecked body, this pile of bones, lived a steel-trap, quick-witted mind bordering on genius. Varina Davis, who knew both Georgians well, believed Toombs, his big best friend, loved him "with a tenderness that was almost pathetic."[13] Toombs said of Stephens that he "carried more brains and more soul for the least flesh of any man God Almighty ever made."[14]

When Stephens spoke on the floor of Congress, his voice was an "ear-piercing pipe," sharp, shrill, and high pitched, but musical. It was a voice that startled with its "penetrating tones."[15] He could orchestrate this screech from low to loud and shoot it bullet-like at audiences. There was always the concern, however, that "the cadaverous speaker might not live to finish the speech."[16]

Some remarked that when aroused, his tongue became "a whip of scorpions."[17] When he thought he was right, which was most of the time, he was fearless, with an acute sense of personal honor. Five times in his life he issued challenges to

10 Pendleton, *Alexander H. Stephens*, 38, 100, 253.

11 The material for these two paragraphs of description of Stephens I owe to Schott, *Alexander H. Stephens of Georgia*, 19-21, 213, and Thompson, *Robert Toombs of Georgia*, 46.

12 Pendleton, *Alexander H. Stephens*, 33.

13 Davis (Varina), *Jefferson Davis*, 1:410.

14 William P. Trent, *Southern Statesmen of the Old Regime* (New York, 1897), 231.

15 Pendleton, *Alexander H. Stephens*, 69.

16 Schott, *Alexander H. Stephens of Georgia*, 19, 31, 56, 81.

17 Pendleton, *Alexander H. Stephens*, 69.

duels, a common practice in the duel-happy South. Those challenges were never answered. Turned sideways, he would have been a tough target to hit.

The Washington journalist, Benjamin Perley Poore, wrote that Stephens gave the impression of a doomed man who "apparently had not a month to live, yet who rivaled Talleyrand, [legendary French politician and diplomat] in political intrigue."[18] He would puzzle everyone by living to the age of seventy-one, dying in his last public office as governor of his state. Since throughout his life many thought he might die at any moment, many obituaries were written over the years, then shelved. It seemed fitting that before he died, he was able to edit his own. When he did at last die, his obituary was published with the title, "The Only True Obituary of Alexander H. Stephens, Corrected by Himself."[19]

The Rebel Trumpet

Robert Toombs was big-shouldered, imposing, boisterous, overbearing, profane, and over six feet tall. Seen together, as they often were, he and Stephens were akin to Jonathan Swift's Gulliver and a Lilliputian.

Shakespeare's Falstaff was said to be one of Toombs's favorite characters in literature, and there was a lot of Falstaff in him.[20] He was fiery, erratic, maverick-minded, impulsive, and a noisy rhetorical time bomb apt to explode at any moment. Someone said he "disagrees with himself between meals."[21]

In the antebellum years, Toombs served in both houses of the Georgia legislature, in the U.S. House of Representatives, and Senate. Wherever he was, he was a dogged and intractable champion of frugality, a conservative skinflint about public finance.[22]

Varina Davis liked him, describing him about as well as anybody did. She said, "one could scarcely imagine a wittier and more agreeable companion . . . (a) university man" who "kept up his classics." She believed his personal habits were those of "a fine gentleman [barring an affinity for getting drunk] . . . his diction was good, his wit keen, and his audacity made him equal to anybody in the heat of debate."[23]

18 Poore, *Perley's Reminiscences*, 1:317.

19 Pendleton, *Alexander H. Stephens*, 384.

20 Phillips, *The Life of Robert Toombs*, viii.

21 Thompson, *Robert Toombs of Georgia*, 66.

22 Thompson, *Robert Toombs of Georgia*, 17-18, 129, 179.

23 Von Abele, *Alexander H. Stephens*, 194.

Robert Toombs

Library of Congress

Varina was particularly taken with his "long glossy black hair," which he tossed about when speaking, like a mop on the end of a long handle. His teeth were "brilliantly white," his mouth "somewhat pendulous," his eyes "magnificent, dark and flashing." He had "a certain lawless way of ranging about that was indicative of his character." His hands were "beautiful," Varina thought, "kept like those of a fashionable woman." His voice was "like a trumpet."[24]

Describing Toombs giving a speech, Benjamin Perley Poore, the newsman and author in Washington, noted "his black, uncombed hair standing out from his massive head, as if charged with electricity, his eyes glowing like coals of fire, and his sentences rattling forth like volleys of musketry."[25] The *Augusta Chronicle* called Toombs "Richard the lion-hearted, with his strong arm and ponderous battle axe."[26] The *Athens Southern Watchman* called him the "burly blusterer."[27] The *Atlanta Constitution* said he spoke rapidly, "his tongue . . . [running] like a bell clapper."[28] It was said that like lawyers addressing juries, Toombs "commanded," while Stephens "persuaded."[29]

Although he voted for Georgia to secede, Toombs didn't believe Southern secession would lead to war. Many Southerners thought that. Former U.S. Senator James Chesnut, Jr, Mary Boykin Chesnut's husband, said he would drink all the blood that would be shed if the South seceded. It was more commonly said in the South that "a lady's thimble" would hold all the blood lost.[30]

In some things, however, Toombs could foresee the future clearly. It horrified him to hear that the young Confederacy was contemplating firing on Fort Sumter in April 1861. "The firing on that fort," he trumpeted, "will inaugurate a civil war greater than any the world has yet seen. . . . [I]t is suicide, murder, and will lose us every friend at the North. You will wantonly strike a hornet's nest which extends from mountains to ocean; and legions, now quiet, will swarm out and sting us to death. It is unnecessary; it puts us in the wrong. It is fatal."[31]

His foreboding was a bullseye, but few listened. And it was indeed hard not to listen when that big-bodied Falstaff spoke. When he spoke, his closet friend, the very thin Alexander Stephens, always listened, usually agreeing. That is what this pair of best-friend Georgia boys did.

24 Davis (Varina), *Jefferson Davis*, 1:409-10.

25 Poore, *Perley's Reminiscences*, 1:360.

26 Augusta Chronicle, Oct. 16, 1851.

27 *Athens Southern Watchman*, Sep. 8, 1859.

28 Quoted in Thompson, *Robert Toombs of Georgia*, 249.

29 Pendleton, *Alexander H. Stephens*, 37.

30 James M. McPherson, *Battle Cry of Freedom: The Civil War Era* (New York, 1988), 238.

31 Phillips, *The Life of Robert Toombs*, 232, 234-35.

Chapter 11

Thorns in Lincoln's Bosom

After being re-elected president in 1864, Lincoln told serenaders in Washington, "So long as I have been here I have not willingly planted a thorn in any man's bosom."[1]

That was not a two-way street. Innumerable others had willingly planted thorns in his bosom. From that legion, here are three of the most notable: Horace Greeley, influential editor of the *New York Tribune*; Adam Gurowski, self-appointed critic of everything in Washington; and Peter Cartwright, Lincoln's Methodist-for-life Democratic opponent, in their run against one another for Congress in 1846. These three gadflies had the additional merit of also being very eccentric.

Rare Bird in the Rookery

The tall, gawky man on the badly set frame was probably, after Abraham Lincoln, the most recognizable figure of Civil War times. "He was," one observer said, "the most public character in the country . . . celebrated and exaggerated in print and caricature . . . one of the sights of New York and would have been recognized at any crossroad in the United States."[2]

The sight of him walking the streets of New York recalled shambling dishevelment. Everything he wore seemed to trail after him rather than go with him. He was seen with necktie awry, in a long white duster with pockets stuffed

1 Lincoln, *CW*, 8:101.

2 Albert E. Pillsbury, "Memorial to Horace Greeley," *Address on the Centenary Observation of Horace Greeley at Amherst, New Hampshire*, Feb. 3, 1911 (Boston, 1911), 69.

Horace Greeley

Library of Congress

with newspapers, and one leg of his shapeless trousers snagged on a boot top. On his round head, thought to be rather too large, he wore a broad brimmed white straw or felt hat and toted an umbrella.

That was Horace Greeley, editor-publisher of the *New York Tribune*. To the world, he presented a childlike and clean-shaven face with a deceptively sweet and earnest smile. He had owl-like crystal blue eyes that looked small behind his round, gold-rimmed glasses. A thin ration of flaxen hair curled half-heartedly under the hat. A collar of flaxen floating hair swooped under the cherubic face and upward on either side, giving him the appearance of a sunflower. He was an eccentric, stooped and myopic with a shrieking voice to match a talented and shrieking pen.[3]

Greeley was the editor and publisher of the most circulated, politically potent newspaper in the divided country. He wanted that country back undivided. He prodded Lincoln constantly to work out a compromise with the Confederacy to end the war with the slaves freed. Lincoln wanted that too, but he also knew it was going to take time. Greeley was the rabbit to Lincoln's turtle.

Greeley began early as a thorn in Lincoln's bosom. He seldom agreed with Lincoln on any important measure, and criticized him boldly, bitterly, and constantly. Greeley was aggressive, impulsive, and often ill-advised, keeping him in constant conflict with Lincoln while still supporting the war effort.

Greeley wielding his pen in his office in the Old Rookery on the third floor of the *Tribune* building was just as riveting as his shambling gait. He worked at a desk nearly chin-high, his myopic eyes riveted to the paper, manufacturing illegible editorials at racehorse speed. As he finished a sheet, he let it slip to his lap or onto the floor, to be scooped up by a copy boy and rushed to the composing room where puzzled stares would study it.

John C. Robinson, an employee who could supernaturally decipher Greeley's hen scratches, was often called in to translate. Robinson would study the text, then read it off as if it was already in print. When Robinson wasn't around, the typesetters flew blind, taking the mysterious text for what they thought it said.

Notoriously absentminded to begin with, Greeley became oblivious when in his writing mode. Once, his office boy watched him pounding out an editorial at his desk, utterly unconscious of a water leak dripping steadily down on him.[4]

But his influence with his army of readers was unmatched by any other editor of his day. He had a knack for reporting that is illustrated in his coverage of an

3 This description of Greeley leans, with some intercessions by me, on a troop of nine other writers and historians: George W. Bungay, *Off-Hand Takings, or Crayon Sketches of the Noticeable Men of Our Age* (New York, 1854), 237, 239-40; John Callan O'Laughlin, "Lincoln and the Press," in *Abraham Lincoln Association Papers* (Springfield, IL, 1931), 38; *As God Made Them: Portraits of Some 19th Century Americans* (Boston, 1929), 134; John G. Shortall, "Horace Greeley," typescript, Horace Greeley Papers, Manuscript Division, Library of Congress, Washington, D.C., 2-3; Don Carlos Seitz, *Horace Greeley, Founder of the New York Tribune* (repr., New York, 1970), 1-3, 24, 75; Henry Luther Stoddard, *Horace Greeley: Printer, Editor, Crusader* (New York, 1946), xi; Jester Allen Isley, *Horace Greeley and the Republican Party* (Princeton, NJ, 1947), 10-11; Carpenter, *Six Months at the White House*, 152; J. Cutler Andrews, *The North Reports the Civil War* (Pittsburgh, 1955), 10.

4 This picture of Greeley at work is distilled from Seitz, *Horace Greeley*, 17-18, 10; Shortall, "Horace Greeley," 2; Bungay, *Off-Hand Takings*, 243.

evening sermon by the Reverend William Henry Channing. Channing was a celebrated clergyman, writer, and philosopher. Greeley wanted to cover the sermon and do a story for the next day's newspaper. But he simply could not stay awake in church, any church. So, he took his friend Oliver Johnson along, begging him to keep him awake by any means.

Arriving early, Greeley nodded off immediately, despite Johnson's elbow tattooing his ribs, trying to keep him awake. It was a fruitless assignment. That the two sat in a pew not six feet from the pulpit irked Channing.

After the sermon, Greeley and Johnson returned to the Rookery, where a somewhat groggy Greeley began reporting on what the preacher had said. It took up a little less than a column in the next morning's paper. An astounded Channing asked Johnson if Greeley had actually written it. When Johnson verified it was truly Greeley's handiwork, Channing exclaimed, "Why, I could not myself have made so accurate an abstract of my own discourse. He has not only given the substance of what I said, he has followed my line of thought, and remembered not a little of my language."[5]

Greeley was more than he appeared. An unforgiving memory, "as retentive as Pascal's," offset his absentmindedness.[6] He had the talent of holding grudges forever. His friend Alexander McClure thought him "one of the best haters I have ever known."[7] Yet there was another side of pure kind-heartedness and selfless philanthropy. He was a soft touch for a handout or a loan to almost anybody, within limits. However, solicited to subscribe to "a cause which will prevent a thousand of our fellow-beings from going to hell," Greeley snapped, "I will not give you a cent. There don't half enough go there now."[8]

In his heart, Greeley didn't really want to be the heavy-hitting editor he became. He said, "I should have become a farmer."[9] Or a politician, which in reality he already was. But he had to settle for being what he became in the end, an "ink-slinger," as he described himself.[10]

5 This story is told by Johnson in "Horace Greeley in Church," Greeley Papers, Archives and Manuscripts Division, New York Public Library.

6 Seitz, *Horace Greeley*, 8.

7 McClure, *Abraham Lincoln and Men of War Times*, 291.

8 Bradford, *As God Made Them*, 144-45.

9 Greeley, *Recollections of a Busy Life*, 295.

10 James H. Trietsch, *The Printer and the Prince: A Study of the Influence of Horace Greeley upon Abraham Lincoln as Candidate and President* (New York, 1955), 248.

He slung plenty, to the edification of many, the amusement of some, and the annoyance of others, including Abraham Lincoln. Though impatient, Greeley, in hindsight, did write this about Lincoln:

> He was simply a plain, true, earnest, patriotic man, gifted with eminent common sense, which in its wide range, gave a hand in shrewdness on the one hand, humor on the other, and which allied him intimately, warmly, with the masses of mankind.[11]

As with Channing's sermon, Greeley got that right.

Critic of Everybody

No thorns were more poison-tipped than those hurled by Count Adam Gurowski, a Polish exile born to insurrection. Venom pronouncements flew from his daily diary in all directions.

The favored target was "that sham" Abraham Lincoln, the "most mediocre of mediocrity,"[12] who ran the war squarely into Gurowski's disapproval. The president's slow-acting, careful style infuriated him. "Lincoln and Company," he raged, "make me lose my mind."[13]

"You can not," Gurowski raged, "change Lincoln's head, you can not fill his small but empty skull with brains." Lincoln, he charged "never yet boldly faced events and emergencies, never seized the hour by the forelock or the bull by the horns."[14] Gurowski's bombs landed elsewhere and exploded visibly. The Pole poured all his rancor into a diary, and worse, had it published as he was writing it.

All politicians were to Gurowski, "gnats and musquitoes . . . the race of hell." Lincoln's cabinet was "a violent mixing . . . of inimical and repulsive forces."[15] Of Union generals: "There they parade in splendid array, the starred ones! misnamed generals. . . . Marses who very well know how not to do it. All of them bats, not eagles."[16]

As the race of hell was convening to nominate Lincoln for a second term in 1864, Gurowski wrote: "As the Washington winds raise clouds of dust filled with atoms of offal putrified in the streets and alleys, so in all parties . . . election and

11 Joel Benton, *Greeley on Lincoln* (New York, 1893), 25.

12 Adam Gurowski to John Andrew, Mar. 27, and Apr. 27, 1864, in John Andrew Papers. Massachusetts Historical Society, Boston.

13 Adam Gurowski to John Andrew, Jun. 20, 1862, Ibid.

14 Gurowski, *Diary*, 1:207, 209.

15 Ibid., 1:16.

16 Ibid., 3:58.

Adam Gurowski

National Portrait Gallery

re-election fill the air with all kinds of foetid miasma. All the worst and meanest passions are stirred and they rise like gasses to the surface."[17]

Born in Poland in September 1805, Gurowski descended from a noble Polish family that traced back to the Crusades. He started early in life, getting in trouble

17 Ibid., 1:59.

with his mouth, his convictions, and his incendiary bent. The Imperial Russian Government expelled him from school for advocating Polish patriotism. He participated in the Polish uprising of 1830 against Russian rule. His role in an unsuccessful plot to kidnap Czar Nicolas I landed him a death sentence in absentia. For several years, with a noose hanging over him, he drifted around Europe as something of a *persona non grata*. Disillusionment drove him from the Old Country to America to become a gadfly disillusioned by Lincoln's running of the war.

Few exiles were as highly educated or experienced as Gurowski. He had been in his rebellious life a Polish patriot, a Russian civil servant, a protagonist of Pan Slavism, and in America, a lecturer on Roman law and a journalist for Horace Greeley. One of his friends was the poet, Henry Wadsworth Longfellow, who after spending several hours with Gurowski, said, "We all feel as if a huge garden-roller had gone over us."[18] Longfellow and the other victims that day likely suffered a double whammy at Gurowski's hands. As another friend explained, Gurowski often demonstrated friendship "very much in the way in which the tenderness of a bear is sometimes manifested, by a bear hug which seems almost fatal to the subject of it."[19]

With his experience and political savvy, Gurowski had hoped to land a major policy-making role in Washington. The best he could manage was a job as a translator in the State Department. From there, however, he became the unasked-for observer and critic of the Lincoln administration and its conduct of the war. Like many of Lincoln's critics, he was a Republican Radical, a hardline abolitionist opposed to Lincoln's forgiving view of life. He wrote his cranky observations in his diary, and when published, he was fired. But he had talent and connections in high places. He was a mostly unwelcome presence in Washington, constantly intruding on others' privacy, and interrupting important meetings.

He was visually perhaps the most colorful figure in Washington. He was of a burly build, medium height, with a pendulous paunch and side whiskers ringing a large round head full of his incendiary ideas. His most notable accessory was a pair of battered blue goggles with side blinkers. He had fallen on a pocketknife in his boyhood, injuring an eye. He wore the goggles to keep out irritating sunrays and to shroud the mutilation. Gurowski donned a long, flowing Old World-tailored black cloak topped by a broad brimmed, bell-shaped hat. His title of Count came legitimately, a rank the King of Prussia in 1787 had given Gurowski's grandfather and all his descendants, all genders, forever.

18 Samuel Longfellow, ed., *Life of Henry Wadsworth Longfellow: With Extracts from His Journals and Correspondence*, 3 vols. (1887; repr., Chicago, 2003), 2:183-84.

19 Quoted in LeRoy H. Fischer, *Lincoln's Gadfly, Adam Gurowski* (Norman, OK, 1964), 260.

Gurowski, who never lost a talent for violence, carried a pocket pistol, and drew it on occasions where things were not going his way. In July 1864, when a raid by Confederate Gen. Jubal Early had penetrated to Washington's outskirts, Gurowski drew his pistol on a fire brigade, to prod them along. They imprisoned him in the firehouse and charged him five dollars.

This side of his character and his outspoken mouth kept him under strict police surveillance since Lincoln's inaugural in March 1861. Gurowski's character did not escape notice by Lincoln. The president never gave much credit to threats on his life, but with Gurowski, he made an exception. "So far as my personal safety is concerned," he told his friend and bodyguard, Ward Hill Lamon, "Gurowski is the only man who has given me a serious thought of a personal nature. From the known disposition of this man, he is dangerous wherever he may be. I have sometimes thought he might try to take my life. It would be just like him to do such a thing."[20]

John Hay didn't give Gurowski that much credit. Although Hay called him "the venomous old count," he thought him merely "an undertone of nuisance."[21]

The Count, however, was Washington's loose cannon with crusading in his genes, revolution in his blood, havoc in his heart, and fire in his pen.

Shaking for the Lord

When Lincoln ran for Congress as a Whig in 1846, his Democratic opponent violated the separation of church and state.

The opponent was Peter Cartwright. He was a long-time circuit riding Methodist preacher, a revival-tent legend, who had for years been plowing the sinful prairies of Illinois for the Lord. Cartwright was a formidable figure of compelling charisma, popular everywhere he preached. He was an unconventional, Bible-thumping eccentric, capable of leaving believers and unbelievers shaking in a holy hysteria. Cartwright could get over 500 worshipers trembling at once and declaring for Jesus. It was said that "sinners fell before him like men slain in battle."[22]

He was physically as well as scripturally charismatic. He was five feet, ten inches tall, burly, and powerfully built with a "crowning foliage of luxuriant black hair wreathed into long, but rough and curling ringlets" on "a head that looked

20 Quoted in Lamon, *Recollections of Abraham Lincoln*, 274.

21 Hay, *Inside Lincoln's White House*, 192, 78.

22 Peter Cartwright, *Autobiography of Peter Cartwright*, W. P. Strickland, ed. (New York, 1857), 48.

Peter Cartwright

A Youth's History of Kentucky for School and General Reading

by Ed Porter Thompson

as large as a half bushel."[23] Some claim he had "an arm of flesh as well as a word of power, and who at times believed in the dispensation of muscular Christianity as well as a dispensation of the Holy Ghost."[24]

More than once in his long ministry, he put his sermon on hold to restore order in the audience. "The roughs and bruisers at camp-meetings and elsewhere," one observer noted, "stood in awe of [his] brawny arm, and many anecdotes are told of his courage and daring that sent terror to their ranks. He felt that he was one of the Lord's breaking plows, and that he had to drive his way through all kinds of roots and stubborn soil."[25]

He was as old in 1846 as Lincoln's father. He said, "I was born [in Viginia in 1785] in a cane brake . . . to escape the tomahawks of savage Indians; I was rocked in a bee-gum for my cradle, and my graduation degrees were taken from, and in, life's thunderstorms."[26]

Cartwright, who was a wild oat-sowing youth, converted and joined the Ebenezer Methodist Episcopal Church in Kentucky when he was sixteen. A born exhorter, he gained his license at seventeen to exercise that God-given gift. He became a deacon at twenty-one, an elder at twenty-three, and a presiding elder at twenty-seven. Cartwright had been felling sinners ever since.

He fell in love with Frances Gaines and married her in 1808, the year before Lincoln was born. She was nineteen, and he was twenty-three. Together they produced two boys and seven daughters, all good Methodists.

He was uncultivated in a book-learning way, like most Methodist circuit riding preachers of the time. He said, "We could not, many of us, conjugate a verb

23 *Illinois Daily Journal*, Jan. 30, 1850; Arthur C. Boggess, *The Settlement of Illinois, 1778-1830* (repr., Freeport, NY, 1970), 191.

24 Phillip M. Watters, *Peter Cartwright* (New York & Cincinnati, 1910), 443; John Mack Faragher, *Sugar Creek: Life on the Illinois Prairie* (New Haven, CT, 1986), 161.

25 Boggess, *The Settlement of Illinois*, 191-92.

26 Quoted in Henry B. Rankin, *Personal Recollections of Abraham Lincoln* (New York, 1916), 282.

or parse a sentence, and murdered the King's English almost every lick."[27] But, he could "mount a stump, a block, or old log, or stand in the bed of a wagon, and without notes or manuscript, quote, expound and apply the word of God to the hearts and consciences of the people."[28]

Alas, Cartwright had a secular weakness for politics, if not necessarily a gift for it. A lifelong Jackson Democrat, he was elected twice to the Illinois state legislature. But he did not present the vivid figure there as he did in a revival tent. He left no fellow legislators jerking and shaking.

In 1846, he raised his political sights to run for Congress, a seat for which Abraham Lincoln was also running. They were opponents, Lincoln the Whig versus Cartwright the Democrat.

Cartwright suspected Lincoln was an infidel, belonging to no organized church. He let that politically deplorable charge be broadcast around the district, prompting Lincoln to issue urgent denials. It was political suicide then for any politician to be an unbeliever. Still is.

During the campaign, Cartwright held one of his camp meetings in Springfield, and Lincoln dropped in to listen. As some sinners jerked toward the mourner's bench to accept the Lord as their savior, Cartwright noticed Lincoln in the audience and urged him forward, bellowing, "If you are not going to repent and go to Heaven, Mr. Lincoln, where are you going?" Lincoln slowly rose to his feet, and said, "I am going to Congress, Brother Cartwright."[29] So he was. Lincoln won the election with fifty-six percent of the vote, despite Cartwright's popularity.

Foiled in politics, Cartwright went back to the revival tent. He continued to excel there and was a beloved figure until he died in 1872 at age eighty-seven. When he left this earth, he left 129 direct descendants, kids, and grandkids to mourn his going. His preaching career began at the beginning of the nineteenth century and stretched for seventy years. In that lifetime, he preached enough miles in Illinois to circle the globe multiple times. During those seventy years, he converted 12,000 of the quaking faithful, and preached 15,000 sermons. But he never got to Congress.

Despite his charisma, he did not depart in quite the style of his wife, Frances, who survived him by four years. In a religious meeting at Bethel Chapel, a mile from her home, Frances was called on to give testimony. She testified for the Lord with great feeling, ending with: "The past three weeks have been the happiest of

27 Cartwright, *Autobiography*, 7.

28 Quoted in Faragher, *Sugar Creek: Life on the Illinois Prairie*, 160-61.

29 This story is told in Ida M. Tarbell, *Abraham Lincoln and His Ancestors* (1924; repr., Lincoln, NE, 1997), 270-71.

my life; I am waiting for the chariot." When the meeting broke up, Frances failed to rise with the rest of the congregation, as she always did.

The minister announced, "The chariot has arrived."[30]

30 Carl Sandburg told this true story in a poem, "Waiting for the Chariot" in *Harvest Poems, 1910-1960* (New York, 1960), 29.

Chapter 12

Six Beauties

Civil War era women, until recently, have mostly been absent from mainline Civil War history. This is a damn shame.

With a few rare exceptions, women didn't fight on the battlefields. However, thousands were nurses or wives, mothers, or sisters of the men and officers who did. We cannot measure their impact, but it would have been enormous.

Many took over their husbands' responsibilities at home, following the plow. Some, wives of famous generals and politicians, became influential behind-the-scenes advisers to their husbands. Several kept diaries and journals, writing letters that later made it possible for mostly male historians to write the history we have left them out of. Thousands of Civil War women endlessly sewed, knitted, cooked, and baked for the men who fought. A rare few became spies or soldiers incognito. Some women became famous in their day, only to have faded from memory.

Fortunately, this historic neglect is being corrected. A new generation of prominent historians are emerging and are writing about women in the war. Here are six women special to the era, whom I have met and fallen in love with.

Richmond's Super Belle

Gen. Winfield Scott finally met his match, on the battlefield of love. The Captain of the Age met and married Maria Mayo, the Richmond Belle of the Age. It was probably Scott's hardest fought campaign.

They were a huge physical mismatch. He was colossal for his time, six feet, four-and-a-quarter inches tall, topping off at a massive 300-plus pounds. She was

Maria Mayo

GRANGER

an abyss shorter, vastly slimmer, and 200 pounds lighter. She was the product of wealth and prestige, the shimmering ornament of one of the First Families of Virginia. Her grandfather, William Mayo, a brilliant civil engineer, had laid out the city of Richmond on its seven hills. Her father, John Mayo, had been its mayor.

Scott was a famous hero of the War of 1812, a young, often-promoted general of vast military talent but with an unimpressive pedigree. The groom's fame did not impress the father-in-law, who reluctantly, finally accepted the marriage.

Maria was an absolute knockout, unquestionably the leading belle of Richmond. She was a gifted harpist, pianist, and linguist, with a singing voice to complement her beauty and intelligence. She was a protégé of Dolly Madison and was also a virtuoso at turning down wedding proposals. It was said that she rejected at least 100 proposals of marriage, including a multiple number by Scott. Only after a long and intensive siege by this military genius did she finally say yes. Even then, a friend remarked, "So you married Captain Scott after all." She replied, "No—I refused Captain Scott to the last. I accepted the general."[1]

They married in late March 1817, in her reluctant father's residence in Belleville, Virginia. Scott was thirty-one, and she was twenty-seven. He was America's most eligible bachelor; she was the country's most desired catch. For the first five years, they lived in one of her father's residences in Elizabethtown, New Jersey, across the river from Scott's headquarters in New York City. Scott was too busy for them to honeymoon at the time of the wedding. Three months later, he took Maria to Niagara Falls, proudly showing her all the major sites of his heroism in the War of 1812.

Maria finally said yes to this big man, but never did she knuckle under to him. It was not a model marriage. They often got into domestic rows in public. It was a union of strong with strong. She didn't hesitate to define ennui, boredom, as "a tallow candle, a game of whist, and General Scott."[2] When the question of Scott's massive size came under discussion, Maria supposedly said, "Nobody but his wife ever knew how little he was."[3]

Despite this, Scott would sire, with her obvious participation, seven children, five girls and two boys. Only three survived to adulthood. Scott and Maria had more than their share of common sorrow. They were often separated for long periods, he on the nation's business, or she in Europe with the children. Their longest time

1 Chesnut, *Mary Chesnut's Civil War*, 283-84.

2 Henry Heth, *Memoirs of Henry Heth, Contributions in Military History*, no. 6, James L. Morrison, Jr., ed. (Westport, CT, 1974), 76.

3 Chesnut, *Mary Chesnut's Civil War*, 126-27.

apart was the years from 1838 to 1843, after the death of their youngest daughter. Maria retreated across the Atlantic without him.

Maria deplored Washington, describing it as "an ill-contrived, ill-arranged, rambling, scrambling village." "You see nothing but dust, hear nothing but political discussions and . . . the weather is sultry enough to make a dog mad," she complained.[4] She was fluent in French, and loved Paris, where she was a hit in the highest social circles. Maria was celebrated as "la Princess Sauvage," after she showed up at a high society fancy dress ball in the costume of an American Indian.[5]

There was not the slightest hint or complaint of marital infidelity by Scott in these long separations. He prided himself on his faithfulness to Maria. "I have never," he said, "violated my marriage vow, nor did I ever give a human being cause to imagine that I desired to violate it. I pledge my soul, my honor and my life that all I say now is strictly true."[6]

When apart, they kept in touch. In 1859, Scott departed on a tedious months-long 7,000-mile ocean journey to Oregon Territory aboard the steamer *Star of the West*, to pacify a Northwest border dispute with Great Britain. Maria wrote a *l'envoi* to him that ended:

Sail on gallant Scott! True discipline of virtue!

Whose justice and faith every danger will breast you,

There are angels on guard 'round the "Star of the West."[7]

Suffering from a lifelong chronic "epidemic sore throat" and failing eyesight, Maria died in Rome in 1862. Scott brought her body home and buried her next to their eldest daughter, Maria, in the West Point cemetery. Four years later, he would join them there.

Erasmus D. Keyes, a West-Pointer on Scott's personal staff, said that he had known "many of the grandest and most gifted dames of all the Christian nations of the world," but "remembered none who in breeding and accomplishment were the superior of Mrs. Scott."[8]

4 Maria Scott to Mrs. John H. Bernard, Apr. 13, 1843, William and Mary College Library, typescript, Virginia Historical Society, Richmond, VA., 127.

5 Allan Peskin, *Winfield Scott and the Profession of Arms* (Kent, OH, 2003), 81.

6 Keyes, *Fifty Years' Observation of Men and Events*, 29, 34.

7 Scott, *Memoirs*, 2:606-7.

8 Keyes, *Fifty Years' Observation of Men and Events*, 29.

Her Father's Spin Doctor

Mary Lincoln warned her husband to be wary of Kate Chase, the delectably desirable daughter of Lincoln's Secretary of the Treasury, Salmon Portland Chase.

Kate's father, considering himself more able, hungered to be president instead of Lincoln, his boss. Kate, his eldest daughter (he had two, Kate and the younger Nettie) was as ambitious for her father to sit in the nation's preeminent seat as he was.

No pile-driving daughter ever came in a more attractive package. Kate was devastating, a host unto herself, a phalanx of dazzling enchantment and beauty that regularly laid waste to all of Washington society. The British newspaper correspondent, William Howard Russell, described her as "very attractive, agreeable and sprightly." That was like calling the stunning Taj Mahal a pretty good-looking building. She, and not Mary Lincoln, was the real queen of wartime Washington society.

Kate was statuesque, tall like her father, and slender, wavy, and willowy. Her skin was the color of moonlight, her hair a rich chestnut with tones of red-gold, copper, and mahogany. Her dark eyes, flecked with green, were large, languid, proud, and enquiring, with long black lashes under crescent eyebrows. Kate's voice was a melody, low and magical.[9]

Her beautiful head rested on an elegant neck. She moved with a swan's delicacy and majesty. The German-born politician-general, Carl Schurz, seeing her in motion, said she glided into rooms, letting herself down on chairs "with the graceful lightness of a bird that, folding its wings, perches upon the branch of a tree."[10] This swanlike beauty was imperial and captivating, a mover of men's imaginations.

What set this daughter of a politician apart, besides her beauty, was her own wondrous gift for politics. In her teens in Ohio, the daughter of the then-governor, she possessed one of the most astute political minds in the state. When she moved to Washington with her father, first when he was a senator and then secretary of the treasury, she again became one of *its* most astute politicians.

But it was neither Kate Chase's beauty nor her mind that was most remarkable. It was her mindset. Few women ever have been more their father's daughter. Her father trusted her political acumen unconditionally. He called her "Katie" and for him she harbored an absolute, unswerving love and a dedication that gave new meaning to the Fourth Commandment.

9 Carl Schurz, *The Reminiscences of Carl Schurz*, Frederic Bancroft & William A. Dunning, eds., 3 vols. (New York, 1907-1908), 2:1:69; Ishbel Ross, *Proud Kate: Portrait of an Ambitious Woman* (New York, 1953), 32.

10 Schurz, *Reminiscences*, 2:169.

Kate Chase

Library of Congress

Tall, influential, and commanding, this father-daughter pair was the most handsome in Washington. Kate longed for the White House, perhaps more intensely than her father. There she would be *de jure* to what she already was *de facto*: the social divinity of Washington. She would be the official hostess in the White House. Her father, unlucky in love and marriage, had buried three wives all of whom had died young. He had not since remarried, and Kate would see that he wouldn't.

Kate, however, would marry. In November 1863, she wed Rhode Island Senator William Sprague. The Chases were not wealthy, but Sprague was one of the richest men in America, and money was necessary for the Chase's presidential ambitions. Some cynics presumed the marriage was not a love match as much as a money match.

In the end, Chase's not so covert campaign to unseat Lincoln in the election of 1864 ended. Later that year, Lincoln would name Chase the Chief Justice of the Supreme Court. It was a lofty elevation, but not lofty enough for the Chases.

Chase would rise no higher and his daughter's end would be tragic. A stormy divorce ended her marriage to Sprague in 1882. Her husband had problems with alcohol and women, and Kate was caught having an affair with New York Senator Roscoe Conkling. After the divorce, she lived for a time with her three daughters. After her son, who was living with his father, committed suicide in 1890, she became a recluse and died in poverty of Bright's disease on July 31, 1899.

The *Cincinnati Enquirer* said of her when she died, "No Queen has ever reigned under the Stars and Stripes, but this remarkable woman came closer to being Queen than any American Women has."[11] It was hardly an overstatement.

Caught Between Two Lovers

Two pals, George B. McClellan and A. P. Hill, learned all about triangles at antebellum West Point, where mathematics was the reigning terror. When the hormones were flying in the mid-1850s, after graduating, they found themselves on two sides of one of those triangles.

Both men fell in love with the same beauty, an enchantress, Mary Ellen Marcy of Hartford, Connecticut. Mary Ellen, nicknamed Nelly, was, like Kate Chase, a stunner, with blue eyes, blonde tresses, and a gentle winning smile. She was sprightly, loving, lovable, tender, and desirable.

It ensnared the two pals in love in a many-sided competition. More than just the two pals loved her, or wished they could. Many officers, in exile on the western

11 *Cincinnati Enquirer*, July 31, 1899.

Mary Ellen Marcy

Library of Congress

frontier in the 1850s, were losing their hearts to her on the eastern seaboard. But she had strength of character. She knew the word "no" and how to use it, breaking many hearts.

But the two pals soon had the inside track. She would fall in love with one and marry the other. The situation was complicated.

The *bête noir* to this triangle was Mary Ellen's father, army Captain Randolph B. Marcy, one of the premier soldier-explorers on the far western frontier. He figured he had the right of veto over Mary Ellen's love life. That's the way things worked back then. Daddy didn't want her to marry a soldier and live in a remote fort without necessities, or be left alone, for weeks, months, or years. He could cite his own often-away career as a prime example. Besides, he wanted Mary Ellen to aim higher socially and financially. He wanted her to snag wealth and social standing.

That meant that he didn't approve of the suitor she first fell in love with, A. P. Hill. He had no noticeable prospects besides being a soldier. If it had to be a soldier, Marcy much favored the other pal, George McClellan. McClellan had served under Marcy for a time on a frontier exploration and Marcy thought highly of him. Besides, McClellan had prospects, being the son of a famed physician in the upper elevations of Philadelphia society. And he possessed an overall talent that stirred envy.

Before his pal Hill won Mary Ellen's heart, McClellan, utterly smitten, had asked her to marry him and she had exercised her devastating "no" word. It was a shocking turndown for McClellan, who had rarely heard the word used against him before. He had never failed at anything. But when Hill asked her, Mary Ellen's eyes shone, and she said "yes." They became engaged, and he gave her a ring with "*le t'aime*" etched inside. *Le t'aime* was not the word for her father's reaction. Marcy raged against the match, forcing Mary Ellen to call off the engagement and give back the ring.

This didn't mean, however, that she would now say yes to McClellan. Although her parents loved him, she didn't. But McClellan, being permanently smitten and an admirer of sieges, laid siege to her affections, with the active connivance of her mother. It took half a decade. Only after he left the army and became a much praised, highly paid superintendent of a great railroad line, the Illinois Central, did her hard heart soften. On May 22, 1860, less than a year before a great civil war would change everybody's lives, they were married in New York City. It was one of the fashionable weddings of the season, loaded with a Who's Who in America in attendance.

The beautiful but elusive Mary Ellen grew to truly love her second-choice husband and became a model wife. She also lent staunch support to McClellan during his troubled generalship in the upcoming war. In that war, the two pals went separate ways, Hill with the Confederacy and McClellan with the Union.

There is a story about what the Union soldiers thought of all this, when Hill's soldiers of the famed Confederate Light Division one early morning attacked McClellan's Union army with vengeance. One of Stonewall Jackson's young staff members telling the story, said, "The long roll was beaten, there was commotion and confusion and a rush to arms, during which one hardened old Union veteran unrolled himself from his blanket and in a tone of weariness and disgust, cried out, 'My God, Nelly, why didn't you marry him!'"[12]

The Actress and Her Cross-Eyed Cuttlefish

It is perhaps because looks in a mate don't seem as important to women as it is to men that Sarah Hildreth would marry a cross-eyed man.

But she did, marrying the stunningly cross-eyed Benjamin F. Butler. For behind those crossed eyes, Sarah saw one of the most shrewdly calculating intelligences, a perfect fit for her own shrewd mind. Butler became a lawyer, a natural calling. A judge who knew him called him "the smartest damned rascal that ever lived."[13] Those two words, "smartest" and "rascal," defined Butler. He had been a smart damned rascal with a questionable reputation from childhood. In his neighborhood, he was "the dirtiest, sauciest, lyingest child on the road."[14]

That opinion didn't wash with Sarah. In adulthood, in peace and in war, her husband was a powerhouse. He was a Massachusetts lawyer-politician with a reputation as an "infamous arch demagogue" and a "political scoundrel."[15] He was a hard man to beat in a courtroom, talented at getting evidence in and keeping it out, an art that makes for judicial success.

During the Civil War, Lincoln made Butler a Union major general. His legal and political qualifications were unquestioned. His military qualifications were dubious, at best. He was the very worst general in the entire war, on either side. That fact didn't offend Sarah, for Butler was recognized by all as a political heavyweight who had clout and lasting power. That trumped his ineptness on

12 Douglas, *I Rode with Stonewall*, 177-78.

13 Hay, *Lincoln and the Civil War*, 115.

14 Robert S. Holzman, *Stormy Ben Butler* (New York, 1954), 5.

15 Benjamin F. Butler, *Butler's Book: Autobiography and Personal Reminiscences of Major-General Benj. F. Butler* (Boston, 1892), 108.

Sarah Hildreth

Butler's Book, *by Benjamin F. Butler*

a battlefield. Lincoln suggested that, being cross-eyed, Butler "didn't see things as other people did."[16]

Likely, the smartest thing Butler ever did in his lifetime was to marry Sarah. She saw things in him, qualities that hid behind those crossed eyes. She loved him dearly. She believed him to be a man who liked the tempest and evoked the thunder and the flashing lightning, a man given to high drama.

Sarah was attracted to high drama herself. She was the daughter of a Massachusetts physician, Dr. Israel Hildreth, a very scholarly and literary father. He was an admirer of the great English and Scottish poets, Shakespeare and Robert Burns. Dr. Hildreth taught Sarah, his second daughter, Shakespeare, stirring in her a passion for the stage.

At sixteen, she went to Boston to train as a dramatic actress. Soon she appeared with brilliant success in leading roles at the Tremont Theater in Boston and the Park Theater in New York. She became one of the most acclaimed stage actresses of her day. Invited to a Thanksgiving feast in 1836, Butler met her for the first time. "I was very much impressed," he later wrote, "with her personal endowments, literary attainments, and brilliancy of mind."[17]

For the next six years, "a most cordial intimacy was maintained between us," Butler claims, whatever that meant. In the spring of 1843, he visited her in Cincinnati, where she was being honored as a stage star. Now established enough in his profession, they became engaged. They married on May 16, 1844, and Sarah left the stage. They set out together, producing and raising a family of four children.[18]

16 Richard C. Evarts, "Colonel Richardson and the Thirty-Eighth Massachusetts," in *Cambridge Historical Publication*, vol. 39—Proceedings for the Years 1961–1963 (Cambridge, 1964), 11.

17 Butler, *Butler's Book*, 78.

18 Ibid., 79.

Sarah was beautiful and smart. She was popular with politicians and soldiers, a political asset and counterweight for her often-grating husband. Butler said, proudly, "She took her place in society, when at Washington, and maintained it with such grace, dignity, and loveliness of character that no one ever said an unkind or a disparaging word of her."[19] As for Butler, a fellow Union general had it right when he described Butler as "a cross-eyed cuttlefish swimming about in waters of his own muddying."[20]

Butler was astute enough to know how smart his wife was, at least as bright as he. Loving her as much as she loved him, he confided in her broad, lucid intelligence. She became for him "an adviser, faithful and true, clear-headed, conscientious and conservative, whose conclusions could always be trusted."[21]

He wanted her at his side throughout the war, and often she was, "with a devotion that was quite unparalleled." He explained: "In the mere military movements, although she took full note, she never interfered by suggestion, for in regard to them I relied upon the opinions of my valued, accomplished, and efficient staff officers." In other matters, Butler admitted, "all that she agreed to was right and for the best; and if there is anything in my administration of affairs that may be questioned, it is that in which I followed the bent of my own opinions."[22] Now we know why Butler was such a flop as a general. In hindsight he should have been, after all, holding staff meetings with her instead of his officers.

The union of a drama star and a cross-eyed lawyer-politician-general is rare. This one worked, a match made in heaven.

What's Not to Love?

In 1848, Sara Agnes Rice, a Virginia beauty, married Roger Pryor, son of a preeminent Presbyterian minister. Roger was to become a prominent Southern newspaper editor and firebrand preaching Southern secession.

It became apparent early that Sara with no effort on her part had a gift for attracting the notice of famous men. The first great man she charmed was Henry Clay, the preeminent Kentucky senator. She was just a child and the great man was passing through Richmond, again campaigning, vainly, to be president. Admirers thronged him, so she was lifted to her Uncle Samuel Hargraves's shoulders for a better look. A space between them cleared for a moment, much as the Red Sea

19 Ibid., 85.

20 Lew Wallace, *Lew Wallace, an Autobiography*, 2 vols. (New York, 1906), 2:674.

21 Butler, *Butler's Book*, 82.

22 Ibid.

Sara Agnes Rice

Virginia Museum of History & Culture (E415 .7 P98 1904)

must have parted for Moses, and Clay spotted her. He smiled, lifted his hat, and gallantly bowed.[23]

In the 1850s, she was grown and married to Roger, when Illinois Senator Stephen A. Douglas, Lincoln's great political rival, came to Virginia where Roger edited an influential newspaper. Douglas had just returned from a visit to Europe where he had met Eugenie, the dazzling consort of Napoleon III, and therefore Empress of France. Eugenie was the foremost beauty of mid-nineteenth century Europe. Douglas was quick to notice how the charmer in Virginia looked so like the one in Paris, and he told her so.[24]

Several years later, at a crowded Washington ball, Douglas approached Sara carrying two glasses and a bottle of champagne. "I need no introduction, madam," he told her. "I am sure you cannot have forgotten the man who met you a few years ago in the little Petersburg hotel and how like you are to the Empress Eugenie. No? I thought not." Jostled by the crowd, Douglas accidentally poured a cascade of champagne down Sara's cleavage. "Don't worry about the gown!" Douglas said helpfully. "You have an excuse now to buy another."[25]

What she did not need to buy was any more magnetism. Before the war, she became a friend of the bachelor president, James Buchanan. At a wedding reception on December 20, attended by the president and the cream of Washington society, it was Sara who told the already overwhelmed president that she had heard that South Carolina had just seceded from the Union. It likely meant there was to be a civil war.

During the war, after Roger became a brigadier general in the Confederate army, and went to fight Yankees, Sara lived a precarious nomadic life with two of her children. Toward the war's end, in besieged Petersburg, she charmed Robert E. Lee, who often rode past her cottage on the way to the trenches. Roger had become a scout for Lee, captured by Yankees, released, and sent back South just as the war was ending.

After the war, the Pryors eventually left the war-devastated South with their seven children and moved to New York, "into arms of the enemy."[26] There, they built a new and successful life. Roger became a respected lawyer, then a judge on New York's highest court, and worked as hard for reunion as he had for separation before the war. Renowned for her personality, intelligence, and compassion, Sara

23 Mrs. Roger A. Pryor, *My Day: Mrs. Roger* (New York, 1909), 35.

24 Ibid., 84-85.

25 Mrs. Roger A. Pryor, *Reminiscences of Peace and War* (New York, 1904), 67-68.

26 *New York Times*, Feb. 16, 1912.

kept charming distinguished men, old high-level friends in the South, and new high-level friends in the North.

Among them was Gen. Phil Sheridan, Grant's trusted cavalry commander during the war. After Petersburg and Richmond fell and Lee surrendered to Grant at Appomattox Court House, Sheridan commandeered Sara's house in Petersburg for his adjutants. Despite being inconvenienced, she charmed him as well.

After the war, Sara met Sheridan again at a reception in Gen. and Mrs. Grant's home in New York. At first, Sheridan was too astonished to speak. "He had hardly supposed," Sara later wrote, "when he parted from me in the house where . . . I had been kept by him literally in durance vile, that our next meeting would be in the drawing rooms of the wife of his commander. I gave him time to realize all this, and then I asked him gently, 'Do you remember me, General Sheridan?' In a moment, both hands grasped mine. 'Indeed, indeed I do, dear lady!'"[27]

Few men who met her ever forgot her. The man that she charmed for a lifetime was Roger. When she died in New York at 84, he, who would live to age 90, said, "I have lost the sweetheart of my life."[28]

An admirer said, "She was as harmonious as music, as gentle as a summer's breeze, as steadfast as a star. There was no place in her heart where fear or meanness or envy lurked. Bravely, tenderly, hopefully she lived through great events."[29]

Four years before she died, Sara wrote this short verse in a longer poem:

I have lost my rose, forgotten my song,
But the true heart that loved me is mine always;
The stars are alight—the way not long—
I had my day.[30]

For many men who met her, famous and not so famous, she made their day. She repeatedly made mine when I was researching for a book about how she, Roger, and their children survived the Civil War. I fell in love with her, too, but what was not to love about Sara Pryor?

27 Mrs. Pryor, *My Day*, 376-77.

28 *New York Law Journal*, Mar. 18, 1919.

29 Willcox, "A Light is Out!" 6.

30 Mrs. Pryor, in a prelude to *My Day*, ii, written Nov. 8, 1908.

The Unquiet Quaker

Anna Elizabeth Dickinson did what few women did in Civil War times. She spoke in public, a no-no in the patriarchal America of the nineteenth century.

It hadn't been intentional. At eighteen, she was an obscure Quaker teenager working in the United States mint in Philadelphia. Nobody knew of the oratorical volcano raging with rhetorical lava within. It erupted, uninvited, one evening in early 1860 at a meeting of the Association of Progressive Friends. A male speaker had made a case for female inferiority and it lit Anna's fuse. To everybody's astonishment, and perhaps her own, she rose from her seat and bombarded the offending man with a brash oratorical cannonade.

Before she knew it, she was in rocketing demand as a part time speaker at local Quaker and antislavery meetings around Philadelphia. People began flocking to hear and see this novelty. She was something to see and hear. Anna's nose was Grecian, and her chin firmly set. Her eyes were large, gray, and flashing. Her hair was black and wavy, curling slightly and tossing as she shifted gears to oratorical climaxes. She was medium height and slender, with a full, graceful figure. Her voice was a strong contralto "of remarkable power and sweetness,"[31] one reporter wrote, which she wielded as a lash.

William Lloyd Garrison, the editor of *The Liberator*, the leading abolitionist newspaper of the times, heard her for the first time at a speech at the annual meeting of the Pennsylvania Anti-Slavery Society in October 1861. He was stunned and dazzled as everybody was by this teenager's "remarkable oratorical fluency."[32]

Garrison became her mentor, and under his guiding hand, Anna went national on the antislavery speech circuit. Her flying mane of hair, rapid-fire delivery, withering sarcasm, beauty, and the heresy of a girl among the male orators left audiences gasping. Not an original thinker, she was fed ammunition by the abolition leaders. She launched assaults that were charged with highly immoderate, unladylike statements.

They fired her from her job at the mint after her withering criticism of Union Gen. George B. McClellan. Few laggards escaped her venom, not even Abraham Lincoln, who she praised when she thought he was doing right and lambasted when she thought he wasn't. When he dragged his feet on emancipation, she called him "an Ass . . . for the Slave Power to ride."[33]

31 Wendy Hammond Venet, *Neither Ballots nor Bullets: Women Abolitionists and the Civil War* (Charlottesville, VA, 1991), 55.

32 James Harvey Young, "Anna Elizabeth Dickinson and the Civil War: For and Against Lincoln," *MVHR* 31 No.1 (Jun. 1944), 60.

33 Ibid., 62.

Anna Dickinson

Library of Congress

By this time, her admirers were calling her "this most charming of female Demosthenes," the new Joan of Arc, Portia, Pythia, Evangeline, Juliet, and Cassandra.[34] She had become a prophetess, and a star voice, not only of abolitionism, but of Radical Republicanism. This, of course, prompted Democrats, who were prime victims of her venom, to call her "that spiritual medium," that "political witch," that "parrot," or that "crowing hen."[35]

An invitation from the United States Congress to deliver a public lecture led to her crowning hour. On January 16, 1864, she would deliver her remarks in the hall of the House of Representatives. Lincoln had received her at the White House earlier in the day, and he and Mary attended the lecture that evening with 2,500 other curious or enthralled listeners, friends, and critics.

This was unprecedented. No woman had ever been invited to speak in the halls of Congress, much less a girl who had just turned twenty-two. After taming her stage fright, which always visited her before a speech, she began snapping her verbal whip. She was a vision in her black silk gown with its red velvet furbelows and long train. Her rise on the national oratorical circuit had graduated her from simple Quaker wear to this sort of glittering garb. A London correspondent called her a "crazy Jane in a red jacket."[36] Traditional, devout Quakers must have looked at how she dressed and blanched.

Noah Brooks, the Washington correspondent for a California newspaper, listening to her that evening, thought he had her pegged. "She will flash out her brief and splendid career," Brooks predicted, "and then subside into the destiny of all women and be heard of no more."[37]

Brooks was wrong. Anna remained one of the nation's most celebrated and popular lyceum speakers for nearly a decade after the war. When her speaking career ebbed, she went into acting, living to age 90, a third of the way into the twentieth century.

In her glory years, hardly more than a girl, she demonstrated more brash speech-making power than most men. In time, fortunately, following Anna's lead, other women would stand on public platforms with like power and brashness.

34 Venet, *Neither Ballots nor Bullets*, 55.

35 Young, "Anna Elizabeth Dickinson and the Civil War," 66.

36 Ibid., 70.

37 Brooks, *Mr. Lincoln's Washington*, 281-82.

Chapter 13

A Pair of Wackos

War is not funny. But some soldiers can be so different from the norm that they are funny, often without knowing it. Confederate Maj. Gen. Richard Stoddart Ewell qualifies. The way he looked, talked, and acted combined to present a noteworthy eccentric. Another is Capt. George Horatio Derby, unofficially considered the looniest West Pointer ever, and the funniest officer in the Old Army. Yet, besides being eccentric, these two wackos were also excellent soldiers.

The Sometimes Looney General

Confederate Lt. Gen. Richard Stoddert Ewell was a West Pointer, Indian fighter, and sometime looney.

He was born on February 8, 1817, into a prominent Virginia family, giving him a leg up in life. He was the son of a doctor, and on his mother's side, the grandson of the first U.S. Secretary of the Navy. The Ewell family members were bright and highly competent. That was the upside. The downside was that they were chronic inbreeders. The norm was cousins marrying cousins. That had worked to make the entire extended family somewhat wacko, and they knew it.

Before the Civil War, Ewell and his older brother Ben, a professor of mathematics and President of William & Mary College, visited the Eastern Lunatic Asylum in Williamsburg, Virginia. There, Ewell ventured the thought that "there might be

Richard Stoddert Ewell

Library of Congress

many worse things than a berth in the asylum." Ben nodded, saying it might be a good place for their entire family.[1]

1 This visit of the Ewell brothers to the insane asylum is retold in Donald C. Pfanz, *Richard S. Ewell: A Soldier's Life* (Chapel Hill, NC, 1998), 60.

Ewell was a chip off that wacky block. Yet many considered him to be the sanest of the bunch. That doesn't mean that he was not eccentric. Oh, no. His eccentricity began with his appearance. He was nearly bald. His nickname besides "Old Dick" was "Old Bald Head."[2] Ewell's nearly hairless dome was bomb-shaped, and he had bright prominent eyes, an aquiline nose and a lush beard, his chin apparently the only place where hair could grow. Some compared his appearance to a woodcock. That was from his nervous, hyperactive, hippity-hop temperament and birdlike habit of cocking his head to one side while delivering utterances in a lisp. He didn't talk so much as he chirped.[3]

Ewell was a trim and gaunt five feet, ten-and-a-half inches tall, weighing 140 pounds, a spare body hardened by years on the western frontier fighting Indians. One of his most remarkable features was his bright restless eyes. They were constantly in motion, roaming everywhere as he talked or listened,[4] perhaps a nervous reflex from his frontier days.

Ewell not only looked like a woodcock, with his darting eyes and cocked head, but he swore like a mule driver. A man who met him in the 1850s wrote that he "could swear the scalp off an Apache."[5] His genius for swearing was phenomenal. Ewell's cavalry commander in the Civil War, Tom Munford, said he could swear "in a style that defies description."[6] "His profanity," another officer marveled, "did not consist of single or even double oaths, but was ingeniously wrought into whole sentences. It was profanity which might be parsed, and seemed the result of careful study and long practice."[7]

A preacher once said, while perhaps covering his ears, that Ewell "did not confine himself to the dull neutralities of undecorated speech."[8] Ewell's cussing was a talent that would cause Stonewall Jackson to say, "Ewell, that was well done, and I don't see how a man of your habits and who uses language like yours can do his work so well."[9]

2 Percy Gatling Hamlin, "Richard S. Ewell: His Humanity and Humor," in *Cavalcade* (Autumn, 1971), 10.

3 Taylor, *Destruction and Reconstruction*, 36; G. Moxley Sorrel, *Recollections of a Confederate Staff Officer* (1905; repr., Dayton, OH, 1978), 53.

4 Richard Stoddert Ewell Papers, Manuscripts Division, Library of Congress, Washington, D.C.; Pfanz, *Ewell*, 334.

5 J. Ross Browne, *Adventures in the Apache Country: A Tour Through Arizona and Sonora, with Notes on the Silver Regions of Nevada* (New York, 1869), 156.

6 Thomas Taylor Munford, "A Confederate Officer's Reminiscences" (Ft. Reno, OK, 1892), 523.

7 George Cary Eggleston, *A Rebel's Recollections* (Bloomington, IN, 1969), 136.

8 Quoted in Pfanz, *Ewell*, 168.

9 Wise, "Stonewall Jackson as I Knew Him," 144.

Ewell was fearless in battle. Bravery was his flagship trait from childhood.[10] In the Arizona Territory in the 1850's, he was happiest when there was the prospect of a bloody encounter with the Apache. When a fight seemed likely, he always rode at the head of the patrol.[11] That is also where he would ride in the Civil War, at the head of his division and later, his corps.

Ewell graduated from West Point in 1840, in the same class as William Tecumseh Sherman, the famed Union general-to-be, who was his best friend. George H. Thomas and Bushrod Johnson, two other notable commanders in the war, were also classmates. Ewell graduated thirteenth in a class of forty-two, one file behind Thomas.

Sent to the Western frontier before and after the Mexican War, in which he fought gallantly under Gens. Zachary Taylor and Winfield Scott, Ewell became one of the premier Indian fighters in the old army. Some thought him "without a superior as a cavalry captain."[12] Phillip St. George Cook, Ewell's commander when he was still a lieutenant, reported that he "has had during the fall a command—that of a squadron—much above his rank, but not above his merit."[13]

Ewell was to earn his Indian fighting reputation in Southern Arizona. It was the most desolate and dangerous part of the country, alive with unfriendly Apache, gunslingers, outlaws, and killers. Tucson, its largest settlement (and my hometown a century later), held the graves of forty-seven white men. Only two had died of natural causes.[14] The gun was the final decider in most such cases.

Ewell was highly regarded by the locals on this frontier of mayhem. In his most celebrated achievement, he negotiated the rescue of a kidnapped white girl from the Apache. The jubilant citizens of Tucson poured into the town square to cheer and bless him when he rode in with the rescued girl. In their gratitude, the citizens named one of the territory's original four counties after Ewell.[15] The name would not stick on the county, but it showed how popular he was in Tucson.

Ewell's fellow Indian fighters also admired him. After joining a military posse with the legendary Kit Carson to head off outlaws intending to rob a wagon train,

10 Elizabeth Ewell to Benjamin Stoddert Ewell, May 12, 1832, Benjamin Stoddert Ewell Papers, College of William and Mary, Williamsburg, VA.

11 Richard Stoddert Ewell to W. A. Nichols, May 22, 1856, National Archives, Washington, D.C.

12 Sorrel, *Recollections*, 53.

13 William E. Connelly, ed., "A Journal of the Santa Fe Trailin," in *MVHR* 12 (1925), 253-54.

14 Browne, *Adventures in Apache Country*, 22.

15 Hubert Howe Bancroft, *History of Arizona and New Mexico*, 1530-1888, Vol. 17 (San Francisco, 1889), 507n.

he and Carson become longtime friends.[16] Even Cochise, the most famous and terrorizing of the Apache chiefs, was friendly with Ewell, when not fighting him. When Ewell commanded the garrison at Fort Buchanan, Cochise visited at least twice, returning livestock that native warriors of another tribe had stolen.[17]

Until the Civil War, Ewell had rarely commanded anything in battle larger than a company, and even after given larger commands in the war, he occasionally still thought small. When there had been a need to go foraging for his 7,500-man division he had gone out, returning late in the day proudly leading a single bull. One of his brigadiers said it was a truly impressive animal but would hardly feed 7,500 men.

"Ah," chirped Ewell, "I was thinking of my fifty dragoons."[18]

Ewell hated the Civil War. He later confessed, "If there were anything I had to dread & regret it was this war."[19] When war became reality, in April 1861, he resigned from the old army with a heavy heart. "It is hard to account for my course, except from a painful sense of duty," he mourned. "I say painful because I believe few were more devoted to the country than myself."[20] But like many other Southerners, it was a choice; either you were for your state and family, or for the Union. Like so many others in those days, the state trumped the Union for Ewell's loyalty. But it was loyalty sadly given.

Ewell felt he had everything to lose and nothing to gain in the Civil War. It was "sacrificing every earthy hope for principle . . . like death to me."[21] However, he was more than welcome in the Confederacy. Like many West Pointers North and South, Ewell shot overnight from captain to general, passing multiple ranks in an army that instantly needed high level commanders trained for battle on a large scale.

Ewell, in conversation, would abruptly utter incomprehensible thoughts pulled out of nowhere. Once, he asked one of his brigadiers, "General Taylor! What do you suppose President Davis made me a major-general for?"[22] He referred

16 Richard Stoddert Ewell to Benjamin Stoddert Ewell, Feb. 25, 1854, Richard Stoddert Ewell Papers, Library of Congress, Washington, D.C.

17 Richard Stoddert Ewell to Lizinka Campbell Brown, Apr. 23, 1862, ibid.

18 Taylor, *Destruction and Reconstruction*, 38.

19 T. Harry Williams, ed., "General Ewell to the High Private in the Rear," *The Virginia Magazine of History and Biography* 54, No.2, (April 1946), 159.

20 Ibid.

21 Ibid.

22 Taylor, *Destruction and Reconstruction*, 37.

to himself for some time after as "a mere ephemeral production of the president."[23] There were often such unexpected lispings as this one to a young lieutenant: "Come and eat a cracker with me, Lieutenant. We will breakfast together here and dine together in hell."[24]

Many thought Ewell was the "oddest, most eccentric genius in the Confederate Army." He augmented his eccentricity with a volcanic temper, and a razor-sharp tongue loaded with cuss words that could cut unmercifully.[25] "No man," one of his brigadiers said, "had a better heart or a worse manner of showing it. He was in truth as tender and sympathetic as a woman, but, even under slight provocation he became externally as rough as a polar bear, and the needles with which he pricked sensibilities were more numerous and keener than porcupines' quills."[26] One officer said the men who were victims "were a great deal more afraid of him than of Yankees."[27]

Another of Ewell's brigadiers said, "Virginia had never produced a truer gentleman, braver soldier, more lovable—or odder man."[28] His brother Tom said he had "the sharpest tongue and softest heart," of anyone he knew.[29]

At the battle of First Manassas in July 1861, Ewell noted artillery booming up the Confederate line. He was expecting an order from P. G. T. Beauregard at any moment, directing him to lead an assault on the Union left. But the order didn't arrive. It was lost, but Ewell didn't know that. In suspense, he mounted his horse one moment, dismounted it the next, and stalked to and fro, muttering to himself, "No orders! No orders!"[30]

Ewell's own written orders were models of accuracy and clarity. But his verbal orders, at times, came directly from Babel. They were understandable by no man in any tongue, especially when he was under intense excitement. At such times, his brain outraced his tongue. His thoughts leaped across great chasms, which

23 Richard Stoddert Ewell to Lizinka Campbell Brown, Apr. 13, 1862, Richard Stoddert Ewell Papers, Library of Congress, Washington, D.C.

24 Gordon, *Reminiscences*, 39.

25 Ibid., 38.

26 Ibid.

27 Frank M. Myers, *The Comanches: A History of White's Battalion, Virginia Cavalry* (1871; repr., Marietta, GA, 1956), 37.

28 Taylor, *Destruction and Reconstruction*, 89.

29 Gordon, *Reminiscences*, 38.

30 Ibid.

his words could never hope to span. Woe to the man who failed to understand a thing he said.[31]

At First Manassas, while Ewell was awaiting Beauregard's orders, he sent for a trooper to act as a courier. When the young man arrived, Ewell machine-gunned him with some of the most rapid-fire, incomprehensible, garbled instructions ever uttered on a battlefield.

"Do you understand, Sir?" Ewell demanded when he was finished.

When the dazed subaltern, who had not understood a word, asked for more explicit directions, Ewell waved him away impatiently. "Go away from here," he roared, "and send me a man who has some sense."[32]

At that same battle, a young Virginia beauty, around seventeen years old, caught between the lines, heard information that needed reporting to the Confederates. She rode up to Ewell in a flutter of excitement. She had plenty of intelligence about the Yankees. Ewell listened, then pointed to the Union batteries being placed on the opposite hill.

"Look there, look there, Miss!" he chirped. "Don't you see those men with the blue clothes on, in the edge of the woods? Look at those men loading those big guns. They are going to fire, and fire quick, and fire right here. You'll get killed. You'll be a *dead damsel* in less than a minute. *Get away from here! Get away!*"

The young lady cast a quick, but disinterested glance toward the great danger, and turned again to Ewell, pressing once more, oblivious to the pending doom. Ewell stared at her in mute wonder. Turning abruptly to one of his officers, he said, "Women—I tell you sir, women would make a grand brigade—if it were not for snakes and spiders! They don't mind bullets—women are not afraid of bullets; but one big black-snake would put a whole army to flight."[33]

During the war, on May 26, 1863, Ewell would marry one of those divine creatures who didn't mind bullets. She was born Elizabeth, but was called Lizinka, after the wife of Czar Alexander I, of Russia, whom her parents knew personally.

Ewell's Lizinka was a beauty, highly educated, rich, fond of talking, and a bit on the bossy side. Of course, in the Ewell custom, she was a cousin. Ewell had loved her for years, but she had married a man named James Percy Brown.

31 Ibid., 38-39.

32 Ibid., 40.

33 This anecdote about the wannabe teenage spy and the nature of women, snakes, spiders, and bullets is from Ibid., 41-42.

Brown mistreated her and fortuitously, committed suicide in 1844, leaving her a 24-year-old widow.[34]

A few years later, she began to communicate with Ewell. After a long correspondence, Ewell's wish came true, better late than never. He worked up courage he never lacked in battle to ask Lizinka to marry him. She said yes. A rigid Episcopalian, she was to give her new husband religion: he was to start putting God in his dispatches and to saddle-break his foul language. Some would insist she ruined him. He would introduce her to his friends after their marriage as, "My wife, Mrs. Brown."[35]

In early 1862, this quaint man was ordered to join Stonewall Jackson, in the Shenandoah Valley, as his second in command. Ewell rode to Jackson, as usual, in advance of his 7,500-man division, just as he rode at the head of his fifty dragoons in the West. When he arrived, he was soon convinced that it was Jackson who was the looney one. Jackson believed that one arm and leg were heavier than the other, and on the battlefield, he would raise his arm straight to heaven to let the blood run back into his body to relieve the excessive weight. Ewell wondered how anybody who believed that could be anything but crazy.

It could be argued that Ewell was as crazy as Jackson. He was also a victim of mysterious internal maladies. Jackson wouldn't eat pepper and sucked on lemons to cure himself. Ewell was known to confine his diet to a pasty, inedible mishmash made from wheat. He once said his "stomach [was] not provided with brains to know what [was] sufficient for the health of the other parts."[36] His nervous nature also often prevented him from sleeping normally. Instead, he would pass nights curled around a campstool.[37]

When Ewell arrived at Conrad's Store at the eastern edge of the Valley, Jackson left with his command. He did not give Ewell any notion about where he was going, what he was going to do when he got there, or when he would return. Stonewall, some said, wouldn't tell the buttons on his coat where he was going.[38] "The truth is," one of Ewell's young staff officers later explained, "Ewell never knows anything about Jackson's plans until they are fully developed."[39] After several months with

34 Elizabeth Stoddert Ewell to Benjamin Stoddert Ewell, Mar. 11, 1850, Benjamin Stoddert Ewell Papers, College of William and Mary, Williamsburg, VA.

35 Taylor, *Destruction and Reconstruction*, 89.

36 Richard Stoddert Ewell to Elizabeth Stoddert Ewell (Lizzie), Richard Stoddert Ewell Papers, Library of Congress, Washington, D.C.

37 Taylor, *Destruction and Reconstruction*, 37.

38 Douglas, *I Rode with Stonewall*, 234.

39 Jones, "Stonewall Jackson," 174; see also Jones, "Port Republic," 363-64, and "Career," 84-85.

Jackson, Ewell would say, "I pledge you my word that I do not know whether we are to march north, south, east or west, or whether we are to march at all or not."[40]

Jackson was going across the Valley, where he would fight the battle at McDowell in the mountains of western Virginia, without Ewell. En route, he would occasionally send Ewell, whom he had directed to keep an eye on Gen. Nathaniel Banks's Union army, cryptic and enigmatic notes that utterly failed to lessen Ewell's misgivings.[41]

When Col. James A. Walker, one of Ewell's regimental commanders, came on business, Ewell asked as he walked into his tent: "Colonel Walker, did it ever occur to you that General Jackson is crazy?"

"I don't know, General," Walker replied, "we used to call him 'Fool Tom Jackson' at the Virginia Military Institute, but I don't suppose he is really crazy."

"I tell you, sir," Ewell protested, "he is crazy as a March hare. He has gone away, I don't know where, and left me here with some instructions to stay until he returns, but Banks' whole army is advancing on me and I haven't the most remote idea where to communicate with General Jackson. I tell you, sir, he is crazy and I will just march my division away from here. I do not mean to have it cut to pieces at the behest of a crazy man."[42]

Ewell came to call Jackson the "enthusiastic fanatic."[43] Richard Taylor, son of former President Zachary Taylor, and one of Ewell's most trusted lieutenants, later said Ewell "never saw one of Jackson's couriers approach without expecting an order to assault the North Pole."[44]

Often looniness is in the eye of the beholder. Ewell's brother, Ben, no straight arrow himself, said philosophically, "Most of us by the estimation of our best friends are more or less eccentric. So, Taylor and Ewell thought Jackson, and so Taylor thought Ewell, and so Ewell thought Taylor, and I have no doubt that if Jackson's mind hadn't been full of more important matters he would have thought so of Ewell and Taylor."[45]

When Jackson returned from McDowell and headed down the pike toward Front Royal, Strasburg, Winchester, and Harpers Ferry in his stunning

40 Douglas, *I Rode with Stonewall*, 235.

41 *OR*, Ser. 1, vol, part 3, 884; Jedediah Hotchkiss, *Make Me a Map of the Valley: The Civil War Journal of Stonewall Jackson's Topographer*, Archie McDonald, ed. (Dallas, 1973), 34-35.

42 Hamlin, "Old Bald Head," 84.

43 Richard Stoddert Ewell to Elizabeth Stoddert Ewell (Lizzie), May 13, 1862, Richard Stoddert Ewell Papers, Library of Congress, Washington, D.C.

44 Taylor, *Destruction and Reconstruction*, 37.

45 Benjamin Stoddart Ewell, "Jackson and Ewell" in Benjamin Stoddert Ewell Papers, Manuscript and Rare Books Department, Swern Library, College of William and Mary, Williamsburg, VA, 32-33.

Valley campaign, Ewell was finally called to his side. Together, the two generals fought brilliantly, and Ewell began to see what wonders were going on under Jackson's faded kepi.

Jackson learned that he could always depend on Old Bald Head. Ewell was perhaps the only general under Jackson that Jackson never saw any need to have arrested. Jackson, of course, gets the credit as the mastermind of the Valley campaign. But Ewell was more than just another lieutenant. Some viewed it as a partnership, a co-venture. When Abraham Lincoln, perplexed, frustrated, and disgusted, spoke of the Confederate force in the Valley, he called it "Jackson & Ewell."[46]

So what if Jackson was an enthusiastic fanatic? What if Ewell looked like a woodcock and swore like a mule driver, lisping strange, incomprehensible orders? Together, they created a military masterpiece in the Shenandoah Valley.

The *Richmond Daily Enquirer*, assessing Ewell's contribution to Jackson's campaign, wrote, "In sixteen days they fought seven battles and in every instance were victorious. . . . It is the first time that General Ewell has had an opportunity of showing in battle how skillfully and bravely he could handle an army. Never defeated, never surprised, always at the right place at the right time, he has earned and well merits the title of General."[47]

"Plain in his dress," a fellow officer wrote, "quick . . . in his orders, prompt in execution, almost reckless in his courage, and stubborn and unyielding in holding any position assigned him, he was just the man Jackson needed, in whom he seemed to have the utmost confidence, and to whom he was certainly indebted for much of his splendid success."[48]

At the end of the Valley campaign, before they set out to help Gen. Lee drive Union Gen. McClellan from the gates of Richmond, Ewell spoke to Tom Munford again. "Look here, Munford, do you remember a conversation we had one day at Conrad's Store about Jackson? I take it all back, and will never prejudge another man. Old Jackson is no fool; he knows how to keep his own counsel, and does curious things; but he has a method in his madness; he has disappointed me entirely."[49] Later asked about Jackson in the Valley campaign, Ewell said, "Well, sir, when he commenced it, I thought him crazy; before he ended it I thought him inspired."[50]

46 For instance, see Lincoln, *CW*, 5:232, 233, 245, 246. Lincoln was known also to have called them "Ewell and Jackson," 246.

47 *Richmond Daily Enquirer*, Jun. 18, 1862.

48 Jones, "Reminiscences," 187.

49 Munford, "Reminiscences," 530.

50 Jackson, *Memoirs*, 287.

After Ewell was wounded at Groveton, at Second Manassas, and lost a leg, he convalesced at a cousin's house thirty miles from where the epic and bloody battle was raging across Antietam Creek at Sharpsburg, Maryland. Ewell fretted, saying he "could not listen to the sounds of the battle without fearing the loss of General Jackson, believing his preservation important and necessary to the success of the Confederate cause."[51]

Jackson also had an opinion of Ewell that ran deeper than never having to have him arrested. After the Valley campaign and after they had helped drive McClellan from the Peninsula, Jackson told a friend he believed 60,000 Confederates could march into Maryland and threaten Washington. Wishing this view were laid before President Davis, he would, to avoid self-seeking, not lead it himself, but follow Lee, or "the gallant Ewell."[52] This was high praise from Jackson.

These two quaint men would not remain a team much longer after the Valley campaign and the Seven Days battles on the Peninsula. At Second Manassas in the late summer of 1862, Ewell was wounded. By the time he was able to fight again, Jackson would be dead, shot accidentally at Chancellorsville by a regiment of his own corps, dying a week later of pneumonia. Ewell would replace him at the head of the Army of Northern Virginia's Second Corps. It was said that Jackson's deathbed wish was that Ewell succeed him in command.[53]

As Jackson's successor, Ewell would leave a mixed resume. He conducted a brilliant campaign to recapture Winchester, Virginia, on the way to Gettysburg in the summer of 1863. He was Jacksonian in skill, maneuver, and audacity.

He is viewed as being less than brilliant at Gettysburg. On the first night of that battle, vigorously urged by his chief lieutenants to capture lightly defended Cemetery Hill, he hesitated. Lee had ordered him not to bring on a general engagement until the entire army had arrived. Not until Lee himself changed that order and commanded him to assault the hill if he "could do it to advantage," did Ewell look to do it. By then it was too late.[54] Federal forces had rushed heavy reinforcements to Cemetery Hill. Had Ewell not hesitated, it likely may have been a game changer. A mix-up in the Confederate army's coordination, and timing on the second and third days of the Gettysburg campaign, assured failure. Ewell did not come out looking good.

51 Ewell, "Jackson and Ewell," 30.

52 Robert Lewis Dabney, *The Life and Campaigns of Lieut.-Gen. Thomas J. Jackson* (New York, 1866), 486-87.

53 McGuire in an article labeled "Anonymous" in the *Richmond Daily Enquirer*, May 13, 1862; Hamlin, "Old Bald Head," 135-36.

54 Ewell's testimony, in *OR*, Ser 1, vol.27, part 2, 445.

Some argue that if Jackson had still been in command of the Second Corps, he would not have hesitated, no matter what caution Lee had advised. He would have assaulted the hill early, taken it, and the Confederates would have likely won the battle, and perhaps the war. But it might not have happened that way. Ewell would later confess to a fellow officer that "it took a dozen blunders to lose Gettysburg, and he had committed a good many of them."[55]

Ewell was brilliant, back in form, in the battle of the Wilderness in May 1864. He was less impressive at the struggle for the Muleshoe at Spotsylvania. Lee, though praising Ewell as "a brave old soldier, ready to attempt anything," relieved him of command of the Second Corps, on grounds that he was too ill to continue.[56] He was assigned to command of rebel forces in Richmond. It was Lee's way of putting him on the shelf.

There, a Richmond reporter wrote, Ewell, with his wooden leg, was a familiar sight in the city, "the spectacle of a worn and mutilated man looking prematurely old."[57] Sometimes Ewell drove the streets in a dilapidated sulky. "It was a sorrowful picture," the reporter wrote, "but a nearer view disclosed a man remarkable even in the ruin of health and constitution, whose gray eye was as sharp and fierce as ever, and whose precise conversation showed that the vigour of his mind was as yet untouched."[58]

Ewell engineered one last brilliant moment in September 1864. There, with an unimpressive force of teamsters, prisoners, and what troops he could muster, he beat back a Federal breakthrough across the James River. In effect, he saved Richmond. He was later to regard this as his greatest accomplishment in the war.[59]

Lee ordered Ewell to abandon the city he had saved when Petersburg fell on April 1, 1865. Ewell joined the main army, trying to break out of the closing Federal trap and escape to Danville on the North Carolina border. Ewell got only as far as Little Saylor's Creek. On April 6, Federal troops cut off, fought, beat, and then captured him, six other rebel generals, fourteen pieces of artillery, and a third of Lee's army.

55 Eppa Hunton, *Autobiography of Eppa Hunton* (Richmond, 1933), 98.

56 Longstreet, *Manassas to Appomattox*, 645; *OR*, Ser 1, p, 46, part 2, pp. 1259-60; H. E. Wood, "More of the Last Defense of Richmond," in *Confederate Veteran* 16 (1908), 397.

57 Edward A. Pollard, *Lee and His Lieutenants: Comprising the Early Life, Public Services, and Campaigns of General Robert E. Lee and His Companions in Arms, with a Record of Their Campaigns and Heroic Deeds* (New York, 1867), 461-62.

58 Ibid.

59 Richard Stoddert Ewell, Letterbook, Manuscript Department, William R. Perkins Library, Duke University, Durham, NC.

Ewell, now in Union hands, was shipped to Fort Warren, the Federal prison for Confederate generals in Boston Harbor. On the way, news arrived that Lee had surrendered the Army of Northern Virginia to Grant at Appomattox Court House. Ewell threw up his arms and said, "The jig is up!"[60] While on the train, he learned Lincoln was assassinated at Ford's Theater, and he wept. "My God!" he cried, "I am sorry for that; it is the worst thing that could happen to the South."[61]

After his release from Fort Warren, Ewell would never again be a soldier. He would become instead a farmer, one of the most successful in the South. He settled in Tennessee where he ran Lizinka's considerable land holdings; a huge stock farm, one of the largest in Tennessee, and two plantations in Mississippi, which Lizinka had inherited when her father, her first husband, and her brother died. Lizinka was one of the wealthiest women in the country. When she died, the value of her real estate holdings approached a quarter-million dollars.[62]

She and Ewell continued to work together, love each other, and bond closer than ever, until January 1872. Early that month, Ewell fell ill with pneumonia, following Jackson's path to death. By mid-January, as he lingered, Lizinka, constantly at his bedside, caught his illness. She began a rapid decline. On January 22, she died first. He began to fail rapidly, breathing his last three days later, on January 25. In two weeks, he would have been fifty-five years old. They buried Ewell and "Mrs. Brown" together in the Old City Cemetery in Nashville, Tennessee.

So, what can we conclude about Dick Ewell? He was a soldier for a quarter of a century, nearly half of his life. He had participated in two major mounted expeditions in the West, fought in two wars, and risen in grade from second lieutenant to lieutenant general. Ewell was wounded three times, and at Groveton, he lost a leg. Once he had almost died. Five horses were shot from under him. But not once did he fail to do his duty, as he saw it.

For a time, he thought Jackson was nutty as the Mad Hatter. Some sources believed he was one of the mourners who accompanied Jackson's remains from Richmond to Lexington to be buried. Whether or not he did, Ewell left Jackson to the ages. He, a nutcase, had been intimately associated in war with another nutcase who was also a military genius.

I believe that Ewell was a more worthy commander than history makes him out to be. Except for his lapse at Gettysburg, and his so-so generalship at Spotsylvania,

60 Samuel P. Bates, *History of the Pennsylvania Volunteer, 1861-1865*, 5 vols. (Harrisburg, PA, 1869-71), 2:677; *OR*, Ser 1, vol. 46, part 3, pp. 692-93.

61 Butler, *Butler's Book*, 908.

62 See Pfanz, *Ewell*, p. 607, note 27. Pfanz's biography of Ewell, is the standard on the subject, an excellent book.

we might consider him brilliant today. He was a gallant and brave man, one of the old army's finest and most fearless Indian fighters and a courageous soldier. I think, despite a pair of mediocre showings in command of the Second Corps, he was one best generals in the Confederate army.

And better for laughs than any of them.

The Wacko from West Point

The West Point Class of 1846 was the largest and arguably the most star-studded of the antebellum years. Its fifty-nine graduates produced over twenty generals in the Civil War, names that have come rolling down through the decades: Stonewall Jackson, George McClellan, A. P. Hill, George Pickett, and more. These men were household names in their time, and have left indelible benchmarks in our history and on our memories.

In that distinguished class was also George Horatio Derby, graduating in fifth place. Very likely, you have never heard of him. The highest rank he ever reached in the army was captain of topographical engineers. He only barely made it to the Civil War. He died just as it was beginning, in May 1861, a month after the firing on Fort Sumter. But no cadet in the class left a sharper mark on West Pointer memories than he. There was not one of them who wouldn't swear that he was an absolute looney, in the best sense of the word.

Like many of them, he would become famous and make the *Dictionary of American Biography*. Unlike them, he would make it not as a soldier, which he was, but as an American writer of comic sketches, one of the earliest and best. That and mapping terrain were not all that Derby did well. He engineered pranks that were legendary. When the entire Academy was rousted out in the middle of the night in full equipment to put out a fire that didn't exist, Derby was, without question, and justifiably, believed to be behind it. When the drawing of a water pump on the blackboard looked strikingly like the professor himself, you can bet Derby drew it. He spoke of himself in the plural. At West Point he had picked up the nickname Squibob and therefore referred to himself as "Derby and I."[63]

Like most of his classmates, Derby went to the Mexican War the year he graduated, fought heroically, and was wounded at the battle of Cerro Gordo.

The story is told, doubtless apocryphal, but in character, that the commanding general of the American army, the heroic Winfield Scott, found Derby, one of his valued topographical engineers, lying bleeding on the field.

"My God, Darby," exclaimed the great general, "you're wounded!"

63 George H. Derby to H. W. Halleck, Apr. 16, 1853, in Papers of George Horatio Derby, Bancroft Library, University of California, Berkeley.

George Horatio Derby

The Bancroft Library

And Derby replied, "Yes, General Scatt."

To which Scott replied, "My name is Scott, not Scatt."

To which Derby replied, "And my name is Derby, not Darby."[64]

After graduating from West Point with the class of 1846, Derby took his weird sense of humor with him into the regular army. An early celebrated story, also unlikely to have happened but circulated and attached to Derby, was of the circular-shooting cannon. Derby, the account goes, was at army headquarters in Washington shortly after graduating, waiting to be received by a well-known general.

"Good morning, Mr. Derby," said the old campaigner, "happy to see you sir! Take a seat."

Derby bowed and took the offered seat, his face wearing its customary joyless expression.

"Anything new?" the general asked.

"Well, no sir!" said Derby. "Nothing particular—excepting that remarkable gun, invented by Captain ———, of the artillery." Derby looked modestly down at his cap, turning it shyly in his hands.

New gun? What new gun? the general asked, as he hadn't heard about any new gun. Could Derby describe it?

The general and several staff officers of various ranks leaned forward, expectantly. Derby rose respectfully, laid his cap on the chair, and looked inquiringly toward the table that held the drawing materials. The general nodded and Derby took materials and illustrated the principle of the ingenious new weapon. His gifted

64 This story is told in a letter by Bessie Derby, February 3, 1933, in the Derby Family Records, Betsey B. Creekmore Special Collections and University Archives, The University of Tennessee, Knoxville.

hands deftly sketched a diagram. His eager auditors gathered around, the old general foremost.

"Now, sir," Derby said, holding up his detailed and lucid sketch. "This is Captain ——'s invention for throwing projectiles in a curved line, to sweep them around and behind intervening objects."

The old general, who had been scrutinizing the illustration with the utmost interest, now turned a searching gaze on the young lieutenant. Derby explained the principle of the weapon, the shape of the projectile, its motion and effect. Letter A, the muzzle of the gun; Letter B, the line describing the arc of the missile, its course, and so on. His explanation was fluent and plausible, his words clear, distinct, and knowledgeable, his use of artillery terms precise and exact, his drawings illuminating. It all made sense.

"Has the principle been tested?" the general asked when the young subaltern finished his presentation.

"Yes, sir," Derby said. "Sergeant McCue fired the gun off yesterday morning."

"What was the result?" the general asked.

"The shot passed entirely around the barracks, striking the gunner in the os coccyges [tailbone]," Derby replied.

The general now turned squarely on the young officer, so that he could see him more distinctly through his spectacles. There was a long and stony silence and an uneasy shifting of the auditors as the general continued to stare at the poker-faced young scapegrace. Then, in a burst of hearty forgiving laughter, the old veteran clapped a fatherly hand on the young officer's shoulder. "Mr. Derby, remember that it is only once in a lifetime, and under peculiar circumstances, that such a thing would be overlooked."[65]

Derby's, or Darby's, ultimate destiny lay in a universe as quirky as his own, California.

When gold was discovered in the Sacramento Valley in 1849, the army discovered that not only did the hoards flocking to the gold fields need protection from Indians and one another, but that the Gold Rush country also needed mapping. So, it sent Derby, a topographical engineer, one of the best in the army. There could not have been a better match. California and George Derby were made for each other. It was in California that he began writing quirky sketches for local newspapers.

Quickly, he became an instantly recognizable fixture on the streets of San Francisco. He had merry blue eyes, a round figure getting rounder, and a face as

65 This story is told in T. A. Barry & B. A. Patton, *Men and Memories: In the Spring of '50* (1873; repr., Whitefish, MT, 2007), 148-51.

grave as a gravedigger. Derby's physiognomy was noteworthy. When delivering his rankest pun, concocting his most cockamamie story, or pulling his most outrageous hoax, he never cracked a smile. The merriment was there in his eye, but the rest of his face remained a phiz of dejected marble. Think of the early film slapstick comedian Buster Keaton, poker-faced through every disastrous adversity, and you have George Derby.

From an early age in Medfield, Massachusetts, where he was raised in a matriarchy composed of his divorced mother, two maiden aunts, and a grandmother, little George had a different perspective from most kids. His drum banged to an entirely different beat.

It was not the everyday looney who would think to substitute the real menu at San Francisco's exclusive Tehama House with one featuring roast mule, kangaroo cutlets, and rat-tail soup.[66] It was not the everyday maniac who would introduce two friends, whispering to each that the other was hard of hearing, and then sit back and listen to them shout at one another.[67]

It wasn't an ordinary stage director who, when staging a production of *Romeo and Juliet* for the military garrison at Monterey, cast himself and a strapping 200-pound German soldier's wife as the star-crossed lovers. Juliet's Teutonic accent and ample figure alone convulsed the audience. But when the stage construction collapsed in the middle of the balcony scene, it added just the right touch.[68]

Derby was said by one contemporary to be "a wag from the womb," pulling off practical pranks before he could walk.[69] One friend said, "What other men would sacrifice for ambition, for love, for the attainment of fortune or personal aggrandizement, he would sacrifice for fun—his best friend would have no more chance of escape than his worst enemy."[70]

Soon after arriving in California, after the Mexican War, he added a third name—John Phoenix—to his persona. I call this pile-up of made-up names, "Derby and We." On the one hand, he was Lt. Derby, military and correct, the most active topographical army engineer in California, mapper of the gold fields, and the first white man to explore the mouth of the Colorado River. The nickname Squibob remained. And to readers of local publications, for which he began to

66 George R. Stewart, Jr., John Phoenix, Esq., *The Veritable Squibob: A Life of Captain George H. Derby* (New York, 1937), 4-5.

67 George H. Derby, *Squibob: An Early California Humorist*, Richard Derby Reynolds, ed. (San Francisco, 1990), 56.

68 From an unidentified newspaper in the Derby Family Records.

69 Derby, *Squibob*, 14.

70 From *Reminiscences*, in Manuscript by Mrs. Charles M. Hitchcock, typed copy in possession of Floride Green of San Francisco.

write humorous sketches, he was John Phoenix, the funniest man in California, the state wit.

His army persona was admirable. In the early years of the 1850s, he commanded four path–breaking map-making expeditions, three in the Gold Rush country, and the fourth to the mouth of the Colorado. For his eight years in the West, he claimed to have done little but travel through California and Oregon at the head of pack trains. During that time, he said he saw over 4,000 mules loaded with over 800,000 pounds of goods, and heard them addressed by upwards of 4 million oaths and profanities.[71]

Derby took his humor to the highest echelons in the War Department. He would manage on at least two occasions to offend the secretary of war himself, who in Derby's time, in the 1850s, was Jefferson Davis. Davis had decided there should be a new army uniform, and to that end he solicited suggestions from officers. That was a serious mistake, as Derby responded with a fully illustrated proposal.

The main characteristic of Derby's newly proposed uniform, which had several unique features, was a hook sewed into the seat of every pair of trousers. Joined to a companion hook on the cantle of a saddle, the device could hold the drunkest dragoon securely in place. Soldiers could hang camp kettles and other necessities from these same hooks, and with a deficiency of mules, employ themselves for draught purposes. At bedtime, the soldiers could simply hang themselves from their hooks on fence rails. In battle, company commanders with long poles and compatible hooks could wheel their troops into position by the seats of their pants. If a soldier attempted to skedaddle, the officer could simply catch him by the hook in the seat of his pants and grapple him back into line.[72]

Reports say that the unsmiling secretary of war did not take this proposal in the proper spirit. Davis would have court-martialed Derby if cooler, more fun-loving heads hadn't prevailed. If so, Secretary Davis must also have enjoyed Derby's proposal for the rotary mule howitzer.

Derby devised this unique weapon to satisfy the need for a lightweight, rapidly firing gun in tight, hard-to-get-to places. The proposal, as formally submitted to the War Department, and fetchingly illustrated, called for two howitzers to be packed on a common mule. One gun was lashed to the beast's back, its muzzle pointed toward the tail, the other to its belly and aimed between its two front legs. Five artillerymen were assigned to each mule, two to each piece. The fifth member of the team, called the "persuader," stood by the side of the mule with a

71 George Horatio Derby (John Phoenix), *The Squibob Papers* (New York, 1865), 245.

72 Poore, *Perley's Reminiscences*, 1:492-93. Derby's new uniform proposal illustrated by him, is pictured in Derby, *Squibob*, 50-52.

twin sausage-stuffer stuffed with oats. When targets appeared, the mule, by a crank movement of the tail, was limbered to the front. It didn't matter which way the mule faced. One gun was always pointed to the front in either case.

At the command, "Fire!" the top howitzer boomed, and the recoil threw the mule over on its back, bringing the second gun into position. This was fired, jerking the mule back onto its feet, to have its throat quickly swabbed out with oats by the persuader and the guns reloaded. Derby's illustrations pictured the rotary mule in several attitudes, looking serene and smilingly content.

Some of Derby's best works were neither written nor drawn, but simply perpetrated. One of his classic outrages occurred soon after his arrival in California, in the spring of 1850. Derby was killing time in Barry & Patten's Saloon, a favorite hangout of wits, literati, and savants on San Francisco's Montgomery Street. It was a fine spring morning and Derby, a regular at the establishment, raised his grave, thoughtful eyes just in time to see a horse and wagon passing on the street. EAGLE BAKERY was painted on its side in heavy capital letters. He rushed out, waving his arms frantically.

"Hi! hallo you!" he shouted.

The driver, a phlegmatic German baker, rested his stolid gaze on the lieutenant, and turned his horse reluctantly to the curb.

"Vat you vants?" he demanded.

"I'll take a baked eagle!" Derby said.

"Eh? Vat's dat?"

"A baked eagle," Derby repeated, stamping impatiently. "Don't you understand?"

"I pakes pread," protested the indignant driver.

"Stop!" commanded Derby as the "pread paker" started to drive away. "You're an imposter! How dare you deceive the public in this way? Here have I been for six weeks trying to get a baked eagle, which my medical adviser prescribes for my health, and you have raised hopes only to deceive me."

The befuddled baker's attention was directed to the lettering on the side of his wagon.

"If you don't have those words—that falsehood—painted out immediately," Derby threatened, "I'll have you put under arrest and court-martialed!"

The baker stared, uncomprehending.

"Away!" Derby said, waving him off with impatience and disgust, and stomping indignantly back into Barry & Patten's.[73]

73 Stewart, *John Phoenix, Esq.*, 77.

On another day, Derby hailed yet another passing team, with even more enigmatic results. He dashed out of a house into the street and called to the driver so urgently that the horses were flung back on their haunches.

"Do you go to the mission?" Derby demanded urgently.

"Yes!" the driver shouted.

"I thought so," Derby said, and nonchalantly turned and walked back into the house.[74]

Derby was as skilled at switching objects to the befuddlement of his victims as he was at hailing down wagons. Shoes, for example. He would switch his beat-up old pair for his roommate's new pair. His most notorious alleged switch stirred widespread civic consternation in Sonoma. It was the custom at the annual gala ball in that town for the mothers to leave their bundled–up babies in the same room where they left their cloaks. As they danced the night away, somebody switched all the sleeping babes in their bundles. It was a jumbled situation that went unnoticed by the tired, but happy mothers when they came to reclaim their infants.

When they arrived home, however, they found that the swaddling clothes were theirs, but the swaddled babies within were not. There was an indignant simultaneous outcry from all over town and a chaotic scramble with the babies back to the dance hall. They did not conclusively pin the prank on Derby, but nobody doubted for a moment that it was his doing.[75]

Derby employed puns indiscriminately and without letting up. But they were only fillers for his more serious humor. Pranks such as the Sonoma baby exchange were far more soul-satisfying. Full-scale hoaxes were best of all, and his specialty. In the first half of the 1850s, when he was writing for local publications in California, readers hardly knew if they could believe what they were reading. Every ridiculous thing John Phoenix and Squibob wrote sounded plausible, if a little off-center. Derby's pen was as deadpan as his face.

When the sewing machine first came on the market, Phoenix was ready with his remarkable "Feline Attachment," available by mail order. Like many great inventions, it operated on a remarkably simple principle. An upright shaft was connected to the machine by a cogwheel and pinion, supported below by a suitable framework. Two projecting arms were attached to the shaft. To one of these, a large cat—the feline attachment—was connected by a light harness, and from the other, a living mouse was suspended by the tail. As the cat sprang forward to seize the mouse, the latter moved, rather like a greyhound chasing a rabbit. This caused the

74 Ibid., 108.

75 The baby switch is told in Edwin A. Sherman, "Personal Reminiscences of a California Pioneer of 1849," manuscript, Bancroft Library, Pasadena, CA.

machine to spin rapidly. The prodigious velocity produced by the rapacity of the cat in its vain pursuit of the mouse could only be imagined by those who had not seen the attachment in actual operation.

To stop the machine, a handkerchief was simply thrown over the mouse and the cat at once stopped in disgust. When the handkerchief was removed, the cat sprang forward with renewed ardor, and the machine continued. Phoenix claimed he had seen one cat make eighteen pairs of men's trousers, two dozen regular shirts, and seven stitched shirts before dropping from exhaustion.[76]

Gadgets fascinated Derby. So Squibob and John Phoenix conjured up several, such as the Feline Sewing Machine. He also enjoyed science, which caused John Phoenix to write a two-part Lecture on Astronomy which he prepared to be delivered before the Lowell Institution in Boston. But it was never delivered "owing to the unexpected circumstance of the author's receiving no invitation to lecture before that institution." In his lengthy lecture, Derby was perhaps the first scientist ever to describe what would happen if the world was suddenly to stop spinning:

> The earth moves around the sun from west to east in a year, and turns on its axis in a day; thus moving at the rate of 68,000 miles an hour in its orbit, and rolling around at the tolerably rapid rate of 1,040 miles an hour. As our readers may have seen when a man is galloping a horse over a smooth road, if the horse from viciousness or other cause suddenly stops, the man keeps on at the same rate over the animal's head; so we, supposing the earth is suddenly arrested on its axis, men women, children, horses, cattle and sheep, donkeys, editors and members of Congress, with all our goods and chattels, would be thrown off into the air at a speed of 173 miles a minute, every mother's son of us describing an arc of a parabola which is probably the only description we should ever be able to give of the affair.[77]

During a stay in San Diego, Derby was persuaded by the editor of the local newspaper to edit the sheet in his absence. It was near election time, and there was a critical gubernatorial race underway. The paper was ardently Democratic. Within days, Derby had turned it into an unrepentant Whig sheet, throwing local politics into chaos, and nearly tipping the election in an unintended direction.[78]

It was about the time of the newspaper hoax that Derby got married. And it wasn't one of his pranks as usual; it was one of hers.

76 Derby, *Squibob*, 229-30.

77 George Horatio Derby, "Lectures on Astronomy," in *Phoenixiana, or Sketches and Burlesque* (New York, 1856), 62. The text of the two lectures can be found on pages 51-66 and 236-53.

78 The sketch of Phoenix being installed as temporary editor of the *San Diego Herald* and its consequences are in Ibid., 95-115.

Mary Angeline Coons was a 24-year-old beauty from a prominent St. Louis family when she met Derby in 1853 in San Francisco. He courted her. They suffered a lover's quarrel, and Derby left in a huff, vowing not to return to San Francisco until the Coonses had cleared out of California. It was a terrible sacrifice, for Derby loved San Francisco, and San Francisco loved him.

Mary Coons also loved him, and she was a woman who could give as good as she got in the pranks department. In a move worthy of her intended, she falsely listed her and her mother's names at the head of the manifest of a steamer bound for the East. The newspaper published the manifest; Derby read it some days later in San Diego, as she knew he would. Believing the coast was clear, Derby returned to San Francisco, and found her waiting. There was nothing left then but to marry her, and she knew that, too. They married in January 1854. Derby called her "Molly," and they were very much in love.[79]

In the autumn of 1856, the Derbys and their baby daughter left California for good. For half a decade, Derby had been the army's topographical engineer in Gold Rush country. Derby by now had not only California, but most of the rest of the country in stitches. His works had been published in a collection, titled *Phoenixiana, or Sketches and Burlesques*, edited by his old friend, the editor of the Democratic newspaper that Derby had switched to Whig in San Diego. It was one of the worst-edited books of the time but became a bestseller and the witty engineer became recognized as an American humorist of the first rank. A second volume of his writings, *The Squibob Papers*, would one day follow. The Derby style of extravagant expression and thought would influence later satirists, including a young and rising humorist who called himself Mark Twain.

But the laughter ended for Derby in early 1861. He was dying, just as the Civil War was aborning. His eyes had been bothering him for years. Now he was going blind. Rheumatism, carbuncles, and other ailments racked his ample frame, causing him to lose weight alarmingly. He was by now a captain of engineers, designing and building lighthouses along the Gulf. In Florida he suffered sunstroke. It was the beginning of the end.

On May 16, 1861, a month after Fort Sumter was fired on and the armies of the Union and Confederacy were building to fight a great civil war, Derby died in New York City. Had he lived, he probably would have become a Union general. On the other hand, it was just as well. The war of brothers would have been too serious for Derby and We.

"Derby is dead!" cried the *San Francisco Times* in its anguish:

79 The courtship is described in Stewart, *John Phoenix, Esq.*, 131-33.

> The sword of the soldier is rusting in its sheath, the pen of the writer waits in vain for the master's hand, the pencil of the artist no longer transfers to the paper the visions of a creative brain. At the sound of the great reveille the gallant spirit has marched to headquarters. For him no shrill tones of the fife, no roll of the stirring drum, no sound of battle, will ever come again. He belongs to the grand army of the dead, he is in the rear guard of eternity. Earthly epaulettes and plumes, sash and button are changed for the wreaths of immortality. The man of wit, of humor, of genuine originality, walks no more with us, educing pleasant thoughts from the most barren subjects, winning golden ideas from the very dust of the desert.[80]

Derby sleeps eternally today "in a green and narrow bed"[81] in the West Point cemetery. Most of the other memorials that surround him are standard. But over Derby looms a large shapeless lump of granite boulder. Not five paces away, under a glistening white monument ringed by a wrought-iron fence, rests his old friend, Gen. Scatt. It is indeed fitting.

So Squibob had played his last prank. John Phoenix had perpetrated his last hoax. George Derby had written his last sketch, drawn his last map, designed his last bridge, built his last lighthouse, and cursed his last mule.

80 *San Francisco Times*, May 15, 1861; *Shasta* (California) *Courier*, June 15, 1861.

81 From the Civil War Song, final verse, "The Vacant Chair," by George F. Root.

Bibliography

Primary Sources

Manuscript Collections

Andrew, John A. Papers. Massachusetts Historical Society, Boston.

Chase, Samuel P. Papers. Library of Congress. Washington, D.C.

Churchill, Winston. Speech to House of Commons, in praise of Neville Chamberlain, November 12, 1940.

Davis, Jefferson. Papers. Museum of the Confederacy, Richmond, VA.

Derby, George Horatio. Papers, 1846-1870. Bancroft Library, University of California-Berkley.

_____. Family Records. Betsey B. Creekmore Special Collections and University Archives, The University of Tennessee, Knoxville.

Ewell, Benjamin Stoddert. Papers, Manuscript and Rare Books Department, Swem Library, College of William and Mary, Williamsburg, VA.

Ewell, Richard Stoddert. Papers. Manuscript Division Library of Congress Washington, D.C.

Greeley, Horace. Papers. Manuscript, and Archives Division. New York Public Library.

_____. Papers. Manuscript Division, Library of Congress.

Hay, John. Papers. Brown University, Providence, RI.

Meriwether Family. Papers. 1737-circa 1880's. Southern Historical Collection at the Louis Round Wilson Special Collections Library, University of North Carolina, Chapel Hill, NC.

Morton, John W. Papers. Spring of 1861 to November 5, 1864. In Special Collections, Jean and Alexander Heard Library, Vanderbilt University, Nashville, TN.

Outlaw, David. Papers. 1847-1855, 1866. Southern Historical Collection, Chapel Hill Library, University of North Carolina, Chapel Hill, NC.

Reminiscences, in manuscript by Mrs. Charles M. Hitchcock, typed copy in possession of Floride Green of San Francisco.

Scott, Maria to Mrs. John H. Bernard, April 13, 1843. Typescript. William and Mary College Library, Richmond: Virginia Historical Society.

Sherman, Edwin A. "Personal Reminiscences of a California Pioneer of 1849." Manuscript. Bancroft Library, Pasadena, CA.

Tidball, John C. Papers. U. S. Military Academy Library, West Point, NY.

Tilton, Theodore. Papers. Buffalo, NY, Buffalo Public Library.

Published

Books

Allan, William. *History of the Campaign of Gen. T. J. (Stonewall) Jackson*. 1880. Reprint, Dayton, OH: Morningside, 1987.

Arnold, Isaac Newton. *The Life of Abraham Lincoln*. 6th ed. Chicago: Jansen, McClurg, 1893.

Barnes, Thurlow Weed. *Memoir of Thurlow Weed*. Boston: Houghton, Mifflin, 1884.

Barry, T. A. & Patten, B. A. *Men and Memories of San Francisco: In the "Spring of '50."* 1873. Reprint, Whitefish, MT: Kessinger Publishing Rare Reprints, 2007.

Bates, Edward. *The Diary of Edward Bates, 1859-1866*. Edited by Howard K. Beale. *Annual Report of the American Historical Association for 1930*. Vol. 4. Washington, D.C.: Government Printing Office, 1933.

Bates, Samuel P. *History of the Pennsylvania Volunteers, 1861-5*. 5 vols. Harrisburg, PA: B. Singerly, 1869-71.

Benton, Thomas Hart. *Thirty Years' View: or a History of the Workings of the American Government for Thirty Years, from 1820 to 1850*. 2 vols. 1856. Reprint, New York: Greenwood Press, 1968.

Bierce, Ambrose. *The Devil's Dictionary*. 1911. Reprint, New York: Thomas Y. Crowell, 1979.

Boggess, Arthur C. *The Settlement of Illinois, 1778-1830*. 1908. Reprint, Freeport, NY: Books for Libraries Press, 1970.

Boykin, Laura Nesbit. *Shinplasters and Homespun: The Diary of Laura Nesbit Boykin*. Mary Wright Stock, ed. Rockville, MD: Printex, 1975.

Brooks, Noah. *Mr. Lincoln's Washington: Selections from the Writings of Noah Brooks, Civil War Correspondent*. P. J. Staudenraus, ed. South Brunswick, NJ: Thomas Yoseloff, 1967.

_____. *Washington in Lincoln's Time*. Herbert Mitgang, ed. New York & Toronto: Rinehart, 1958.

Browne, Frances Fisher. *The Everyday Life of Abraham Lincoln: A Narrative and Descriptive Biography with Pen-Pictures and Personal Recollections by Those Who Knew Him*. Chicago: Browne & Howell, 1913.

Browne, J. Ross. *Adventures in the Apache Country: A Tour through Arizona and Sonora, with Notes on the Silver Regions of Nevada*. New York: Harper & Brothers, 1869.

Bungay, George W. *Off-Hand Takings, or Crayon Sketches of the Noticeable Men of Our Age*. New York: DeWitt & Davenport, 1854.

Butler, Benjamin F. *Butler's Book: Autobiography and Personal Reminiscences of Major-General Benj. F. Butler*. Boston: A.M. Thayer, 1892.

Carpenter, Francis B. *Six Months at the White House with Abraham Lincoln: The Story of a Picture*. New York: Hurd and Houghton, 1867.

Cartwright, Peter. *Autobiography of Peter Cartwright, the Backwoods Preacher*. W. P. Strickland, ed. New York: Carlton & Porter, 1857.

Casler, John O. *Four Years in the Stonewall Brigade.* 1893. Reprint, Dayton, OH: Morningside House, 1982.

Chase, Salmon P. *Inside Lincoln's Cabinet: The Civil War Diaries of Salmon P. Chase.* David H. Donald, ed. New York: Longmans, Green, 1954.

Chesnut, Mary. *Mary Chesnut's Civil War.* C. Vann Woodward, ed. New Haven, CT: Yale University Press, 1981.

Clark, Walter A. *Under the Stars and Bars: Memories of Four Years of Service with the Oglethorpes of Augusta, Georgia.* Augusta: Chronicle Printing, 1900.

Cleveland, Henry. *Alexander H. Stephens, in Public and Private.* Philadelphia: National, 1866.

Colton, Calvin. *Life, Correspondence and Speeches of Henry Clay.* 6 vols. New York: A. S. Barnes, 1857.

Cooke, John Esten. *Stonewall Jackson and the Old Stonewall Brigade.* Richard Barksdale Harwell, ed. Charlottsville: University of Virginia Press, 1954.

Crist, Lynda Lasswell, et. al., eds. *The Papers of Jefferson Davis.* 14 vols. Baton Rouge: Louisiana State University Press, 1971-2015.

Dabney, R. L. *Life and Campaigns of Lieut-Gen. Thomas J. Jackson.* 1865. Reprint, Boston: Sprinkle Publications, 1983.

Davis, Varina Howell. *Jefferson Davis, Ex-President of the Confederate States of America: A Memoir by His Wife.* 2 vols. 1890. Reprint, Freeport, NY: Books for Libraries Press, 1971.

Derby, George Horatio. *Phoenixiana, or Sketches and Burlesque.* New York: D. Appleton, 1856.

_____. *Squibob: An Early California Humorist.* Richard Derby Reynolds, ed. San Francisco: Squibob Press, 1990.

_____. (John Phoenix). *The Squibob Papers.* New York: Carlton, 1865.

"Diary of a Public Man." In the *North American Review* August-November 1879, and later as a book: *The Diary of a Public Man: And a Page of Political Correspondence—Stanton to Buchanan.* Foreword by Carl Sandburg. Prefatory Notes by F. Lauriston Bullard. New Brunswick, NJ: Rutgers University Press, 1946.

Douglas, Henry Kyd. *I Rode with Stonewall. 1899.* Reprint, Chapel Hill: University of North Carolina Press, 1940.

Douglass, Frederick. *The Frederick Douglass Papers.* John W. Blassingame, ed. Series 1 Vols. 1-5. New Haven: Yale University Press, 1979-1982.

_____. "Your Late Lamented Husband": An Unpublished Letter of Frederick Douglass to Mary Todd Lincoln. New York: The Gilder Lehrman Institute of American History, 2000.

Eggleston, George Cary. *A Rebel's Recollections.* Bloomington: Indiana University Press, 1969.

Ellis, John B. *Sights and Secrets of the National Capital.* Chicago: Jones, Junkin, 1869.

Emerson, Ralph Waldo. *The Complete Essays and Other Writings of Ralph Waldo Emerson.* Edited with biographical introduction by Brooks Atkinson. New York: Modern Library, 1940.

Fehrenbacher, Don E., & Virginia Fehrenbacher. *Recollected Words of Abraham Lincoln.* Stanford, CA: Stanford University Press, 1996.

Free Soil Songs for the People. Boston: Wright's Steam Press, 1848.

French, Benjamin Brown. *Witness to the Young Republic: A Yankee's Journal 1828-1870.* Donald B. Cole & John J. McDonough, eds. Hanover, NH: University Press of New England, 1989.

Gilder, Richard Watson. *The Poems of Richard Watson Gilder.* Boston & New York: Houghton Mifflin, 1908.

Grant, Ulysses S. *Personal Memoirs of Ulysses S. Grant.* 2 vols. in 1. 1894. Reprint, New York: AMS Press, 1972.

Greeley, Horace. *The Autobiography of Horace Greeley, or Recollections of a Busy Life.* New York: E. B. Treat, 1872.

_____. *Recollections of a Busy Life.* New York: J. B. Ford, 1868.

Gurowski, Adam. *Diary.* 3 vols. 1862-1866. New York: Burt Franklin, 1968.

Hay, John. *At Lincoln's Side: John Hay's Civil War Correspondence and Selected Writings.* Michael Burlingame, ed. Carbondale: Southern Illinois University Press, 2000.

_____. *Inside Lincoln's White House: The Complete Civil War Diary of John Hay.* Michael Burlingame & John R. Turner Ettlinger, eds. Carbondale: Southern Illinois University Press, 1997.

_____. *Lincoln and the Civil War: In the Diaries and Letters of John Hay.* Selected by Tyler Dennett. New York: Dodd Mead, 1939

Helm, Katherine. *The True Story of Mary, Wife of Lincoln.* New York: Harper, 1928.

Hendrick, Burton J. *Lincoln's War Cabinet.* Boston: Little, Brown, 1946.

Henry, Robert Selph, ed. *As They Saw Forrest: Some Recollections and Comments of Contemporaries.* 1956. Reprint, Wilmington, NC: Broadfoot, 1987.

Heth, Henry. *The Memoirs of Henry Heth.* James L. Morrison, Jr., ed. Contributions in Military History, No. 6. Westport. CT: Greenwood Press, 1974.

Hilliard, Henry W. *Politics and Pen Pictures at Home and Abroad.* New York: G. P. Putnam's Sons, 1892.

Hotchkiss. Jedediah. *Make Me a Map of the Valley: The Civil War Journal of Stonewall Jackson's Topographer.* Archie P. McDonald, ed. Dallas, TX: Southern Methodist University Press, 1973.

_____. *Virginia.* Vol. 4 of *Confederate Military History, Extended Edition.* Clement A. Evans, ed. 1899. Reprint, Wilmington, NC: Broadfoot, 1987.

Hubbard, John Milton. "Private Hubbard's Notes." In *As They Saw Forrest.* Robert Selph Henry, ed. Wilmington, NC: Broadfoot, 1987.

Hunton, Eppa. *Autobiography of Eppa Hunton.* Richmond: William Byrd Press, 1933.

Imboden, John D. "Stonewall Jackson in the Shenandoah." Vol. 2 of *Battles and Leaders.* 4 vols. 1887. Reprint, Secaucus, NJ: Castle, n.d.

Jackson, Mary Anna. *Memoirs of Stonewall Jackson.* 1895. Reprint, Dayton, OH: Press of Morningside Bookshop, 1985.

Julian, George Washington. *Political Recollections, 1840 to 1872.* Chicago: Jansen, McClurg, 1884.

Keyes, Erasmus Darwin. *Fifty Years' Observation of Men and Events.* New York: Charles Scribner's Sons, 1884.

Kimball, Nathan. "Fighting Jackson at Kernstown." In Vol. 2 of *Battles and Leaders.* 4 vols. 1887. Reprint. Secaucus, NJ: Castle, n.d.

Lamon, Ward Hill. *Recollections of Abraham Lincoln,* 1847-1865. Dorothy Lamon Teillard, ed. 1985. Reprint, Lincoln: University of Nebraska Press, 1994.

Lee, Jr., Robert E. *Recollections and Letters of General Robert E. Lee.* New York: Doubleday, Page, 1909.

Life and Reminiscences of Jefferson Davis By Distinguished Men of His Time. Baltimore: R. H. Woodward, 1890.

Lincoln, Abraham. *Collected Works of Abraham Lincoln.* Roy P. Basler, ed. 8 vols. New Brunswick, NJ: Rutgers University Press, 1953.

Long, A. L. *Memoirs of Robert E. Lee*. Collected and edited by Marcus J. Wright. 1886. Reprint, Secaucus, NJ: Blue and Grey Press, 1983.

Longfellow, Samuel, ed. *Life of Henry Wadsworth Longfellow: With Extracts from His Journals and Correspondence*. 3 vols. 1887. Reprint, Chicago: Sequoyah Books, 2003.

Longstreet, James. *From Manassas to Appomattox*. 1895. Reprint, New York: Great Commanders Collection, 1994.

McClellan, George B. *The Civil War Papers of George B. McClellan: Selected Correspondence, 1860-1865*. Stephen W. Sears, ed. New York: Ticknor & Fields, 1989.

McClure, Alexander K. *Abraham Lincoln and Men of War Times: Some Personal Recollections of War and Politics during the Lincoln Administration*. Philadelphia: Times Publishing, 1892.

McGuire, Hunter H. & Christian, George L. *The Confederate Cause and Conduct in the War Between the States*. Scott's Valley, CA: Create Space Independent Publishing Platform, 2014.

Maury, Dabney H. *Recollections of a Virginian: In the Mexican, Indian, and Civil Wars*. New York: Charles Scribner's Sons, 1894.

Miers, Earl Schenck, Editor in Chief. *Lincoln Day By Day, A Chronology 1809-1865*. 3 vols. Washington: Lincoln Sesquicentennial Commission, 1960.

Military Annals of Tennessee: Confederate: First Series, Embracing a Review of Military Operations, with Regimental Histories and Memorial Rolls. John Berrien Lindsley, ed. Nashville: J. M. Lindsley, 1886.

Morison, Elting E. et. al., eds. *Letters of Theodore Roosevelt*. 8 vols. Cambridge: Harvard University Press, 1954.

Morton, John W. "A Soldier Sums Up." In *As They Saw Forrest*. Robert Selph Henry, ed. Wilmington, NC: Broadfoot, 1987

Nicolay, John G. & John Hay. *Abraham Lincoln: A History*. 10 vols. New York: Century, 1890.

_____. *An Oral History of Abraham Lincoln: John G. Nicolay's Interviews and Essays*. Michael Burlingame, ed. Carbondale & Edwardsville, IL: Southern Illinois University Press, 1996.

Oh, I'm a Good Old Rebel. Song. Words by Adelbert Volck or Innes Randolph, music to the tune of *Jim Bowers*, by R. Bishop Buckley. In Willard A. & Porter W. Heaps. *The Singing Sixties: The Spirit of Civil War Days Drawn from the Music of the Times*. Norman: University of Oklahoma Press, 1960.

Opie, John Newton. *A Rebel Cavalryman with Lee, Stuart, and Jackson*. Chicago: W.B. Conkey, 1899. E. B. Treat, 1867.

Pollard, Edward A. *Lee and His Lieutenants: Comprising the Early Life, Public Services, and Campaigns of General Robert E. Lee and His Companions in Arms, with a Record of Their Campaigns and Heroic Deeds*. New York, E. B. Treat, 1867.

Poore, Benjamin Perley. *Perley's Reminiscences of Sixty Years in the National Metropolis*. 2 vols. Philadelphia: Hubbard Brothers, 1886.

Pryor, Mrs. Roger A. *My Day: Reminiscences of a Long Life*. New York: Macmillan, 1909.

_____. *Reminiscences of Peace and War*. New York: Macmillan, 1904.

Publications of the Buffalo Historical Society. Vol. 10. Millard Fillmore Papers. Vol 1. Frank H. Severance, ed. Buffalo, NY: Buffalo Historical Society, 1907.

Rambaut, Gilbert V. "Forrest at Shiloh." In *As They Saw Forrest*. Robert Selph Henry, ed. Wilmington, NC: Broadfoot, 1987.

Rankin, Henry B. *Personal Recollections of Abraham Lincoln*. New York: G. P. Putman's Sons, 1916.

Rice, Allen Thorndike, ed. *Reminiscences of Abraham Lincoln by Distinguished Men of His Time.* New York: North American Review, 1885.

Root, George F. "The Vacant Chair." Song. Cleveland: S. Brainard's Sons, 1861.

Schurz, Carl. *The Reminiscences of Carl Schurz.* Frederic Bancroft and William A. Dunning, eds. 3 vols. New York: McClure, 1907-1908.

Scott, Winfield. *Memoirs 1864.of Lieut.-General Scott, LLD.* 2 vols. 1864. Reprint, Freeport, NY: Books for Libraries Press, 1970.

Seward, Frederick William. *Seward at Washington, as Senator and Secretary of State: A Memoir of His Life, With Selections From His Letters, 1846-1861.* New York: Derby & Miller, 1891.

Stoddard, William O. *Inside the White House in War Times.* New York: Charles L. Webster, 1892.

Stone, William Leete. "John Hay, 1858." In *Memories of Brown University.* John M. Hay Library, Brown University. Providence, RI.

Strong, George Templeton. *The Diary of George Templeton Strong: The Civil War 1860-1865.* Edited by Allan Nevins & Milton Halsey Thomas. New York: Macmillan, 1952.

Taylor, Richard. *Destruction and Reconstruction: Personal Experiences of the Late War.* New York: D. Appleton, 1883.

Townsend, George. *Rustics in Rebellion: A Yankee Reporter on the Road to Richmond 1861-1865.*1866. Reprint, Chapel Hill: University of North Carolina Press, 1950.

Truth, Sojourner. *The Narrative of Sojourner Truth: By Sojourner Truth-Illustrated.* 1850. Reprint, Mineola, NY: Dover Publications, 1997.

Van Tyne, C. H, ed. *The Letters of Daniel Webster.* New York: McClure, Phillips, 1902

Wallace, Lew. *Lew Wallace, An Autobiography.* 2 vols. New York: Harper & Brothers, 1906.

Weed, Thurlow. *Autobiography of Thurlow Weed.* Harriet A. Weed, ed. Boston: Houghton, Mifflin, 1884.

Welles, Gideon. *Diary of Gideon Welles, Secretary of the Navy under Lincoln and Johnson.* 3 vols. Boston: Houghton Mifflin, 1911.

Wentworth, John. *Congressional Reminiscences: Adams, Benton, Clay, Calhoun, and Webster.* Chicago: Fergus, 1882.Morningside Bookshop, 1976.

Witherspoon, William. "Tishomingo Creek or Bryce's Cross Roads." In *As They Saw Forrest.* Robert Selph Henry, ed. Wilmington, NC: Broadfoot, 1987.

Wolesley, Garnet. "General Viscount Wolseley on Forrest." In *As They Saw Forrest.* Robert Selph Henry, ed. Wilmington, NC: Broadfoot. 1987.

Young, John Preston, *The Seventh Tennessee Cavalry (Confederate): A History.* 1890. Reprint, Dayton, OH: Press of Morningside Bookstore, 1976.

Young, John Russell. *Around the World with General Grant.* 2 vols. 1879. Reprint, Baltimore: Johns Hopkins University Press, 2002.

_____. *Men and Memories: Personal Reminiscences.* May D. Russell Young, ed. 2nd edition. New York: F. Tennyson Neely, 1901.

Government Documents

Buchanan, James. Fourth Annual Message to Congress on the State of the Union, December 3, 1860.

Pierce, Franklin. First Annual Message to Congress on the State of the Union. December 5, 1853.

Scott, Winfield to William Marcy, May 21, 1846, *Senate Documents*, no. 378, 29th Cong, 1st sess., 1846.

U.S. Congress. Forrest testimony in the "Ku Klux Report" of 1872, 2nd sess. 42nd cong. Senate Document no, 41, Vol. 13.

_____. *Senate Documents*, No. 378, 29th Cong, 1st sess.

U.S. War Department. *War of the Rebellion: Official Records of the Union and Confederate Armies*. 128 vols. Washington, D.C.. 1880-1901.

Periodical Collections

Anderson, Charles W. "My Last Meeting with Gen. Forrest." *Confederate Veteran* 4, no. 11 (November 1896): 387.

Binckley, J. W. "The Leader of the House." *Galaxy* 1 (July 1866): 493-500.

Brand, W. H. "Lieutenant-General N.B. Forrest." In *The Land We Love*. Vol 1, No. 4 (August 1866): 263-75.

Century Magazine

Conant, Jasper "A Visit to Washington in 1861-62." In *Metropolitan Magazine*. 33 (June 1910), 313.

Confederate Veteran

Congressional Globe

Douglass's Monthly, October, 1862. University of Rochester. Frederick Douglass Project in the Department of Rare Books and Special Collections and the Frederick Douglass Institute.

Evans, T. C. "Personal Reminiscences of John Hay: By a Veteran Journalist." In *New York Times*, July 16, 1905.

Ewell, Richard C. "Colonel Richardson and the Thirty-Eighth Massachusetts." In *Cambridge Historical Society: Publication, Vol. 39—Proceedings for the Years 1961-1963*. Cambridge: Cambridge Historical Society, 1964.

Gardner, William Montgomery. "The Memoirs of Brigadier-General William Montgomery Gardner." Elizabeth McKinne Gardner, ed. Typescript copy of a series of articles in the *Memphis Commercial Appeal*, 1912. U.S. Military Academy Library, West Point, NY.

Hill, Daniel Harvey. "The Real Stonewall Jackson." *Century Magazine* 47 (February 1894): 623-28.

Hosea, Lewis Montgomery. *Some Sidelights on the War for the Union: Paper Read Before the Ohio Commandery of the Loyal Legion at Cleveland, Ohio, October 9, 1912.*

Jones, John William. "Down in the Valley after 'Stonewall's Quartermaster'." *Southern Historical Society Papers Vol 9.* 1881, Reprint, Millwood, NY: Kraus, 1977.

Munford, Thomas Taylor. "A Confederate Officer's Reminiscences." U.S. Cavalry Association, Jan.1,1892. U.S. Cavalry Memorial Research Library. Ft. Reno, OK.

Neill, Edward D. "Reminiscences of the Last Year of President Lincoln's Life." In vol. 1. *A Series of Papers Read before the Minnesota Commandery of the Military Order of the Loyal Legion of the United States*. 1887. Reprint, Wilmington, NC: Broadfoot Publishing, 1992.

Nicolay, John G. "Lincoln's Gettysburg Address." *Century Magazine* 47 (February 1894): 597.

Parmelee, Theodore N. "Recollections of an Old Stager." *Harper's New Monthly Magazine* 45 (August 1872): 445-48, (September 1872): 600-605, (October 1872): 750-53; 46 (December 1872): 92-97, (January 1873): 270-75; 47 (September 1873): 586-91, (October 1873): 753-60; 49 (June 1874): 110-18.

Preston, Margaret Junkin. "Personal Reminiscences of Stonewall Jackson." *Century Magazine* New Ser.10 (October 1886): 927-36.

Quad, M. "Notes and Queries: A Federal Soldier's Opinion of Stonewall Jackson." *Southern Historical Society Papers* 10, no. 7 (July 1882): 334.

"Reminiscences of Washington." *Atlantic Monthly* 46 (December 1880): 799-810; 47 (February 1881): 234-50, (April 1881): 538-47, (May1881): 658-66.

Tilton, Theodore. "Our Domestic Relations, or How to Treat the Rebel States." *Atlantic Monthly* 12 (October 1863): 507-29.

Turner, Arlin, ed. "George W. Cable's Recollections of General Forrest." *Journal of Southern History* 21, no. 2 (May 1955), 224-28.

"Washington During the War." *Macmillan's Magazine* 6 (May 1862): 16-29.

Wise, John S. "Stonewall Jackson as I Knew Him." In *The Circle* (March 1908): 143-45. Copy in the Virginia Historical Society Library, Richmond, VA.

Wolesley, Garnet. "General Lee." *McMillan's Magazine* 55 (March 1887), 321-31.

Wood, H. E. "More of the Last Defense of Richmond." *Confederate Veteran* 16 (1908): 397.

Young, J. P. "Monument to Gen. N.B. Forrest." *Confederate Veteran* 13 (September 1905): 389-91.

Newspapers and Magazines

Athens Southern Watchman

Augusta Chronicle

Chattanooga Sunday Times

Chicago Tribune

Christian Science Monitor

Cincinnati Daily Gazette

Cincinnati Enquirer

Illinois Daily Journal

Memphis News-Scimitar

Nashville Banner

New York Herald

New York Law Journal

New York Times

Philadelphia Evening Star

Pittsburgh Dispatch

Richmond Daily Enquirer

Sedalia (Missouri) *Sunday Times*

Shasta (California) *Courier*

Union Springs (Alabama) *Times*

U.S. News and World Report

Washington Union

Secondary Sources

Books

Aaron, Daniel. *The Unwritten War: American Writers and the Civil War.* New York: Alfred A. Knopf, 1973.

Alexander, Holmes. *The Famous Five.* New York: Bookmaker, 1958.

Andrews, J. Cutler. *The North Reports the Civil* War. Pittsburgh: University of Pittsburgh Press, 1955.

Andrews, Marietta M. *Scraps of Paper.* New York: E. P. Dutton, 1929.

Ashdown, Paul & Caudill, Edward. *The Myth of Nathan Bedford Forrest.* Lanham, MD: Rowman & Littlefield, 2005.

Baker, Carlos. *Emerson Among the Eccentrics: A Group Portrait.* New York: Viking, 1996.

Baker, Jean H. *James Buchanan.* New York: Henry Holt, 2004.

_____. *Mary Todd Lincoln: A Biography.* New York: W. W. Norton, 1987.

Bancroft, Hubert Howe. *History of Arizona and New Mexico, 1530-1888.* Vol. 17. San Francisco: History Company, 1889.

Barzun, Jacques. *Lincoln the Literary Genius.* Evanston, IL: Schori Private Press, Evanston Publishing Company, 1960.

Basler, Roy P. "An Appreciation of the Gettysburg Address." In *A Touchstone for Greatness: Essays, Addresses, and Occasional Pieces about Abraham Lincoln.* Westport, CT: Greenwood Press, 1973.

_____. "Lincoln's Development as a Writer," in *A Touchstone for Greatness: Essays, Addresses, and Occasional Pieces about Abraham Lincoln.* Westport, CT: Greenwood Press, 1973.

Belden, Thomas Graham & Marva Robins Belden. *So Fell the Angels.* New York: Little, Brown: 1956.

Benton, Joel. *Greeley on Lincoln.* New York: Baker and Taylor, 1893.

Bradford, Gamaliel. *As God Made Them: Portraits of Some 19th Century Americans.* Boston: Houghton Mifflin, 1929.

Brodie, Fawn M. *Thaddeus Stevens: Scourge of the South.* New York: W. W. Norton, 1959.

Bruce, Henry. *Life of General Houston 1793-1863: The Portal to Texas History.* New York: Dodd, Mead, 1891.

Carden, Allen & Thomas J. Ebert. *John George Nicolay: The Man in Lincoln's Shadow.* Knoxville: University of University Press, 2019.

Carman, Harry J. & Reinhard H. Luthin. *Lincoln and the Patronage.* New York: Columbia University Press, 1943.

Carroll, Howard. *Twelve Americans: Their Lives and Times.* 1883. Reprint, Freeport, NY: Books for Libraries Press, 1971.

Cashin, Joan E. *First Lady of the Confederacy: Varina Davis's Civil War.* Cambridge, MA: Belknap Press, *2006.*

Castel, Albert E. *Articles of War: Winners, Losers, (and Some Who Were Both) during the Civil War.* Mechanicsburg, PA: Stackpole Books, 2001.

Curtis, George Ticknor. *Life of James Buchanan Fifteenth President of the United States.* 2 vols. New York: Harper & Brothers, 1883.

Davis, William C. *Jefferson Davis: The Man and His Hour.* Baton Rouge: Louisiana State University Press, 2012.

Dodge, Daniel Kilham. *Abraham Lincoln: The Evolution of His Literary Style.* Carbondale: Southern Illinois University Press, 2000.

Donald, David Herbert. *Charles Sumner and the Rights of Man.* New York: Alfred A. Knopf, 1970.

Durant, Will. *The Story of Philosophy.* New York: Simon & Schuster, 1926.

Dyer, Oliver. *Great Senators of the United States Forty Years Ago.* New York: Robert Bonner's Sons, 1889.

Eisenhower, John S. *Agent of Destiny: The Life and Times of General Winfield Scott.* New York: Free Press, 1997.

Elliott, Charles Winslow. *Winfield Scott: The Soldier and the Man.* New York: Macmillan, 1937.

Faragher, John Mack. *Sugar Creek: Life on the Illinois Prairie.* New Haven, CT: Yale University Press, 1986.

Foote, Shelby. *The Civil War, A Narrative.* 3 vols. New York: Random House, 1958-1974.

Freeman, Douglas Southall. *R. E. Lee: A Biography.* 4 vols. New York: Charles Scribner's Sons, 1935.

Gallagher, Gary W, ed. *Lee the Soldier.* Lincoln: University of Nebraska Press, 1996.

Goodwin, Doris Kearns. *Team of Rivals: The Political Genius of Abraham Lincoln.* New York: Simon & Schuster, 2005.

Green, Constance McLaughlin. *Washington: Village and Capital, 1800-1878.* Princeton: Princeton University Press, 1962.

Hamilton, Holman. *Zachary Taylor, Soldier in the White House.* Indianapolis: Bobbs-Merrill, 1951.

Hamlin, Percy Gatling. *"Old Bald Head" (General R. S. Ewell): The Portrait of a Soldier* and *The Making of a Soldier: Letters of General R. S. Ewell.* (2 books in 1 volume.) Reprint, Gaithersburg, MD: Ron Van Sickle Military Books, 1988.

Hart, Albert Bushnell. *Salmon Portland Chase.* Boston: Houghton Mifflin, 1899.

Heaps, Porter W. & Willard A. Heaps. *The Singing Sixties: The Spirit of Civil War Days Drawn from the Music of the Times.* Norman: University of Oklahoma Press, 1960.

Hearn, Lafcadio. *Occidental Gleanings*, 2 Vols. Edited by Albert Mordell. New York: Dodd, Meade, 1925.

Hendrick, Burton J. *Lincoln's War Cabinet.* Boston: Little, Brown, 1946.

Henry, Robert Selph. *"First with the Most" Forrest.* Reprint, Wilmington, NC: Broadfoot, 1987. Westport, CT: Greenwood Press 1974.

Hofstadter, Richard. *The American Political Tradition and the Men Who Made It.* New York: Vintage Books, 1974.

Holzman, Robert S. *Stormy Ben Butler.* New York: Macmillan, 1954.

Howard, Hamilton Gay. *Civil War Echoes: Character Echoes and State Secrets.* Washington: Howard Publishing, 1907.

Hughes, Nathaniel Cheairs & Roy P. Stonesife, Jr. *Life and Wars of Gideon J. Pillow.* Chapel Hill: University of North Carolina Press, 1993.

Isley, Jester Allen. *Horace Greeley and the Republican Party.* Princeton, NJ: Princeton University Press, 1947.

Johnson, Timothy D. *Winfield Scott: The Quest for Military Glory.* Lawrence: University Press of Kansas, 1998.

Jones, Edgar Dewitt. *Lords of Speech: Portraits of Fifteen American Orators.* Chicago: Willett, Clark, 1937.

Jones, William. *Life and Letters of Robert Edward Lee, Soldier and Man.* New York: Neale Publishing, 1906.

Klapthor, Margaret & Black, Allida. *First Ladies of the United States of America.* New York: Scala Arts Publishers, 2006.

McElroy, Robert. *Jefferson Davis, The Unreal and the Real.* 2 vols. New York: Harper & Brothers, 1937.

McPherson, James M. *Abraham Lincoln and the Second American Revolution.* New York & Oxford: Oxford University Press, 1990 .

_____. *Battle Cry of Freedom: The Civil War Era.* New York: Oxford University Press, 1988.

Miers, Earl Schenck, ed. *Lincoln Day by Day, Chronology, 1809-1865.* 3 vols. Washington, D.C.: Lincoln Sesquicentennial Commission, 1960.

Myers, Frank M. *The Comanches: A History of White's Battalion, Virginia Cavalry.* 1871. Reprint, Marietta, GA: Continental, 1956.

Nevin, David. *The Mexican War.* Alexandria, VA: Time-Life Books, 1978.

Nevins, Allan. *Ordeal of the Union.* 8 vols. New York: Charles Scribner's Sons, 1970.

Nowlan, Robert A. *The American Presidents From Polk to Hayes: What They Did, What They Said & What Was Said About Them.* Denver: Outskirts Press, 2014.

O'Toole, Patricia. *The Five of Hearts: An Intimate Portrait of Henry Adams and His Friends 1880-1918.* New York: Clarkson Potter, 1990.

Painter, Nell Irvin. *Sojourner Truth: A Life, A Symbol.* New York: W. W. Norton, 1996.

Parker, Edward G. *The Golden Age of American Oratory.* Boston: Whittemore, Niles & Hall, 1857.

Parks, Joseph Howard. *General Edmund Kirby Smith, CSA.* Baton Rouge: Louisiana University Press, 1954.

Parton, James. *Famous Americans of Recent Times.* Boston: Ticknor & Fields, 1867.

Pendleton, Louis. *Alexander H. Stephens.* Philadelphia: George W. Jacobs, 1907.

Pfanz, Donald C. *Richard S. Ewell: A Soldier's Life.* Chapel Hill: University of North Carolina Press, 1998.

Peskin, Allan. *Winfield Scott and the Profession of Arms.* Kent, OH: Kent State University Press, 2003.

Peterson, Merrill D. *The Great Triumvirate.* New York: Oxford University Press, 1987.

Phillips, Ulrich B. *The Life of Robert Toombs.* New York: Macmillan, 1913.

Pillsbury, Albert E. "Memorial to Horace Greeley: Address on the Centenary Observation of Horace Greeley at Amherst, New Hampshire," February 3, 1911. Boston: Stetson Press, 1911.

Quarles, Benjamin. *Lincoln and the Negro.* New York: Oxford University Press, 1962.

Roberts, II, John B. *Rating the First Ladies: The Women Who Influenced the Presidency.* New York: Citadel, 2004.

Ross, Ishbel. *First Lady of the South: The Life of Mrs. Jefferson Davis.* New York: Harper, 1958.

_____. *Proud Kate: Portrait of an Ambitious Woman.* New York: Harper & Brothers, 1953.

Rukeyser, Muriel. *The Speed of Darkness.* New York: Random House, 1968.

Sandburg, Carl. *Abraham Lincoln: The War Years.* 4 vols. New York: Harcourt, 1939.

_____. *American Poetry of the Twentieth Century.* Richard Gray, ed. London: Longman Publishing Group, 1990.

_____. *Cornhuskers.* New York: Henry Holt, 1918.

_____. *Harvest Poems, 1910-1960.* New York: Harcourt, Brace, 1960.

Scarry, Robert J. *Millard Fillmore.* 1973. Reprint, Jefferson, NC: MacFarland, 2001.

Schott, Thomas E. *Alexander H. Stephens of Georgia: A Biography.* Baton Rouge: Louisiana State University Press, 1988.

Schuckers, Jacob W. *The Life and Public Services of Salmon Portland Chase.* New York: D. Appleton, 1874.

Segal, Charles M., ed. *Conversations with Lincoln.* New York: G. P. Putman's Sons, 1961.

Seitz, Don Carlos. *Horace Greeley, Founder of the New York Tribune.* 1926. Reprint, New York: AMS Press, 1970.

Shastid, Thomas Hall. *My Second Life,* 1944. Reprint, London: Forgotten Books, 2018.

Smith, Donald V. *Chase and Civil War Politics.* Columbus, OH: F. J. Heer, 1931.

Smith, Elbert B. "Taylor, Zachary." In *Presidencies of Zachary Taylor and Millard Fillmore.* American Presidency Series. Lawrance, KS: University of Kansas Press, 1988.

Smith, William Ernest. *The Francis Preston Blair Family in Politics.* 2 vols. New York: Macmillan, 1933.

Sorrel, G. Moxley. *Recollections of a Confederate Staff Officer.* 1905. Reprint, Dayton, OH: Morningside Bookshop, 1978.

Stauffer, John. *Giants: The Parallel Lives of Frederick Douglass and Abraham Lincoln.* New York and Boston: Twelve Books/Hatchett Book Group, 2008.

Stetson, Erlene & David, Linda. *Glorying in Tribulation: The Lifework of Sojourner Truth.* East Lansing: Michigan State University Press, 1994.

Stewart, George R., Jr. *John Phoenix, Esq., the Veritable Squibob: A Life of Captain George H. Derby, USA.* New York: Henry Holt, 1937.

Stoddard, Henry Luther. *Horace Greeley: Printer, Editor, Crusader.* New York: G. P. Putnam's Sons, 1946.

Tarbell, Ida. *Abraham Lincoln and His Ancestors.* Bison Books Edition. Lincoln, NE: University of Nebraska Press, 1997.

Thomas, Benjamin P. *Abraham Lincoln, a Biography.* New York: Alfred A. Knopf, 1952.

Thompson, William Y. *Robert Toombs of Georgia.* Baton Rouge, LA: Louisiana State University Press, 1966.

Trent, William P. *Southern Statesmen of the Old Regime.* New York: Thomas Y. Crowell, 1897.

Trietsch, James H. *The Printer and the Prince: A Study of the Influence of Horace Greeley upon Abraham Lincoln as Candidate and President.* New York: Exposition Press, 1955.

Turner, Justin G. & Turner, Linda Levitt. *Mary Todd Lincoln: Her Life and Letters.* New York: Alfred A. Knopf, 1972.

Venet, Wendy Hamand. *Neither Ballots nor Bullets: Woman Abolitionists and the Civil War.* Charlottesville: University Press of Virginia, 1991.

Von Abele, Rudolph. *Alexander H. Stephens: A Biography.* New York: Alfred A. Knopf, 1946.

Warden, Robert B. *An Account of the Private Life and Public Services of Salmon Portland Chase.* Cincinnati: Wilstach, Baldwin, 1874.

Warren, Louis A. *Lincoln's Gettysburg Declaration: "A New Birth of Freedom."* Fort Wayne, IN: Lincoln National Life Foundation, 1964.

Watters, Phillip M. *Peter Cartwright.* New York: Easton & Mains; Cincinnati: Jennings & Graham, 1910.

Waugh, John C. *The Class of 1846: From West Point to Appomattox—Stonewall Jackson, George McClellan and Their Brothers*. New York: Ballantine Books, 1999.

Wills, Garry. *Lincoln at Gettysburg: The Words that Remade America*. New York: Simon & Schuster, 1992.

Wilson, Douglas L. & Davis, Rodney O., eds. *Herndon's Informants: Letters, Interviews and Statements about Abraham Lincoln*. Champaign, IL: University of Illinois Press, 1997.

Wilson, Edmund. *Patriotic Gore: Studies in the Literature of the American Civil War*. New York: Oxford University Press, 1962.

Wilson, Rufus Rockwell. *Intimate Memories of Lincoln*. Elmira, NY: Primavera Press, 1945.

Winkler, H. Donald. *The Women in Lincoln's Life*. Nashville, TN: Rutledge Hill Press, 2001.

Woodburn, James Albert. *Life of Thaddeus Stevens*. Indianapolis: Bobbs-Merrill, 1913.

Woodley, Thomas Frederick. *The Great Leveler: The Life of Thaddeus Stevens*. New York: Stackpole Sons, 1937.

Wyeth, John Allan. *That Devil Forrest: Life of General N. B. Forrest*. 1899. Reprint, Baton Rouge, LA: Louisiana State University Press, 1989.

Periodical Articles

Brown, Caroline Owsley. "Springfield Society before the Civil War." In the *Journal of the Illinois State Historical Society*. Vol 15 (April-July 1922): 477-500.

Connelly, William E., ed. "A Journal of the Santa Fe Trail." In *Mississippi Valley Historical Review* 12 (1925): 72-98, 227-55.

Dyer, Brainerd. "Zachary Taylor and the Election of 1848." In *Pacific Historical Review* 9, no. 2 (June 1940): 173-82.

Hamlin, Percy Gatling, "Richard S. Ewell: His Humanity and Humor." *Cavalcade* (Autumn 1971): 10.

Ketchum, Richard M. "Faces from the Past: Zachary Taylor." *American Heritage* 14 (October 1963): 53.

Lloyd, Demarest. "The Home-Life of Salmon Portland Chase." *Atlantic Monthly* 32 (November 1873): 526-38.

Lynch, William O. "Zachary Taylor as President." *The Journal of Southern History*. Vol. 4, no. 3 (August 1938): 279-294.

MacNeil, Neil. "The House Shall Chuse Their Speaker..." *American Heritage* 28 (February 1977): 26-31.

Mabee, Carlton. "Sojourner Truth and President Lincoln." *New England Quarterly* 61 (December 1988): 519-29.

Nordell, Roderick. "The Incomparable Earl." *Christian Science Monitor*, July 12, 1999.

O'Laughlin, John Callan. "Lincoln and the Press." *Abraham Lincoln Association Papers*. Springfield, IL: Abraham Lincoln Association, 1931.

Owen, Robert Dale. "Political Results from the Varioloid: A Leaf of History." *Atlantic Monthly* 35 (June 1875): 660-70.

Remensnyder, Junius B. "With Lincoln at Gettysburg." *Magazine of History with Notes and Queries* 32 (1926): 12.

Riley, Harris D., Jr. "Jefferson Davis and His Health" in the *Journal of Mississippi History*, 49 (August and November 1987): 179-202, 262-287.

Willcox, Louise Collier. "A Light Is Out!" *Harper's Weekly*. February 24, 1912.

Williams, T. Harry, ed. "General Ewell to the High Private in the Rear." *The Virginia Magazine of History and Biography* 54, No. 2 (April 1946): 157-160.

Young, James Harvey. "Anna Elizabeth Dickinson and the Civil War: For and Against Lincoln." *The Mississippi Valley Historical Review*. 31, No.1 (June 1944): 59-80.

Plays

Shakespeare, William. *Loves Labors Lost.*

_____. *Twelfth Night.*

Wilde, Oscar. *Lady Windermere's Fan*. Play first performed February 5, 1893.

Index

About the Author

John C. Waugh spent decades as a journalist and in Washington, D.C. on the staff of Vice President Nelson Rockefeller and as press secretary for Senator Jeff Bingaman. He is the author of many books, including *The Class of 1846: From West Point to Appomattox.* Jack is the father of two children, the grandfather of four, and the great-grandfather of one. He and his wife Kathleen D. Lively live in Pantego, Texas.